Inroads into Burma

'The Nga Mo Yeik *nat* of Rangoon', painting by Noel F. Singer.

Inroads into Burma
A Travellers' Anthology

Compiled and Introduced by
GERRY ABBOTT

KUALA LUMPUR
OXFORD UNIVERSITY PRESS
OXFORD SINGAPORE NEW YORK
1997

Oxford University Press

Oxford New York
Athens Auckland Bangkok Bombay
Calcutta Cape Town Dar es Salaam Delhi
Florence Hong Kong Istanbul Karachi
Madras Madrid Melbourne Mexico City
Nairobi Paris Shah Alam Singapore
Taipei Tokyo Toronto

and associated companies in
Berlin Ibadan

Oxford is a trade mark of Oxford University Press

Published in the United States
by Oxford University Press, New York

© Oxford University Press 1997
First published 1997

British Library Cataloguing in Publication Data
Data available

Library of Congress Cataloging-in-Publication Data
Abbott, Gerry.
Inroads into Burma/compiled and introduced by Gerry Abbott.
p. cm.—(Oxford in Asia paperbacks)
Includes bibliographical references.
ISBN 983 56 0034 1
1. Burma—Description and travel. 2. Burma—Civilization.
3. Burma—Social life and customs. 4. Architecture, Buddhist—Burma.
5. Pagodas—Burma—Pagan. I. Series.
DS527.9.A22 1997
959. 1—dc21

Typeset by Indah Photosetting Centre Sdn. Bhd., Malaysia
Printed by KHL Printing Co. Pte. Ltd., Singapore
Published by Penerbit Fajar Bakti Sdn. Bhd. (008974-T),
under licence from Oxford University Press
4 Jalan Pemaju U1/15, Seksyen U1, 40150 Shah Alam,
Selangor Darul Ehsan, Malaysia

For the Peoples of Burma

Acknowledgements

I must first thank Noel Singer not only for suggesting that I should undertake this project but also for allowing me to reproduce some of the photographs that illustrate his beautiful book *Burmah: A Photographic Journey, 1855–1925*, published by Kiscadale in 1993.

I am indebted to the staff of three libraries. The excellent facilities of the John Rylands Library, University of Manchester were available to me throughout the preparation of this book; the earlier encouragement given by Patricia Herbert of the British Library's Oriental and India Office Collection was invaluable; and the helpfulness of the staff of the Chester Beatty Library in Dublin was most appreciated, as is their permission to reproduce part of a Burmese *parabaik*. At this point I must also express my gratitude to David Griffiths of the School of Education, Manchester University, for his generous help in the preparation of slides and photographs.

I am grateful to the following authors/publishers for permission to reproduce passages (identified below by their numbers in the anthology) from their works:

Michael Aris and Penguin Books Ltd. (36)

James Nisbet & Co. Ltd. (30)

Random House UK Limited (32)

While I have made every effort to ascertain the copyright status of the passages, and to secure the permission of their copyright holders, a few of my attempts have been unsuccessful. I therefore extend my apologies to the copyright holders (if any) who remain unacknowledged.

Finally, I must thank not only my wife, Khin Thant Han, who cheerfully and willingly acted as an unofficial and unpaid editor, but also all those of her compatriots who, during my two years in Burma, gave me such a warm welcome that I set my heart on discovering as much as I could about their beautiful country and its peoples.

ACKNOWLEDGEMENTS

Arrangements have been made for the royalties on all sales of this book to be credited to PROSPECT BURMA, a non-political educational trust for the support of displaced Burmese students.

Manchester   GERRY ABBOTT
September 1996

A Note on Names and Spellings

BURMESE/BURMAN. Within Burma's borders live scores and scores of ethnic groups, all of them *Burmese* by nationality; but it is the *Burman*s, the people of the central lowlands, who predominate. When referring to this one group some writers simply use the adjective *Burmese* while others, including myself, prefer the term *Burman.*

Some of the extracts in this book, especially those written long ago, contain unfamiliar words and spellings. Often such obscurities become clear as one reads on, but even where this is unlikely to happen I have tried as far as possible not to interrupt the passage but to deal with such matters in my introductory notes. At this point, the spelling of Burmese words in roman characters presented various problems which I have tried to overcome by using three sometimes conflicting guidelines: phonetic considerations, conventional spellings, and common sense. The main features to note are as follows:

The use of initial h. This simply indicates that the following consonant is aspirated: *hpaya, hsaya,* and *hti* have the same initial sounds as *pepper, salt,* and *tea* respectively.

The use of accent. This is used to indicate the appropriate stress—for example: the accents in *Pagán, Pegú* show that these places are not pronounced like the English adjective 'pagan' or like 'PEA-goo'.

The use of hyphenation. I have hyphenated some personal and place names between syllables: *Ba-gyi-daw,* for example, helps the reader to see that the name is **not** pronounced *Bag-yid-aw.*

The use of convention. I have followed the long-standing convention by which syllables that are pronounced CHEE and GEE are written *kyi(kyee)* and *gyi(gyee).* Similarly, I refer to *Burma* throughout although the current regime wishes the country to be known abroad as *Myanmar,* and place names are spelt as they were before the introduction of the regime's new and rather cumbersome system of transliteration.

Contents

The Anglo-Burmese Wars

A Few of Burma's Minority Groups

The Independent Women of Burma

Some Elements of Burman Culture

Flora and Fauna

Introduction

GERRY ABBOTT

Though we travel the world over to find the beautiful
we must carry it with us or we find it not.
Emerson, *Essays*, xii.

PEOPLE nowadays who 'travel the world over to find the beautiful' do so at least partly in order to satisfy a curiosity about the world around them. While those who do not travel the easy way find that much of the pleasure of a journey is in the travelling itself, those who prefer the tourist flight or air-conditioned coach find most of the pleasure comes after their arrival. Whichever way our preferences lie, it is usually *difference* that constitutes 'the beautiful'—the difference not only in faces and places, but also in behaviour, dress, food, systems of belief, and so on. If we possess anything worth calling 'curiosity', we shall not be content just to look at people and places. We shall want to know something about how things came to be as they are, how these differences arose. While this selection of extracts attempts to cater for as many tastes as possible, I have tried to give it a historical dimension by starting with some of the first recorded encounters between Europeans and Burmese.

Why just 'Europeans'? Unfortunately, travel writing is, or at least has been hitherto, Eurocentric and even largely Anglo-centric. Looking at the literature it is easy to come away with the impression that most of the world was 'discovered' by western Europeans. However, the peoples of Arabia, India, the Malay Archipelago, and Polynesia all produced skilled navigators and venturesome traders. It may be objected that it was the vast distances sailed by the Europeans, with the attendant perils and hardships eliciting acts of great fortitude and courage, which justifies placing their voyages at the forefront of travel literature. But Chinese junks were plying the sea lanes as far as East Africa long before the arrival in the

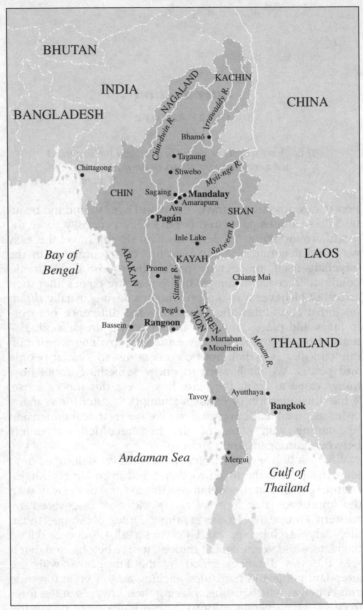

Map of Burma, with places mentioned in the text.

East of the Europeans whose accounts provide us with our opening extracts; and the Polynesians were surely the greatest navigators of their day, having made transoceanic voyages of thousands of miles long before the White explorers dared to do so, but having left us no written records of their feats.

The passages in this book were penned by Western travellers over a span of almost five centuries. The reader may agree neither with Henry Ford that history is bunk nor with the person who first said that history is written by the winners. But a people's history seen entirely through the eyes of foreigners is bound to be somewhat biased. It so happens that Burma suffered defeat at the hands of the British three times, losing territory on each occasion until the whole country was declared part of that British Empire upon which the sun never set. It also happens that many of those who have written about Burma's history were British. Care has been taken to exclude highly prejudiced writings from this book, but some bias may remain and the reader certainly needs to be circumspect when reading other British accounts written in the nineteenth century. Burma has never been well known to Westerners, and the majority will almost certainly know little or nothing about the country's history prior to the Second World War. I have, therefore, concentrated on the accounts of earlier visitors, and most of the works sampled in these pages are either long out of print or distinctly rare.

I have used the word *inroads* in my title in order to highlight the difficulties facing Europeans who over the centuries attempted to penetrate into the interior of the country. The almost constant conflicts between kingdoms were one source of frustration. For example, Hieronimo di Santo Stefano, arriving in Pegú from Italy in 1496, could not go on to the Burmese capital, Ava, because of the violent unrest up-country. The nature of the terrain was another obstacle. Like the Burmese, travellers avoided the rugged ranges and dangerous jungles, preferring to travel by river, but in the days before steam it could take up to two months to push upriver to any one of the successive Burman capitals—Sagaing, Ava, Shwebo, Amarapura, and Mandalay. Extortion and procrastination constituted a further source of difficulty. For instance, when Hieronimo failed to reach Ava he decided to sell his goods in Pegú, but they were so valuable that only the king could afford them, and he kept the merchant waiting eighteen months before paying. The Court convention of keeping visitors waiting was a cultural feature that caused resentment and anger among Western representatives and envoys well into the nineteenth century. During the half-century when Burma was part of the British Empire the country did become open to 'globe-trotters'; but then came the Second World War, followed by internal strife and, finally, a policy of insulation from the outside world that is only now beginning to be relaxed.

Visitors of various kinds—from passing merchants, envoys, tourists and journalists to longer-term residents such as missionaries and expatriate administrators—have left us written records of their time in Burma. Each of these categories is represented in this book. Though it may be objected that resident missionaries and administrators can hardly be called 'travellers' they are nevertheless outsiders, viewing people through the lenses of a very different culture. It is this, coupled with their length of experience in Burma, that makes their accounts valuable to the traveller of today. At the time of writing, unfortunately, tourists still cannot make their own 'inroads' into Burma: they must follow certain limited and pre-specified routes. Nevertheless, it is hoped that the observations and information in the following pages will help modern visitors both to find 'the beautiful' in Burma and to carry it away with them when they leave.

Some Early Travellers

1
Mergui and Pegú

LUDOVICO DI VARTHEMA

Within four years of Vasco da Gama's opening of the sea route from Europe to India, Ludovico di Varthema was on his way eastwards. His outward journey was not around Africa, however, but via Arabia, Yemen, and Persia, and then around India and across the Bay of Bengal to the southern coast of what is now Burma. His round trip spanned the years 1502–8, and he did sail as a passenger round the southern tip of Africa on the return journey.

He was an Italian, probably born in Bologna, perhaps in the 1470s, and he may have been a professional soldier before undertaking his famous travels. On the return voyage he was knighted by the Portuguese for assisting them while they were under siege by Arabs on the Indian coast. That is virtually all that is known about the early part of his life, and his narrative is so spare that we learn little about his character from it. Unlike other travellers of his day, he does seem to have been concerned more with travelling than with arriving, with experience rather than profit; but even by his own account he also appears to have been callous occasionally, even to his friends.

His Itinerario, *the account of his journey, was published in Rome in 1510 to great success. In the next seventy years it ran to many editions not only in Italian and Latin but also in French, Spanish, German, Dutch, and English. Some of his*

*reports are of doubtful accuracy but, if we are to believe him,
he was among other things the first European to go on haj to
Mecca in a pilgrim caravan.*

*In this extract he describes Mergui, a town in the
Tenasserim region (which was actually Siamese territory at
that time), and the Mon kingdom of Pegú to the north, where he
and a Persian companion met King Binnyaran (1481–1526)
before pressing on to Malacca, Sumatra, and the Spice
Islands. The sections on Tenasserim and Pegú contain a mixture of the accurate, the inaccurate, and the tall story. We can
recognize the accuracy of his descriptions of the giant bamboo
of Lower Burma, the hornbill (hardly a bird of prey, though),
and the cock-fighting, for instance. But being ignorant of the
true nature of Buddhism and Hinduism, he apparently con-
fuses the two, calling Buddhist monks or abbots 'Brahmins'
and possibly mistaking the cremation of a monk for an act of
suttee (the burning of a Hindu widow)—though Mergui may
have had a sizeable Hindu community that had retained this
custom. The words 'pagan' and 'the devil' indicate his dis-
missiveness of both religions. The story about the deflowering
of brides is surely just a mariner's yarn. On the other hand, he
is right about the existence of 'Capellan', the ruby-mining district north of Ava, and about the fierce wars between Pegú
and Ava. Also, his account of the audience with Binnyaran,
during which the king gives rubies in exchange for coral, has
the ring of authenticity.*

T HE city of Tarnassari [Mergui] is situated near to the sea:
it is a level place and well watered, and has a good port,
that is, a river on the side towards the north. The king of
the city is a pagan, and is a very powerful lord. He is constantly fighting with the King of Narsinga and the King of
Banghella [Bengal]. He has a hundred armed elephants,
which are larger than any I ever saw. He always maintains
100,000 men for war, part infantry and part cavalry. Their
arms consist of small swords and some sort of shields, some
of which are made of tortoise-shell, and some like those of
Calicut [Kozhikode]; and they have a great quantity of bows,
and lances of cane, and some also of wood. When they go to
war they wear a dress stuffed very full of cotton. The houses
of this city are well surrounded by walls. Its situation is
extremely good, after the manner of Christians, and good

grain and cotton also grow there. Silk is also made there in large quantities. A great deal of brazil-wood is found there, fruits in great abundance, and some which resemble our apples and pears, some oranges, lemons, and citrons, and gourds in great abundance. And here are seen very beautiful gardens, with many delicate things in them.

In this country of Tarnassari there are oxen, cows, sheep, and goats in great quantities, wild hogs, stags, roebucks, wolves, cats which produce the civet, lions, peacocks in great multitudes, falcons, goss-hawks, white parrots, and also other kinds which are of seven very beautiful colours. Here there are hares and partridges, but not like ours. There is also here another kind of bird, one of prey, much larger than an eagle, of the beak of which, that is, of the upper part, they make sword-hilts, which beak is yellow and red, a thing very beautiful to behold. The colour of the said bird is black, red, and some feathers are white. There are produced here hens and cocks, the largest I ever saw, so much so that one of these hens is larger than three of ours. In this country in a few days we had great pleasure from some things which we saw, and especially that every day in the street where the Moorish merchants abide they make some cocks fight, and the owners of these cocks bet as much as a hundred ducats on the one which will fight best. And we saw two fight for five hours continuously, so that at the last both remained dead. Here also is a sort of goat, much larger than ours, and which is much more handsome, and which always has four kids at a birth. Ten and twelve large and good sheep are sold here for a ducat. And there is another kind of sheep, which has horns like a deer: these are larger than ours, and fight most terribly. There are buffalo[e]s here, much more misshapen than ours. There are also great numbers of fish like ours. I saw here, however, a bone of a fish which weighed more than ten *cantari*. With respect to the manner of living of this city, the pagans eat all kinds of flesh excepting that of oxen, and they eat on the ground, without a cloth, in some very beautiful vessels of wood. Their drink is water, sweetened where possible. They sleep high from the ground, in good beds of cotton, and covered with silk or cotton. Then, as to their dress, they go *all' apostolica,** with a quilted cloth of cotton or silk.

---

*Dressed in robes like the Apostles.

Some merchants wear very beautiful shirts of silk or cotton: in general, they do not wear anything on their feet, excepting the Brahmins, who also wear on the head a cap of silk or camelot,* which is two spans long. In the said cap they wear on the top a thing made like a hazel-nut, which is worked all round in gold. They also wear two strings of silk, more than two fingers wide, which they hang round the neck. They wear their ears full of jewels and none on their fingers. The colour of the said race is semi-white, because the air here is cooler than it is in Calicut, and the seasons are the same as with us, and also the harvests.

The king of the said city does not cause his wife's virginity to be taken by the Brahmins as the King of Calicut does, but he causes her to be deflowered by white men, whether Christians or Moors, provided they be not pagans. Which pagans also, before they conduct their wives to their house, find a white man, of whatever country he may be, and take him to their house for this particular purpose, to make him deflower the wife. And this happened to us when we arrived in the said city. We met by chance three or four merchants, who began to speak to my companion in this wise: '*Langalli ni pardesi,*' that is, 'Friend, are you strangers?' He answered: 'Yes.' Said the merchants: '*Ethera nali ni banno,*' that is, 'How many days have you been in this country?' We replied: '*Mun nal gnad banno,*' that is, 'It is four days since we arrived.' Another one of the said merchants said: '*Biti banno gnan pigamanathon ondo,*' that is, 'Come to my house, for we are great friends of strangers'; and we, hearing this, went with him. When we had arrived at his house, he gave us a collation, and then he said to us: 'My friends, *Patanci nale banno gnan penna periti in penna orangono panna panni cortu,*' that is, 'Fifteen days hence I wish to bring home my wife, and one of you shall sleep with her the first night, and shall deflower her for me.' We remained quite ashamed at hearing such a thing. Then our interpreter said: 'Do not be ashamed, for this is the custom of the country.' Then my companion hearing this said: 'Let them not do us any other mischief, for we will satisfy you in this'; but we thought that they were mocking us. The merchant saw that we remained undecided, and said: '*O langal limaranconia ille ocha*

*A soft woollen fabric.

manezar irichenu,' that is, 'Do not be dispirited, for all this country follows this custom.' Finding at last that such was the custom in all this country, as one who was in our company affirmed to us, and said that we need have no fear, my companion said to the merchant that he was content to go through this fatigue. The merchant then said: 'I wish you to remain in my house, and that you, your companions and goods, be lodged here with me until I bring the lady home.' Finally, after refusing, we were obliged to yield to his caresses, and all of us, five in number, together with all our things, were lodged in his house. Fifteen days from that time this merchant brought home his wife, and my companion slept with her the first night. She was a young girl of fifteen years, and he did for the merchant all that he had asked of him. But after the first night, it would have been at the peril of his life if he had returned again, although truly the lady would have desired that the first night had lasted a month. The merchants, having received such a service from some of us, would gladly have retained us four or five months at their own expense, for all kinds of wares cost very little money, and also because they are most liberal and very agreeable men.

All the Brahmins and the king are burnt after death, and at that time a solemn sacrifice is made to the devil. And then they preserve the ashes in certain vases [Martaban jars] made of baked earth, vitrified like glass, which vases have the mouth narrow like a small *scutella* [bowl]. They then bury this vase with the ashes of the burnt body within their houses. When they make the said sacrifice, they make it under some trees, after the manner of Calicut. And for burning the dead body they light a fire of the most odoriferous things that can be found, such as aloes-wood, benzoin, sandal-wood, brazil-wood, storax and amber, incense, and some beautiful branches of coral, which things they place upon the body, and while it is burning all the instruments of the city are sounding. In like manner, fifteen or twenty men, dressed like devils, stand there and make great rejoicing. And his wife is always present, making most exceedingly great lamentations, and no other woman. And this is done at one or two o'clock of the night.

In this city of Tarnassari, when fifteen days have passed after the death of the husband, the wife makes a banquet for all her relations and all those of her husband. And then they go with all the relations to the place where the husband was burnt, and at the same hour of the night. The said woman puts on all her jewels and other objects in gold, all that she possesses. And then her relations cause a hole to be made of the height of a human being, and around the hole they put four or five canes, around which they place a silken cloth, and in the said hole they make a fire of the above-mentioned things, such as were used for the husband. And then the said wife, when the feast is prepared, eats a great deal of betel, and eats so much that she loses her wits, and the instruments of the city are constantly sounding, together with the above-mentioned men clothed like devils, who carry fire in their mouths, as I have already told you in Calicut. They also offer a sacrifice to Deumo [South Indian term, *dêvan*, a godling]. And the said wife goes many times up and down that place, dancing with the other women. And she goes many times to the said men clothed like devils, to entreat and tell them to pray the Deumo that he will be pleased to accept her as his own. And there are always present here a great many women who are her relations. Do not imagine, however, that she is unwilling to do this; she even imagines that she shall be carried forthwith into heaven. And thus running violently of her own free will, she seizes the above-mentioned cloth with her hands, and throws herself into the midst of the fire. And immediately her relations and those most nearly allied to her fall upon her with sticks and with balls of pitch, and this they do only that she may die the sooner. And if the said wife were not to do this, she would be held in like estimation as a public prostitute is among us, and her relations would put her to death. When such an event takes place in this country the king is always present. However, those who undergo such a death are the most noble of the land: all, in general, do not do thus. I have seen in this city of Tarnassari another custom, somewhat less horrible than the before mentioned. There will be a young man who will speak to a lady of love, and will wish to give her to understand that he really is fond of her, and that there is nothing he would not do for her. And, discoursing with her in this wise, he will take a piece of rag well saturated with oil, and will set fire to it, and place it on his arm on the naked flesh, and whilst it is burning he will stand speaking with that lady, not caring about his arm being burnt, in order to show that he loves her, and that for her he is willing to do every great thing.

He who kills another in this country is put to death, the same as in Calicut. With respect to conveying and holding, it is necessary that it should appear by writing or by witnesses. Their writing is on paper like ours, not on the leaves of a tree like that of Calicut. And then they go to a governor of the city, who administers justice for them summarily. However, when any foreign merchant dies who has no wife or children, he cannot leave his property to whomsoever he pleases, because the king wills to be his heir. (And in this country [that is, the natives, commencing from the king] after his death his son remains king.) And when any Moorish merchant dies, very great expense is incurred in odoriferous substances to preserve the body, which they put into wooden boxes and then bury it, placing the head towards the city of Mecca, which comes to be towards the north. If the deceased have children, they are his heirs.

These people make use of very large ships and of various kinds, some of which are made flat bottomed, because such can enter into places where there is not much water. Another kind are made with prows before and behind, and they carry two helms and two masts, and are uncovered. There is also another kind of large ship which is called *giunchi* [junks], and each of these is of the tonnage of one thousand butts, on which they carry some little vessels to a city called Melacha [Malacca], and from thence they go with these little vessels for small spices to a place which you shall know when the proper time comes.

(At this point, having sold some merchandise in Mergui, Ludovico and his Persian friend sailed up to Bengal, where they came across a group of Nestorian Christians. Ludovico's companion engaged them in conversation.)

After a great deal of conversation with these men, my companion at last showed them his merchandise, amongst which there were certain beautiful branches of large coral. When they had seen these branches they said to us, that if we would go to a city where they would conduct us, that they were prepared to secure for us as much as 10,000 ducats for them, or as many rubies as in Turkey would be worth 100,000.

My companion replied that he was well pleased, and that they should depart immediately thence. The Christians said: 'In two days' time from this a ship will sail which goes towards Pego, and we have to go with it; if you are willing to come we will go together.' Hearing this we set ourselves in order, and embarked with the said Christians and with some other Persian merchants. And as we had been informed in this city that these Christians were most faithful, we formed a very great friendship with them. But before our departure from Banghella, we sold all the rest of the merchandise, with the exception of the corals, the saffron, and two pieces of rose-coloured cloth of Florence. We left this city, which I believe is the best in the world, that is, for living in. In which city the kind of stuffs you have heard of before are not woven by women, but the men weave them. We departed thence with the said Christians, and went towards a city which is called Pego, distant from Banghella about a thousand miles. On which voyage we passed a gulf [of Martaban] towards the south, and so arrived at the city of Pego.

* * *

The city of Pego is on the mainland, and is near to the sea. On the left hand of this, that is, towards the east, there is a very beautiful river, by which many ships go and come. The king of this city is a pagan. Their faith, customs, manner of living and dress, are after the manner of Tarnassari; but with respect to their colour, they are somewhat more white. And here, also, the air is somewhat more cold. Their seasons are like ours. This city is walled, and has good houses and palaces built of stone, with lime. The king is extremely powerful in men, both foot and horse, and has with him more than a thousand Christians of the country which has been above mentioned to you. And he gives to each, for pay, six golden *pardai* [ducats] per month and his expenses. In this country there is a great abundance of grain, of flesh of every kind, and of fruits of the same as at Calicut. These people have not many elephants, but they possess great numbers of all other animals; they also have all the kinds of birds which are found at Calicut. But there are here the most beautiful and the best parrots I had ever seen. Timber grows here in great quantities, long, and I think the thickest that can possibly be found. In like manner I do not know if there can be found in the world such thick canes as I found here, of which I saw some which were really as thick as a barrel. Civet-cats are found in this country in great numbers, three or four of which are sold for a ducat. The sole merchandise of these people is jewels, that is, rubies, which come from another city called Capellan [ruby mines district in Burma], which is distant from this thirty days' journey; not that I have seen it, but by what I have heard from merchants. You must know that in the said city, a large pearl and diamond are worth more here than with us, and also an emerald. When we arrived in this country, the king was fifteen days' journey distant, fighting with another who was called King of Ava [Burma]. Seeing this, we determined to go and find the king where he was, in order to give him these corals. And so we departed thence in a ship made all of one piece, and more than fifteen or sixteen paces long. The oars of this vessel were made of cane. Understand well in what manner: where the oar takes the water it was cloven, and they insert a flat piece of board fastened by cords, so that the said vessel went with more power than a brigantine. The mast of it was a cane as thick as a barrel where they put in the provisions. In three days we arrived at a village where we found certain merchants, who had not been able to enter into the said city of Ava on account of the war. Hearing this, we returned with them to Pego, and five days afterwards the king returned to the said city, who had gained a very great victory over his enemy. On the second day after the return of the king, our Christian companions took us to speak with him.

Do not imagine that the King of Pego enjoys as great a reputation as the King of Calicut, although he is so humane and domestic that an infant might speak to him, and he wears more rubies on him than the value of a very large city, and he wears them on all his toes. And on his legs he wears certain great rings of gold, all full of the most beautiful rubies; also his arms and his fingers all full. His ears hang down half a palm, through the great weight of the many jewels he wears there, so that seeing the person of the king by a light at night, he shines so much that he appears to be a sun. The said Christians spoke with him, and told him of our merchandise.

The king replied that we should return to him the day after the next, because on the next day he had to sacrifice to the devil for the victory which he had gained. When the time mentioned was past, the king, as soon as he had eaten, sent for he said Christians, and for my companion, in order that he might carry to him his merchandise. When the king saw such beautiful corals he was quite astonished and greatly pleased; for, in truth, among the other corals there were two branches, the like of which had never before entered India. This king asked what people we were. The Christians answered: 'Sir, these are Persians.' Said the king to the interpreter: 'Ask them if they are willing to sell these things.' My companions answered that the articles were at the service of his highness. Then the king began to say that he had been at war with the King of Ava for two years, and on that account he had no money; but that if we were willing to barter for so many rubies, he would amply satisfy us. We caused him to be told by these Christians that we desired nothing further from him than his friendship,—that he should take the commodities and do whatever he pleased. The Christians repeated to him what my companion had charged them to say, by telling the king that he might take the corals without money or jewels. He hearing this liberality answered: 'I know that the Persians are very liberal, but I never saw one so liberal as this man'; and he swore by God and by the devil that he would see which would be the more liberal, he or a Persian. And then he desired one of his confidential servants to bring him a certain little box which was two palms in length, worked all round in gold, and was full of rubies, within and without. And when he had opened it, there were six separate divisions, all full of different rubies; and he placed it before us, telling us we should take what we wished. My companion answered: 'O, sir, you show me so much kindness, that by the faith which I bear to Mahomet I make you a present of all these things. And know, sir, that I do not travel about the world to collect property, but only to see different people and different customs.' The king answered: 'I cannot conquer you in liberality, but take this which I give you.' And so he took a good handful of rubies from each of the divisions of the said casket, and gave them to him. These rubies might be about two hundred, and in giving them he said: 'Take these for the liberality you have exercised towards me.' And in like manner he gave to the said Christians two rubies each, which were estimated at a thousand ducats, and those of my companions were estimated at about one hundred thousand ducats. Wherefore by this he may be considered to be the most liberal king in the world, and every year he has an income of about one million in gold. And this because in his country there is found much *lacca* [lac], a good deal of sandal-wood, very much brazil-wood, cotton and silk in great quantities, and he gives all his income to his soldiers. The people in this country are very sensual. After some days, the said Christians took leave for themselves and for us. The king ordered a room to be given to us, furnished with all that was requisite for so long as we wished to remain there; and so it was done. We remained in the said room five days. At this time there arrived news that the King of Ava was coming with a great army to make war upon him, on hearing which, this one [of Pego] went to meet him half way with a great many men, horse and foot. The next day we saw two women burnt alive voluntarily, in the manner as I have described it in Tarnassari.

Itinerario de Ludovico de Varthema Bolognese, etc. [The Itinerary of Ludovico di Varthema of Bologna], translated from the original Italian by John Winter Jones in 1863 for the Hakluyt Society, The Argonaut Press, London, 1928, pp. 74–83.

2
The Fair City of Pegú

CESARE DI FEDRICI (CAESAR FREDERICKE)

Cesare di Fedrici was born in Venice into a family that had a long trading tradition. Taking part in a journey to the Orient in 1562, he went to Aleppo, joined an Armenian caravan, proceeded to the Persian Gulf and then sailed to India with the intention of reaching the East Indies. From Ceylon, he sailed first to Sumatra and Malacca and then north to Pegú. In 1569 he decided to return to Italy but through a series of misfortunes lost almost all the profits he had acquired. Undismayed he took up trading again, returning to Pegú and there making good his losses. Returning to Venice via Aleppo, Jerusalem, and Tripoli, he reached home safely in November 1581.

In this extract, Fedrici describes for the benefit of future visitors the strong tidal bore ('Macareo') on the river Sittang and how the boatmen make use of it. Pegú was traditional in that it comprised a palace within a walled city surrounded by spacious suburbs. Fedrici, noting the various types of building including the merchants' godowns, is impressed by the town planning of the inner city and the magnificence of the palace. Details about the capture, training, and use of elephants in warfare lead on to observations on the nature of King Bayinnaung's huge army.

FROM Martavan I departed to goe to the chiefest Citie in the kingdome of Pegu, which is also called after the name of the kingdome, which voyage is made by sea in three or foure daies; they may goe also by lande, but it is better for him that hath marchandize to goe by sea and lesser charge. And in this voyage you shall have a Macareo, which is one of the most marveilous things in the world that nature hath wrought, and I never saw any thing so hard to be beleeved as this, to wit, the great increasing & diminishing of the water there at one push or instant, and the horrible earthquake and great noyse that the said Macareo maketh where it commeth. We departed from Martavan in barkes, which are like to our Pylot boates, with the increase of the water, and they goe as swift as an arrowe out of a bow, so long as the tide runneth with them, and when the water is at the highest, then they drawe themselves out of the Chanell towardes some banke, and there they come to anker, and when the water is diminished, then they rest on dry land: and when the barkes rest dry, they are as high from the bottome of the Chanell, as any house top is high from the ground. They let their barkes lie so high for this respect, that if there should any shippe rest or ride in the Chanell, with such force commeth in the water, that it would overthrowe shippe or barke: yet for all this, that the barkes be so farre out of the Channell, and though the water hath lost her greatest strength and furie before it come so high, yet they make fast their prowe to the streme, and oftentimes it maketh them very fearefull, and if the anker did not holde her prow up by strength, shee would be over-throwen and lost with men and goods. When the water beginneth to increase, it maketh such a noyse and so great that you would thinke it an earthquake, and presently at the first it maketh three waves. So that the first washeth over the barke, from stemme to sterne, the second is not so furious as the first, and the thirde rayseth the Anker, and then for the space of sixe houres while the water encreaseth, they rowe with such swiftnesse that you would thinke they did fly: in these tydes there must be lost no jot of time, for if you arrive not at the stagions before the tyde be spent, you must turne backe from whence you came. For there is no staying at any place, but at these stagions, and there is more daunger at one of these places then at another, as they be higher and lower one then another. When as you returne from Pegu to Martavan, they goe but halfe the tide at a time, because they will lay their barkes up aloft on the bankes, for the reason aforesayd. I could never gather any reason of the noyse that this water maketh in the increase of the tide, and in deminishing of the water. There is another Macareo in Cambaya,* but that is nothing in comparison of this.

By the helpe of God we came safe to Pegu, which are two cities, the olde and the newe, in the olde citie are the Marchant strangers, and marchantes of the Countrey, for there are the greatest doings and the greatest trade. This citie is not very great, but it hath very great suburbes. Their houses be made with canes, and covered with leaves, or with strawe, but the marchants have all one house or Magason, which house they call Godon which is made of brickes, and there they put all their goods of any valure, to save them from the often mischances that there happen to houses made of such stuffe. In the new citie is the pallace of the king, and his abiding place with all his barons and nobles, and other gentlemen; and in the time that I was there, they finished the building of the new citie: it is a great citie, very plaine and flat, and foure square, walled round about and with ditches that compasse the wals about with water, in which diches are many crocodils, it hath no drawe bridges, yet it hath twentie gates, five for every square on the walles, there are many places made for centinels to watch, made of wood and covered or guilt with gold, the streetes thereof are the fayrest

*Previously one of the states in Gujarat.

that I have seene, they are as streight as a line from one gate
to another, and standing at the one gate you may discover to
the other, and they are as broad as 10 or 12 men may ride a
breast in them: and those streetes that be thwart are faire and
large, these streetes, both on the one side and on the other,
are planted at the doores of the houses, with nut trees of
India, which make a very commodious shadowe, the houses
be made of wood and covered with a kind of tiles in forme of
cups, very necessary for their use, the kings palace is in the
middle of the citie, made in forme of a walled castle, with
ditches full of water round about it, the lodgings within are
made of wood all over gilded, with fine pinacles, and very
costly worke, covered with plates of golde.

Truely it may be a kings house: within the gate there is a
faire large court, from the one side to the other, wherein
there are made places for the strongest and stoutest Eliphants
appointed for the service of the kings person, and amongst
all other Eliphants, he hath foure that be white, a thing so
rare that a man shall hardly finde another king that hath any
such, and if this king knowe any other that hath white
Eliphantes, he sendeth for them as for a gift. The time that I
was there, there were two brought out of a farre Countrey,
and that cost me something the sight of them, for they com-
maund the marchants to goe to see them, and then they must
give somewhat to the men that bring them: the brokers of the
marchants give for every man halfe a duckat, which they call
a Tansa, which amounteth to a great summe, for the number
of merchants that are in that citie; and when they have payde
the aforesayde Tansa, they make chuse whether they will see
them at that time or no, because that when they are in the
kings stall, every man may see them that will: but at that time
they must goe and see them, for it is the kings pleasure it
should be so. This King amongst all other his titles, is called
the King of the white Eliphants, and it is reported that if this
king knewe any other king that had any of these white
Eliphantes, and would not send them unto him, that he
would hazard his whole kingdome to conquer them, he
esteemeth these white Eliphants very deerely, and they are
had in great regard, and kept with very meete service, every
one of them is in a house, all guilded over, and they have
their meate given them in vessels of silver and golde, there is

14

one blacke Eliphant the greatest that hath bene seene, and he is kept according to his bignesse, he is nine cubites high, which is a marveilous thing.

It is reported that this king hath foure thousand Eliphants of warre, and all have their teeth, and they use to put on their two uppermost teeth sharpe pikes of yron, and make them fast with rings, because these beastes fight, and make battell with their teeth; hee hath also very many yong Eliphants that have not their teeth sprowted foorth: also this king hath a brave devise in hunting to take these Eliphants when hee will, two miles from the Citie. He hath builded a faire pallace all guilded, and within it a faire Court, and within it and rounde about there are made an infinite number of places for men to stande to see this hunting: neere unto this Pallace is a mighty great wood, through the which the hunts-men of the king ride continually on the backs of the feminine Eliphants, teaching them in this businesse. Every hunter carieth out with him five or sixe of these feminines, and they say that they anoynt the secret place with a certaine composition that they have, that when the wilde Eliphant doeth smell thereunto, they followe the feminines and cannot leave them: when the hunts-men have made provision, & the Eliphant is so entangled, they guide the feminines towards the Pallace which is called Tambell, and this Pallace hath a doore which doth open and shut with engines, before which doore there is a long streigth way with trees on both the sides, which covereth the way in such wise as it is like darkenesse in a corner: the wilde Eliphant when he commeth to this way, thinketh that he is in the woods. At end of this darke way there is a great field, when the hunters have gotten this praye, when they first come to this field, they send presently to give knowledge thereof to the Citie, and with all speed there go out fiftie or sixtie men on horsebacke, and doe beset the fielde rounde about: in the great fielde then the females which are taught in this businesse goe directly to the mouth of the darke way, and when as the wilde Eliphant is entred in there, the hunters shoute and make a great noyse, asmuch as is possible, to make the wilde Eliphant enter in at the gate of that Pallace, which is then open, and assoone as hee is in, the gate is shut without any noyse, and so the hunters with the female Eliphants and the wilde one are all in the Court

together, and then within a small time the females withdraw
themselves away one by one out of the Court, leaving the
wilde Eliphant alone: and when he perceiveth that he is left
alone, he is so madde that for two or three houres to see him,
it is the greatest pleasure in the world: he weepeth, hee
flingeth, hee runneth, he justleth, hee thrusteth under the
places where the people stand to see him, thinking to kil
some of them, but the posts and timber is so strong and great,
that hee cannot hurt any body, yet hee oftentimes breaketh
his teeth in the grates; at length when hee is weary and hath
laboured his body that hee is all wet with sweat, then he
plucketh in his truncke into his mouth, and then hee
throweth out so much water out of his belly, that he sprinck-
leth it over the heades of the lookers on, to the uttermost of
them, although it bee very high: and then when they see him
very weary, there goe certaine officers into the Court with
long sharpe canes in their hands, and prick him that they
make him to goe into one of the houses that is made alongst
the Court for the same purpose: as there are many which are
made long and narrow, that when the Eliphant is in, he cannot turne himself to go backe againe. And it is requisite that
these men should be very wary and swift, for although their
canes be long, yet the Eliphant would kill them if they were
not swift to save themselves: at length when they have gotten
him into one of those houses, they stand over him in a loft
and get ropes under his belly and about his necke, and about
his legges, and binde him fast, and so let him stand foure or
five dayes, and give him neither meate nor drinke. At the
ende of these foure or five dayes, they unloose him and put
one of the females unto him, and give them meate and
drinke, and in eight dayes he is become tame. In my judgment there is not a beast so intellective as are these Eliphants,
nor of more understanding in al the world: for he wil do all
things that his keeper saith, so that he lacketh nothing but
humaine speech.

It is reported that the greatest strength that the king of
Pegu hath is in these Eliphants, for when they goe to battell,
they set on their backes a Castle of wood bound thereto, with
bands under their bellies: and in every Castle foure men very
commodiously set to fight with hargubushes,[*] with bowes

---

[*]Arquebus: a portable long-barrelled gun.

and arrowes, with darts and pikes, and other launcing weapons: and they say that the skinne of this Eliphant is so hard, that an harquebusse will not pierce it, unlesse it bee in the eye, temples, or some other tender place of his body. And besides this, they are of great strength, and have a very excellent order in their battel, as I have seene at their feastes which they make in the yeere, in which feastes the king maketh triumphes, which is a rare thing and worthy memorie, that in so barbarous a people there should be such goodly orders as they have in their armies, which be distinct in squares of Eliphants, of horsemen, of harquebushers and pikemen, that truly the number of them are infinite: but their armour and weapons are very nought and weake as well the one as the other: they have very bad pikes, their swords are worse made, like long knives without points, his harquebushes are most excellent, and alway in his warres he hath eightie thousand harquebushes, and the number of them encreaseth dayly. Because the king wil have them shoote every day at the Plancke, and so by continuall exercise they become most excellent shot: also hee hath great Ordinance made of very good mettall; to conclude there is not a King on the earth that hath more power or strength then this king of Pegu, because hee hath twentie and sixe crowned kings at his commaunde. He can make in his Campe a million and an halfe of men of warre in the fielde against his enemies. The state of his kingdome and maintenance of his army, is a thing incredible to consider, & the victuals that should maintaine such a number of people in the warres: but he that knoweth the nature and qualitie of that people, will easily beleeve it. I have seene with mine eyes, that those people and souldiers have eaten of all sorts of wild beasts that are on the earth, whether it bee very filthie or otherwise all serveth for their mouthes: yea, I have seene them eate Scorpions and Serpents, also they feed of all kinde of herbes and grasse. So that if such a great armie want not water and salt, they wil maintaine themselves a long time in a bush with rootes, flowers and leaves of trees, they cary rice with them for their voyage, & that serveth them in stead of comfits, it is so daintie unto them. This king of Pegu hath not any army or power by sea, but in the land, for people, dominions, golde and silver, he farre exceeds the power of the great Turke in treasure and strength. This king hath divers Magasons ful of treasure, as gold, & silver, and every day he encreaseth it more and more, and it is never diminished. Also hee is Lord of the Mines of Rubies, Safires & Spinels.

Neere unto his royal pallace there is an inestimable treasure whereof hee maketh no accompt, for that it standeth in such a place that every one may see it, and the place where this treasure is, is a great Court walled round about with walls of stone, with two gates which stand open every day. And within this place or Court are foure gilded houses covered with lead, & in every one of these are certaine heathenish idoles of a very great valure. In the first house there is a stature of the image of a man of gold very great, & on his head a crowne of gold beset with most rare Rubies and Safires, and round about him are 4. litle children of gold. In the second house there is the stature of a man of silver, that is set as it were sitting on heapes of money: whose stature in height, as hee sitteth, is so high, that his highnesse exceedes the height of any one roofe of an house; I measured his feete, and found that they were as long as all my body was in height, with a crowne on his head like to the first. And in the thirde house, there is a stature of brasse of the same bignesse, with a like crowne on his head. In the 4. and last house there is a stature of a man as big as the other, which is made of Gansa, which is the metall they make their money of, & this metall is made of copper & leade mingled together. This stature also hath a crowne on his head like the first: this treasure being of such a value as it is, standeth in an open place that every man at this pleasure may go & see it: for the keepers therof never forbid any man the sight thereof.

Richard Hakluyt, *The Principal Navigations, Voyages, Traffiques, & Discoveries of the English Nation*, J. M. Dent, London, 1927, Vol. III, pp. 243–50.

3
Coral, Yes; Republicanism, No!

GASPARO BALBI

Born in the middle of the sixteenth century, Gasparo Balbi was a Venetian jeweller and merchant. For reasons of trade he set out for the East Indies, where he stayed for nine years (1579–88). On his return, he published a detailed description of the countries he had visited, Viaggio delle Indie Orientali, *etc. (Venice, 1590).*

He started out from Aleppo with a caravan of mules and camels which followed the left bank of the Euphrates, reached Baghdad and then continued by boat down the Tigris. He then went by land to Hormuz, where he naturally showed great interest in the local pearl-fishing industry. Embarking on a ship bound for Goa, he then took other ships that sailed round India and across the Bay of Bengal to Negrais, Cosmin, and Dalla[1] (which was later to become a suburb of Rangoon). He arrived at Mecao, a Pegûan port, on 6 November 1583 and so arrived in the city of Pegû.

Like other European visitors of the time, Balbi was impressed by the scale and grandeur of Pegû, comparing its roads and buildings favourably with those of Venice. In this passage we also learn a great deal about the continuing strife between Mon and Burman (the kingdom of Pegû now being part of the Burman empire) and between factions in Pegû and others in Ava. However, the most entertaining episode is the audience with King Nandabayin, who splutters with uncontrollable laughter at the very idea of a republic.

THE second of November we came to the Citie of Dala, where besides other things are ten large roomes full of Elephants: which are kept there by divers servants of the King of Pegu. The day following we came to the faire Citie of Dogon, it is finely seated, and fronted towards the South-west, and where they land are twenty long steps, as from the Pillar of Saint Marke to the Straw-bridge, the matter of them is strong and great pieces of timber, and there are great currents of water both at ebbe and floud, because it is a place neere

---

[1]All three places are in the Irrawaddy delta.

19

Maccareo, which entreth and goeth out of the mouth of Sirian, which is a Sea-port: and alwaies when the water encreaseth, they goe upon the Staires: and when it is ebbe, it discovers all about, and makes it a great way drie land. On both sides the River, at the end of the banke, or at the staires, is a woodden Tigre, very great, and painted after the naturall colour of a Tigre; and there are two others in the midst of the staires, so farre one from another, that they seeme to share the staires equally. They stand with open mouth, shewing their teeth and tongue, with their clawes lifted up and stretched forth, prepared to assaile him that lookes on them. Concerning these they told mee a foolish beliefe which they have, that they stand there to guard, for if any should be so bold to displease the Pagod,* those Tigers should defend him, for he would give them life.

After we were landed we began to goe on the right hand in a large street about fifty paces broad, in which wee saw woodden houses gilded, and adorned with delicate gardens after their custome, wherein their Talapois, which are their Friers, dwell, and looke to the Pagod, or Varella of Dogon. The left side is furnished with Portals and Shops, very like the new Procuratia at Venice: and by this street they goe towards the Varella for the space of a good mile straight forwards, either under painthouses, or in the open street, which is free to walke in. When we came at the Varella, we found a paire of staires of ninety steps, as long in my judgement at the chanell of the Rialto at Venice. At the foot of the first staire are two Tigres, one at the right hand, and the other at the left, these are of stone, and stand in the same fashion that they doe on the shoare-side. The staires are divided into three, the first is forty steps, the second thirty, and the third twenty, and at the top of each of them is a plaine spacious place. On the last step are Angels of stone, each with three Crowns one upon the other; but so, that that which is undermost is the greatest, and that which is next lesser then that, yet greater then the uppermost, which is the least. They have the right hand lifted up, ready to give the benediction, with two fingers stretched out. The other hand of the one is layd upon the head of a Childe, and of the other upon the head of an Ape; those Statues are all of stone. At the right hand is a

*Image in a pagoda.

Varella gilded in a round forme, made of stone, and as much in compasse as the streete before the Venetian Palace, if it were round: and the height may equall Saint Markes Belltower, not the top of it, but the little Pinnaces. At the left hand is a faire Hall carved and gilded within and without. And this is the place of devotion, whither the people goe to heare the Talapois preach: the streete is greater then Saint Markes, at the least larger. And this is a place of great devotion amongst them, and yeerely multitudes of people come by Sea and by Land. And when they celebrate a solemne Feast, the King in person goeth before them all, and with him the Queene, the Prince, and his other sonnes, with a great traine of Nobles and others, who goe to get a pardon. And on this day there is a great Mart where are all sorts of merchandises which are current in those Countries, which they frequent in great multitudes, which come thither not so much for devotion as traffique, and wee may freely goe thither if wee will. Round about this and upon another Varella were Apes running up and downe, the great and small staires also are full of them. After wee had seene this, at the foot of the first staire when I went downe I turned my face to the left side, and with some Portugals which were in my companie found in a faire Hall a very large Bell, which we measured, and found to be seven paces and three hand breadths, and it is full of Letters from the top to the bottome, and so neere together that one toucheth the other, they are very well and neatly made: but there was no Nation that could understand them, no not the men of Pegu, and they remember not whence, nor how it came thither.

At the evening about one of the clocke at night wee went from this place, and about three we came among some Fishers Nets, which almost shipwrackt us, as they did one of our companie, who being entangled in them went under them, and so was sunke, and this was through the negligence of some Fishers, who when they lay forth such Nets, ought to have a barke with a light or fire all the night to give warning to Saylers, that they come not on that side. But praised be God, we freed our selves in the best manner we could; that day after the Sunne was up wee arrived over against the mouth of Sirian, which is on the South side, where with some difficulty we landed, for the violence of the water drew us into Maccareo. Sirian was an Imperiall Citie, where an

Emperour resided, the Walls and Bulwarkes are ruined, by which one may see that it hath beene very strong, and almost impregnable: but Anno 1567, it was subdued by the King of Pegu, who to take it sent a million and an halfe of men; and after he had besieged it two yeeres with the losse of halfe a million of his men, he tooke it by treason. Which when the Emperour understood he poisoned himselfe, and the rest of his familie were carried away prisoners upon Elephants, who returned in great numbers laden with Gold, Jewels, and other precious things: departing from Sirian we followed our Voyage, seeing many inhabited Townes called by divers names.

Finally we came to a place called Meccao, where we disimbarqued to goe by land to Pegu, being about twelve miles. Over against Meccao are certaine habitations where the King of Pegu was then for his disport, who causeth there beautifull gilded vessels to be made, beseeming such a King. From Cosmi* to Meccao we were eleven dayes in our Voyage, sayling alwaies by Rivers of fresh water, which ebbe and flowe, and on both sides there are houses and habitations made upon piles planted in the earth, so that the Tigres cannot molest the Inhabitants, they goe up to them upon Ladders made of light wood, which they draw up. Some of the Inhabitants keepe Bufalos in their houses; for they say, that the Tigres will not come neere the places where these beasts are, by reason of their ill favour: they are in these Countries of unmeasurable greatnesse and thicknesse. For the Voyage of Saint Thomas to Pegu, it is good to carrie Bracelets, which they make of glasse in Saint Thomas, for with these better then with money you may buy victuals, and there in the Citie where you buy them they are sold at a lowe price, but if they are enamelled they sell them deare. The number of Pagods or Varellas which wee saw in this Voyage I write not, for they are innumerable, and in divers shapes; but I onely say, that on the shoare where wee landed to goe to Dogon, which is made of large strong timbers, are two Statues, which resemble two Boyes from the head downewards, their faces after the likenesse of Devils with two wings. There are some Varellas gilded, and set in faire places, to which they come and offer Gold and other mer-

*A port near to, or identical with, Bassein.

chandise in great quantitie, to maintayne their gilding, for the raine spoiles it. About these Varellas are found tyed many Apes of that kinde which resemble Mountain-cats, which wee call Monkeyes; they keepe them very carefully, holding them to be creatures beloved of God, because they have their hands and feet like humane creatures; and therefore their Woods are full of them, for they never take any, except for their Varellas and Statues. ...

After that I was provided of a good Druggerman [interpreter] and Interpreter, the noise of Trumpets was heard, which signified wee should see the King and have audience of him, wee entred within the second gate, whereby they goe into the Court-yard, and the Interpreter and I cast our selves upon our knees on the ground, and with our hands elevated in humble wise, and making a shew three times before we rose of kissing the ground; and three other times we did thus before wee came neere to the place where the King sate with his Semini [council], prostrate on the earth (for no Christian, how neere soever to the King, nor Moorish Captaines, except of this Semini, come in that place so neere the King).

I heard all his Speach, but understood it not: I gave the Emeralds to the Interpreter, who lifted them up over his head, and againe made reverence, of them called Rombee: and as soone as the King saw it, a Nagiran, that is to say, the Lord of his words, or Interpreter, making the like Rombee, tooke the Emeralds, and gave them into the Kings hand, and then went out of his presence, who a little while after called him, commanding him as Lord of his words, that he should aske mee what Countriman I was, how many yeeres it was since I left my Countrie, and what was my name, and from what place I had brought those Emeralds, and I with the accustomed Rombee (for at every word they speake they must make such an obeisance) answered that my name was Gaspar Balbi, that I had beene in my Voyage foure yeeres, and that I brought the Emeralds from Venice to give his Majestie, the fame of whose bountie, courtesie and greatnesse was spread over the world, and especially in our parts, to be the greatest King in the world; all this was written in their letters, and read by the Lord of his words to his Majestie. He commanded to aske me in what parts Venice was seated, and what King governed it; and I told him that it was in the Kingdome of Italie, and that it was a Republike or free State, not governed by any King. When the King heard this, he greatly wondered; so that he began to laugh so exceedingly, that hee was overcome of the cough, which made him that hee could hardly speake to his Great men. Lastly, hee demanded, if that King which last tooke Portugall were as great, and if Venice were warlike. To which I answered, that King Philip that had taken Portugall was the potentest King among the Christians, and that the Venetians were in league with him, but had no feare of any, yet sought friendship with all. And then I reported the overthrow which the Venetians gave the Emperour of the Turkes. Ametbi,* who at that time was at Mecca, confirmed this to be true of the defeat of the Turkish Armado. Then he gave me a Cup of gold, and five pieces of China Damaske of divers colours, and bad them tell me, that he gave me these, and did not so pay me for my Emeralds, for which I should be contented of his publike Terreca, which are his Treasurers. This was holden for novelty with them that saw it, for it was not the Kings custome to present any thing to any. Moreover, the King ordered that for the wares which I had brought, the Decacini† should not make me pay any Taxe or Custome.

* * *

The King of Avva, being subject to the King of Pegu, and Brother to his Father, had a purpose to make himselfe Master of his Nephewes Kingdome, and to make himselfe King, because he was the ancienter of the Royall branch; therefore at the Inauguration of the present King, he would not come to doe him homage as he ought, and as other Kings and Dukes his subjects did; he did not onely absent himselfe, but also kept backe the Present of Jewels which he was wont to give, and restrained also the trade from his Countrie to Pegu, not suffering any Merchant to passe, but sought to conspire with his chiefe Courtiers against the King of Pegu, who as a good Nephew dissembled it, the said King of Avva being recommended to him from his Father before his death. Finally, the King of Pegu, willing to cleare himselfe of the ill will con-

*A companion of Balbi.
†Officers of the King.

24

ceived against the King of Avva his Uncle, sent one of his houshold servants to him, who was slaine by the King of Avva because of the warre, trusting that the Grandes of the Kingdome of Pegu would favour his part, and revolt from their naturall Lord, to set Him in his place.

Therefore the King of Pegu proclaimed warre against Avva, and called to him his Bagnia* and Semini, and gave order to his Decagini that as they came he should put them in prison; which being performed by the Decagini, the King ordained that the morning following they should make an eminent and spacious Scaffold, and cause all the Grandes to come upon it, and then set fire to it, and burne them all alive. But to shew that he did this with justice, he sent another mandate, that he should doe nothing till he had an Olla or Letter written with his hand in letters of gold, and in the meane time he commanded him to retaine all the prisoners of the Grandes families unto the women great with child, and those which were in their swadling clothes, and so he brought them all together upon the said Scaffold; and the King sent the Letter that he should burne them, and the Decagini performed it, and burned them all, so that there was heard nothing but weepings, shrikings, cryings, and sobbings: for there were foure thousand in this number which were so burned great and small, for which execution were publike Guards placed by the King, and all of the old and new Citie were forced to assist them; I also went thither, and saw it with great compassion and griefe, that little children without any fault should suffer such martyrdome, and among others there was one of his chiefe Secretaries, who was last put in to be burned, yet was freed by the Kings order; but his legge was begunne to be burnt, so that he was lame.

And after followed this order from his Majestie, that those other Captaines which remained should come to him, and he said to them, You have seene what we have done to Traitors, but be faithfull, and set in order all the people as you can, for I am a Captaine that warre justly, going without any feare of not overcoming: and so on a sudden, and within few dayes, he gathered together out of both the Cities more then three hundred thousand persons, and encamped without the Citie. Ten dayes after that I saw the King upon an Elephant all over

*Commercial advisers.

25

covered with Gold and Jewels, goe to the warre with great courage, with a Sword after our custome sent him by the Vice-roy of Goa, the hilt whereof was gilded: the said Vice-roy was called Don Luis di Zuida: he left the white Elephants in the Citie.

After that, the King fell sicke of the small poxe, but when he was well, he encountred with the King of Avva, and they two fought body to body without any hinderance of the Armies; who being equally matched, as their use is, combated bravely, as did also the Guard of this King with that of the other, and after the Kings had fought a while hand to hand, first with Harquebusses,* then with Darts, and lastly with the Sword, the Elephant of the King of Pegu brake his right tooth with charging that of Avva, in which furie he so coupled with the other Elephant, that the King of Pegu killed the King of Avva, and he remained lightly wounded on one arme, and in the meane while his Elephant fell dead under him, and the King of Pegu mounted upon that of Avva. But when the Armie of Avva saw their King dead, they ceased to fight, and demanded pardon of the King of Pegu, who with a joyfull countenance praising their valour pardoned them all, and making a muster, found that of three hundred thousand which hee brought from Pegu, there died in that battell more then 200000. and little lesse of those of Avva. After this victorie he ordered that Avva should be destroyed, and all the people made prisoners, among which was the Queene taken prisoner, who was sister of the King of Pegu, and confined, during her life in a large house with many royall attendants; but shee agreed never to goe forth. The rest of the Citizens were banished to live in Woods among Tigres, and other creatures, and this was because the King of Pegu could not finde the great treasure which the King of Avva had. This warre was in the beginning of the moneth of Aprill, when in that Countrie fall great store of raines, causing great cold in a place called Meccao; and the fourteenth day of July, in sixe dayes he returned unexpectedly to Pegu, not finding the Citie with those guards which his Majestie had appointed, but at the request of the Prince his sonne he did no other justice.

At this his arrivall he understood, that when hee was at the warre, there was arrived under excuse to come to his favour

---

*Arquebus: a portable long-barrelled gun.

in the old Citie of Pegu the sonne of the Emperour of Silon (or Siam) with fifty Elephants of warre, and eight hundred Horses, besides Harquebussers, Pikemen, and Souldiers with swords, who were sent towards Avva by the great Brama [the King]; but in stead of taking his way towards that coast he returned to Silon.

In the mean time was brought into Pegu the Elephant of the King of Avva, which was so much discontented, that all the day long he mourned, I my selfe saw him lament, and that hee would eate but very little; and this I saw in the lodging where the King of Pegu was wont to keepe his, where continually were two Semini, that prayed him to eate, and mourne no longer, but be merry, for he was come to serve a King greater then his own. Notwithstanding the said Elephant would not cease from teares, and alwaies in token of sorrow held down his trunk: and thus he continued the space of 15. dayes, and then he began to eate, to the Kings great content.

With the teeth of the Kings Elephant which died in battell by command from his Majestie were made certaine Pagods or Statues, which were layd up to bee kept among the Pagods of gold and silver. After the King made five other of Gonze,* which was a marvellous thing to see, for sitting crosse-legged, they were as high as a strong man could fling a stone, and they were ingraved fairely and curiously: one toe of the foot was greater than a man, and the said Pagods were set in publike before the Palace, and bespangled with gold.

Samuel Purchas (ed.), *Hakluytus Posthumus, or Purchas his Pilgrimes*, Maclehose, Glasgow, 1625; reprinted 1905–7, Vol. X, pp. 153–63.

4

Bargainings and Offerings

RALPH FITCH

In Act 1, Scene 3 of Shakespeare's Macbeth, *the first witch says 'Her husband's to Aleppo gone, master o'the Tiger'. Fifteen years earlier an English merchant, having completed his travels,*

---

*A copper/lead alloy.

had begun his account thus: 'In the yeere of our Lord 1583, I Ralph Fitch of London ... did ship my selfe in a ship of London called the Tyger, *wherein we ... tooke the way for Aleppo ...'. Whether Shakespeare was referring to this particular voyage or not, it is clear that both he and his audience well knew of such ventures.*

Queen Elizabeth I's foreign policy, one of adventurous merchant enterprise, was turning London into the commercial centre of the world. Sir Francis Drake had three years earlier completed his circumnavigation of the globe, but it is to Master Ralph Fitch that much of the credit must go for opening up the trade later developed by the British East India Company. Leaving London with other Levant Company merchants, he went from Aleppo down the Euphrates valley by caravan and boat to become one of the first Englishmen to travel overland to India. Captured by the Portuguese at Ormuz and again at Goa, he escaped, crossed India, and became the first Englishman to visit Burma and Siam. Nevertheless, almost nothing of his personal history has come down to us. It is not even known when he was born or when he died; but we do know that he was still alive in December 1606 because the Minutes of an East India Company meeting held that month show that the Company was still relying on him as an informant.

Fedrici (see Passage 2 above) had preceded Fitch some twenty years earlier, and his account was already widely known. Since parts of Fitch's account appear to owe much to Fedrici's, duplicated information has been removed from the following extract. Like all traders, Fitch was concerned with current and future profits. Like some of the other Western merchants visiting Pegú at this time, he was clearly puzzled by what he saw as a fruitless waste of gold and other commodities by the Buddhist population in their acts of piety. To his credit, however, he seems to have taken a great interest in the processes of entering the monkhood and practising as a 'tallipoie', a life-style that entailed renouncing money and everything that he would have regarded as 'the good life'.

I went from Serrepore [Serampur] the 28. of November 1586. for Pegu in a small ship or foist of one Albert Caravallos, and so passing downe Ganges, and passing by the Island of Sundiva [Sandwip], porto Grande, or the countrie of Tippera [Tripura], the kingdom of Recon and Mogen [Arakan], leaving them on our left side with a faire wind at Northwest: our course was South & by East, which brought us to the barre of Negrais* in Pegu: if any contrary wind had come, we had throwen many of our things over-boord: for we were so pestered with people & goods, that there was scant place to lie in. From Bengala† to Pegu is 90. leagues. We entred the barre of Negrais, which is a brave barre & hath 4. fadomes water where it hath least. Three dayes after we came to Cosmin,‡ which is a very pretie towne, and standeth very pleasantly, very well furnished with all things. The people be very tall & well disposed; the women white, round faced, with litle eies: the houses are high built, set upon great high postes, & they go up to them with long ladders for feare of the Tygers which be very many. The countrey is very fruitful of all things. Here are very great Figs, Orenges, Cocoes, and other fruits. The land is very high that we fall withall, but after we be entred the barre, it is very lowe and full of rivers, for they goe all too and fro in boates, which they call paroes, and keepe their houses with wife and children in them.

From the barre of Nigrais to the citie of Pegu is ten dayes journey by the rivers. Wee went from Cosmin to Pegu in Paroes or boates, and passing up the rivers wee came to Medon, which is a pretty towne, where there be a wonderfull number of Paroes, for they keepe their houses and their markets in them all upon the water. They rowe too and fro, and have all their marchandizes in their boates with a great Sombrero or shadow over their heads to keepe the sunne from them, which is as broad as a great cart wheele made of the leaves of the Coco trees and fig trees, and is very light.

From Medon we went to Dela,§ which is a very faire towne, and hath a faire port into the sea, from whence go many ships to Malacca, Mecca, and many other places. Here are 18. or 20. very great and long houses, where they tame and keep many elephants of the kings: for there about in the wildernesse they catch the wilde elephants. It is a very fruitfull countrey. From Dela we went to Cirion [Syriam],

---

*In the Irrawaddy delta.
†Probably Chittagong.
‡In the Irrawaddy delta.
§Also spelled Dalla; located in the Irrawaddy delta.

'Upstream with the Wind', from R. Talbot Kelly, *Burma*, 2nd. edn., A. & C. Black, London, 1933.

which is a good towne, and hath a faire porte into the sea, whither come many ships from Mecca, Malacca, Sumatra, and from divers other places. And there the ships staie and discharge, & send up their goods in Paroes to Pegu. From Cirion we went to Macao, which is a pretie towne, where we left our boats or Paroes, & in the morning taking Delingeges, which are a kind of Coches made of cords & cloth quilted, & caried upon a stang [pole] betweene 3. or 4. men: we came to Pegu the same day.

Pegu is a citie very great, strong, and very faire, with walles of stone, and great ditches round about it. There are two townes, the old towne and the newe. In the olde towne are all the marchants strangers, and very many marchants of the countrey. All the goods are sold in the olde towne which is very great, and hath many suburbes round about it, and all the houses are made of Canes which they call Bambos, and bee covered with strawe. In your house you have a Warehouse which they call Godon, which is made of bricke to put your goods in, for oftentimes they take fire and burne in an houre foure or five hundred houses: so that if the Godon were not, you should bee in danger to have all burned, if any winde should rise, at a trice. In the newe towne is the king, and all his Nobilitie and Gentrie. It is a citie very great and populous, and is made square and with very faire walles, and a great ditch round about it full of water, with many crocodiles in it: it hath twenty gates, and they bee made of stone, for every square five gates. There are also many Turrets for Centinels to watch, made of wood, and gilded with golde very faire. The streets are the fairest that ever I saw, as straight as a line from one gate to the other, and so broad that tenne or twelve men may ride a front thorow them. On both sides of them at every mans doore is set a palmer tree which is the nut tree: which make a very faire shew and a very commodious shadow, so that a man may walke in the shade all day. The houses be made of wood, and covered with tiles.

The kings house is in the middle of the city, and is walled and ditched round about: and the buildings within are made of wood very sumptuously gilded, and great workemanship is upon the forefront, which is likewise very costly gilded. And the house wherein his Pagode or idole standeth is covered with tiles of silver, and all the walles are gilded with golde. Within the first gate of the kings house is a great large roome, on both sides whereof are houses made for the kings elephants, which be marvellous great and faire, and are brought up to warres and in service of the king. And among the rest he hath foure white elephants, which are very strange and rare: for there is none other king which hath them but he: if any other king hath one, hee will send unto him for it. When any of these white elephants is brought unto the king, all the merchants in the city are commanded to see them, and to give him a present of halfe a ducat, which doth come to a great summe: for that there are many merchants in the city. After that you have given your present you may come and see them at your pleasure, although they stand in the kings house. This king in his title is called the king of the white elephants. If any other king have one, and will not send it him, he will make warre with him for it: for he had rather lose a great part of his kingdome, then not to conquere him. They do very great service unto these white elephants; every one of them standeth in an house gilded with golde, and they doe feede in vessels of silver and gilt. One of them when he doth go to the river to be washed, as every day they do, goeth under a canopy of cloth of golde or of silke carried over him by sixe or eight men, and eight or ten men goe before him playing on drummes, shawmes,[*] or other instruments: and when he is washed and commeth out of the river, there is a gentleman which doth wash his feet in a silver basin: which is his office given him by the king. There is no such account made of any blacke elephant, be he never so great....

The king hath one wife and above three hundred concubines, by which they say he hath fourescore or fourescore and ten children. He sitteth in judgement almost every day. They use no speech, but give up their supplications written in the leaves of a tree with the point of an yron bigger then a bodkin. These leaves are an elle[†] long, and about two inches broad; they are also double. He which giveth in his supplication, doth stand in a place a little distance off with a present. If his matter be liked of, the king accepteth of his present, and granteth his request: if his sute be not liked of, he returneth with his present; for the king will not take it.

---

[*]A wind instrument similar to an oboe.
[†]A unit of measure slightly longer than a metre.

In India there are few commodities which serve for Pegu, except Opium of Cambaia,* painted cloth of S. Thome, or of Masulipatan [Machilipatnam], and white cloth of Bengala, which is spent there in great quantity. They bring thither also much cotton, yarne red coloured with a root which they called Saia, which will never lose his colour: it is very wel solde here, and very much of it commeth yerely to Pegu. By your mony you lose much. The ships which come from Bengala, S. Thome, and Masulipatan, come to the bar of Nigrais and to Cosmin. To Martavan a port of the sea in the kingdome of Pegu come many ships from Malacca laden with Sandall, Porcelanes, and other wares of China, and with Camphora of Borneo, and Pepper from Achen in Sumatra. To Cirion a port of Pegu come ships from Mecca with woollen cloth, Scarlets, Velvets, Opium, and such like. There are in Pegu eight Brokers, whom they call Tareghe, which are bound to sell your goods at the price which they be woorth, and you give them for their labour two in the hundred: and they be bound to make your debt good, because you sell your marchandises upon their word. If the Broker pay you not at his day, you may take him home, and keepe him in your house: which is a great shame for him. And if he pay you not presently, you may take his wife and children and his slaves, and binde them at your doore, and set them in the Sunne; for that is the law of the countrey.

Their current money in these parts is a kinde of brasse which they call Gansa, wherewith you may buy golde, silver, rubies, muske, and all other things. The golde and silver is marchandise, and is worth sometimes more and sometimes lesse, as other wares be. This brasen money doeth goe by a weight which they call a biza; and commonly this biza after our account is worth about halfe a crowne or somewhat lesse. The marchandise which be in Pegu, are golde, silver, rubies, saphires, spinelles, muske, benjamin or frankincense, long pepper, tinne, leade, copper, lacca [lac] whereof they make hard waxe, rice, and wine made of rice, and some sugar. The elephants doe eate the sugar canes, or els they would make very much. And they consume many canes likewise in making of their Varellaes or Idole temples, which are

*Previously one of the states in Gujarat.

33

in great number both great and small. They be made round like a sugar loafe, some are as high as a Church, very broad beneath, some a quarter of a mile in compasse: within they be all earth done about with stone. They consume in these Varellaes great quantity of golde; for that they be all gilded aloft: and many of them from the top to the bottome: and every ten or twelve yeeres they must be new gilded, because the raine consumeth off the golde: for they stand open abroad. If they did not consume their golde in these vanities, it would be very plentifull and good cheape in Pegu.

About two dayes journey from Pegu there is a Varelle or Pagode, which is the pilgrimage of the Pegues: it is called Dogonne, and is of a woonderfull bignesse, and all gilded from the foot to the toppe. And there is an house by it wherein the Tallipoies which are their Priests doe preach. This house is five and fifty paces in length, and hath three pawnes or walks in it, and forty great pillars gilded, which stand betweene the walks; and it is open on all sides with a number of small pillars, which be likewise gilded: it is gilded with golde within and without. There are houses very faire round about for the pilgrims to lie in: and many goodly houses for the Tallipoies to preach in, which are full of images both of men and women, which are all gilded over with golde. It is the fairest place, as I suppose, that is in the world: it standeth very high, and there are foure wayes to it, which all along are set with trees of fruits, in such wise that a man may goe in the shade above two miles in length. And when their feast day is, a man can hardly passe by water or by land for the great presse of people; for they come from all places of the kingdome of Pegu thither at their feast.

In Pegu they have many Tallipoies or priests, which preach against all abuses. Many men resort unto them. When they enter into their kiack, that is to say, their holy place or temple, at the doore there is a great jarre of water with a cocke or a ladle in it, and there they wash their feet; and then they enter in, and lift up their hands to their heads first to their preacher, and then to the Sunne, and so sit downe. The Tallipoies go very strangely apparelled with one camboline or thinne cloth next to their body of a browne colour, another of yellow doubled many times upon their shoulder: and those two be girded to them with a broad girdle: and they have a skinne of leather hanging on a string about their necks, whereupon they sit, bare headed & bare footed: for none of them weareth shooes; with their right armes bare and a great broad sombrero or shadow in their hands to defend them in the Summer from the Sunne, and in the Winter from the raine. When the Tallipoies or priests take their Orders, first they go to schoole untill they be twenty yeres olde or more, and then they come before a Tallipoie appointed for that purpose, whom they call Rowli: he is of the chiefest and most learned, and he opposeth them, and afterward examineth them many times, whether they will leave their friends, and the company of all women, and take upon them the habit of a Tallipoie. If any be content, then he rideth upon an horse about the streets very richly apparelled, with drummes and pipes, to shew that he leaveth the riches of the world to be a Tallipoie.

In few dayes after, he is caried upon a thing like an horsliter, which they call a serion, upon ten or twelve mens shoulders in the apparell of a Tallipoie, with pipes and drummes, and many Tallipoies with him, and al his friends, and so they go with him to his house which standeth without the towne, and there they leave him. Every one of them hath his house, which is very little, set upon six or eight posts, and they go up to them with a ladder of twelve or foureteene staves. Their houses be for the most part by the hie wayes side, and among the trees, and in the woods. And they go with a great pot made of wood or fine earth, and covered, tied with a broad girdle upon their shoulder, which commeth under their arme, wherewith they go to begge their victuals which they eate, which is rice, fish, and herbs. They demand nothing, but come to the doore, and the people presently doe give them, some one thing, and some another: and they put all together in their potte: for they say they must eate of their almes, and therewith content themselves. They keepe their feasts by the Moone: and when it is new Moone they keepe their greatest feast: and then the people send rice and other things to that kiack or church of which they be; and there all the Tallipoies doe meete which be of that Church, and eate the victuals which are sent them. When the Tallipoies do preach, many of the people cary them gifts into the pulpit where they sit and preach. And there is one which sitteth by them to take that which the people bring. It is divided among them. They have none other ceremonies nor service that I could see, but onely preaching.

I went from Pegu to Jamahey [Chiang Mai], which is in the countrey of the Langeiannes [Siamese Laos], whom we call Jangomes; it is five and twenty dayes journey Northeast from Pegu. In which journey I passed many fruitfull and pleasant countreys. The countrey is very lowe, and hath many faire rivers. The houses are very bad, made of canes, and covered with straw. Heere are many wilde buffes and elephants. Jamahey is a very faire and great towne, with faire houses of stone, well peopled, the streets are very large, the men very well set and strong, with a cloth about them, bare headed and bare footed: for in all these countreys they weare no shooes. The women be much fairer then those of Pegu. Heere in all these countreys they have no wheat. They make some cakes of rice. Hither to Jamahey come many marchants out of China, and bring great store of muske, golde, silver, and many other things of China worke. Here is great store of victuals: they have such plenty that they will not milke the buffles, as they doe in all other places. Here is great store of copper and benjamin.

In these countreys when the people be sicke they make a vow to offer meat unto the divell, if they escape: and when they be recovered they make a banket with many pipes & drummes and other instruments, and dansing all the night, and their friends come and bring gifts, cocos, figges, arrecaes [areca nuts], and other fruits, and with great dauncing and rejoycing they offer to the divell, and say, they give the divel to eat, and drive him out. When they be dancing and playing they will cry & hallow very loud; and in this sort they say they drive him away. And when they be sicke a Tallipoy or two every night doth sit by them & sing, to please the divell that he should not hurt them. And if any die he is caried upon a great frame made like a tower, with a covering all gilded with golde made of canes caried with foureteene or sixteene men, with drummes and pipes and other instruments playing before him to a place out of the towne and there is burned. He is accompanied with all his friends and neighbours, all men: and they give to the tallipoies or priests many mats and cloth: and then they returne to the house and there make a feast for two dayes: and then the wife with all the neighbours wives & her friends go to the place where he was burned, and there they sit a certaine time and cry and gather the pieces of bones which be left unburned and bury them, and then returne to their houses and make an end of all mourning. And the men and women which be neere of kin do shave their heads, which they do not use except it be for the death of a friend: for they much esteeme of their haire.

Caplan [Mogok] is the place where they finde the rubies, saphires, and spinelles: it standeth six dayes journey from Ava in the kingdome of Pegu. There are many great high hilles out of which they digge them. None may go to the pits but onely those which digge them.

* * *

The Bramas which be of the kings countrey (for the king is a Brama) have their legs or bellies, or some part of their body, as they thinke good themselves, made black with certaine things which they have: they use to pricke the skinne, and to put on it a kinde of anile or blacking, which doth continue alwayes. And this is counted an honour among them: but none may have it but the Bramas which are of the kings kinred.

These people weare no beards: they pull out the haire on their faces with little pinsons made for that purpose. Some of them will let 16 or 20 haires grow together, some in one place of his face and some in another, and pulleth out all the rest: for he carieth his pinsons alwayes with him to pull the haires out assoone as they appeare. If they see a man with a beard they wonder at him. They have their teeth blacked both men and women, for they say a dogge hath his teeth white, therefore they will blacke theirs.

The Pegues if they have a sute in the law which is so doubtfull that they cannot well determine it, put two long canes into the water where it is very deepe: and both the parties go into the water by the poles, and there sit men to judge, and they both do dive under the water, and he which remaineth longest under the water doth winne the sute.

The 10 of January I went from Pegu to Malacca, passing by many of the ports of Pegu, as Martavan, the Iland of Tavi

[Tavoy], from whence commeth great store of tinne which serveth all India, the Ilands of Tanaseri [Mergui Archipelago], Junsalaon [Penang], and many others; and so came to Malacca the 8 of February, where the Portugals have a castle which standeth nere the sea.

Richard Hakluyt, *The Principal Navigations, Voyages, Traffiques & Discoveries of the English Nation*, J. M. Dent, London, 1927, Vol. III, pp. 298–309.

5
A Rattling Good Tale?

FRANCESCO CARLETTI

Francesco Carletti was born in Florence in or around the year 1573 and died there in 1636. At the age of eighteen he was sent to Sevilla in Spain to learn about maritime trade, and two years later set out for Africa to engage in the slave trade. Having sold his human cargo in South America and prospected unsuccessfully for trade in Peru and Mexico he went on to Japan, where he spent nine months, and then to China, where he stayed for two years. Continuing westwards via Goa, he was just reaching St Helena when the Portuguese ship he was sailing on was captured by the Dutch and he lost all the wealth he had acquired. Arriving in Holland, he spent a considerable time dealing with the consequences of this disaster and other matters. Giving up his plans for a second voyage, he at length returned to Florence where he was welcomed into the court of the Grand Duke of Tuscany, Ferdinando de' Medici, and here he gave an account of his travels. Though he had not set out to do so, Carletti was one of the first men to sail round the globe, albeit as a passenger in several ships rather than as a master mariner.

Though the original manuscript of his Ragionamenti *(Chronicles) is lost, there are other manuscript copies. Scholars agree that the one in Rome's Biblioteca Angelica is the closest to the original, so the passage below is taken from a translation of that text. Carletti's whole account is full of detailed observations on the products and customs of the countries he*

*visited, and this passage is a sort of afterthought inserted into
his account of the year 1599. There is no hard evidence that
he actually entered Burmese territory, so it is possible that in
this extract, despite his assurances, he is reporting what he
had heard and read about rather than what he had seen and
experienced. However, the same subject matter does occur in
other accounts, including those of Balbi and Fitch who are
known to have stayed in Burma. If true, the account throws a
fascinating light on the attitudes of Burman women of the
time; if it is just a mariner's tale, it tells us a great deal about
the European voyagers of the day.*

THOSE people, using an ancient invention designed by a
queen to rule out and render impossible the practicing
of venery in illicit parts of the body even with men,
ordered that each man must have stitched between the skin
and the flesh of his member two or three rattles as large as
large hazelnuts, these made in round or oval shape. And in
these rattles—which I have seen made of gold—there is a
pellet of iron. When these rattles are moved, they give off a
dull sound because they are without holes, being like two
shells fastened together delicately and masterfully. And they
have this little pellet inside, and are called rattles because
they make this sound.

And these rattles, placed, as I have said, under the skin,
which then is sewed together and allowed to heal, have the
result of enlarging the member, as anyone can imagine. And
the women desire them for these reasons and others that are
to be thought of rather than spoken, as being helpful to
pleasure. And that this is an invention by women is proved
particularly by the fact that women are the masters of placing
and adjusting these rattles. And this is confirmed by Nicolò
de' Conti, who, during his voyages, which he described in
the year 1444 by command of Pope Eugenius IV, says that in
the kingdom of Pegú, in the city of Hava, certain old women
had no other calling than that of selling these rattles, which
were of gold, silver, or gilded copper and were as small as
small nuts. (I said that they were large because that was true
of those which I saw, but perhaps in those earlier times they
were content with these small ones or, as he says, placed a
number of them, up to ten or twelve, inside the member, a
thing that does not seem possible.)

And this was done when the youth was at the age to be able to indulge in venery or to marry, performed by the hands of the aforesaid women, who placed these rattles between the flesh and the skin, they being made of gold or of other metals according to the man's station. And without them a man would be rejected, but with them he would be accepted in marriage and to the women's intimacy. The women much fondled men thus equipped, but the contrary with others. And the aforementioned Nicolò says that he was asked if he wished to be equipped with these rattles, but answered that he had no desire to do harm to himself so as to be able to give pleasure to others. And also with regard to this being desired by the women, Amerigo Vespucci, who discovered Brazil, wrote in one of his letters to Piero Soderini that the women of that country, being extremely concupiscent, give the men a certain herb juice to drink so as to increase the size of their members, and that if that juice does not succeed, they had the member bitten or stung by poisonous animals. But I brought some of these rattles as proof, and they also have been taken to Holland by those who travel in those regions. And it is a certain thing and absolutely true that this diabolic invention was made and is used by the women of that country.

My Voyage Around the World, translation by Herbert Weinstock, Methuen, London, 1965, pp. 181–3.

Meeting Burmese Kings and Queens

6
At the Court of Arakan

FATHER SEBASTIÃO MANRIQUE

Father Sebastião Manrique was born in Oporto, Portugal, in the final decade of the sixteenth century. As a boy he was committed to the Augustinian Order. He was later sent to the Portuguese enclave of Goa, where he became a friar. Later, he was transferred to a Portuguese settlement in Bengal close to what is now known as Calcutta. Bengal had been under Muslim rule for four centuries, and the current emperor of India was Shah Jehan. To the east lay Arakan, and it was to this independent kingdom (later to become part of Burma) that Father Manrique was sent in 1629, when he was about forty years old.

By this time the Portuguese freebooters who had harried the shipping and coastline of the Bay of Bengal had settled down and the king of Arakan had taken many into his service, using their seamanship and firepower in the defence of his kingdom, especially against the growing might of Shah Jehan. It was the task of missionaries such as Manrique to provide pastoral care for Portuguese residents and native converts, especially those in whom (as the brave but bigoted friar put it) 'the Devil had renewed the ancient foundations of idolatry', and to introduce Christianity to unbelievers. Manrique sailed from Bengal to Dianga, a port near Chittagong where, suspicious of Portuguese military intentions, King Minzayagyi had in 1607 ordered the massacre of 600 Portuguese settlers. Here in this same port Manrique discovered that an

41

anti-Portuguese cousin of the Arakanese (or 'Magh') king had written to the Court, falsely accusing the Portuguese militia of secretly arranging to allow Shah Jehan's forces to capture Chittagong. If King Thiri-thu-dhamma were to believe this allegation, the consequences could be disastrous not only for the Portuguese community but also for Christian converts in Arakan, and perhaps even for the small group of Japanese Christians residing there as a result of persecution in Japan.

Leaving Dianga on 2 July 1630, the stalwart friar set out through rugged and uncharted country accompanied by a certain Captain Tibao and a local escort. Received by Thiri-thu-dhamma on 1 August, Manrique persuaded the king that the allegation was untrue. From Arakan, Manrique went on to the Philippines and China before returning to Rome. He published his Itinerario *in Rome and he was given important church duties. Twenty years later he was sent on some sort of secret mission to London, where his own Portuguese servant murdered him for his money.*

In this passage we find Manrique in the city of Arakan. Having allayed any fears the king might have had, he now wishes for religious reasons to settle the Christians more closely together as a compact community. At the same time, he does not want the king to think that his purpose might be hostile. The previous king, who ordered the massacre twenty-three years earlier, had married a Burmese princess, a daughter of King Nandabayin. She was known as 'the Pegú Queen'. As step-grandmother of the present king, she would have considerable influence at Court. By coincidence one of the Japanese Christians was able to help smooth Manrique's path and ease his anxieties.

IN the midst of these perplexities I remembered the friendliness of the Japanese, Don Leon Dono. I therefore told him of my intention and the wish to serve God which was urging me to do this. He considered the best line to adopt, and pointed out that it was a very difficult case to settle with such suspicious people as the Maghs, but that as it was in God's service, His Divine Majesty would certainly find a way. He promised to assist me to the utmost, adding that he would talk it over with his wife, who as a native and having the entry of the Palace, as a former servant of the old Queen who had come from Pegu, would devise some way of mentioning the subject to her. He promised to inform me of whatever resulted.

After parting from him I went to our residence in a sufficiently pensive mood. Three days later the Japanese Captain came and told me that his wife had discussed the subject with that Peguan Queen, who had replied that she would use her influence in every way to assist the arrangement. The best way, in her opinion, seeing that I was in the King's good graces, would be for me to find a suitable opportunity and then, without declaring my real object, quietly ask him if he would allow me to engage some *Mangoenes* to serve in the *Varela* of the Christian *Quiay*. I mentioned elsewhere that *Quiay* means God and *Varela* temple, or monastery. The word *Mangoen* is the name for those persons who are appointed by the King to serve any particular person or at any special place. These persons are obliged to serve in turns for one month at a time, without pay, beyond such gifts as they may care to give them. They so divide up the duty among themselves that while some are engaged in serving their Masters, the rest can look after their private interests and livelihood and so are not given daily food.

In telling me this he also said he thought it would be well if I visited this Queen and thanked her for her kindness in assisting the Christians. This advice seemed to me excellent, and I would have at once followed it, the occasion being opportune, but all our curiosities were exhausted and also our Indian and Chinese cloth, owing to the large amount consumed in making various *adias* or presents when we first arrived at this Court. As I have noted before, we were obliged not to make visits empty-handed, under pain of being considered discourteous and being received grudgingly. I was, therefore, obliged to let this good opportunity pass and first do my best to find some adequate gift to present to Her Highness. This gift I obtained through some of the Christians, and at once proceeded to visit the Queen, sending the gift ahead, to act as a lamp and prevent my being received in darkness. Lighted thus, I arrived at a large room, in which Her Highness was waiting. I found the place well lit up, as the result of my gift-lantern, which had preceded me, and I was received graciously and pleasantly, the profound obeisances I had made being recognized with a slight lowering of her head. Those who had accompanied me looked upon this as a mark of unusual favour and honour, not accorded as a rule (they said) to any but Princes or persons of high standing. She had indeed ample justification for such behaviour, as having been Empress of Pegu and also as being a descendant in the male line of the Prechaus Saleus of Sornau,* whom our Portuguese style Emperors of Siam, whose origin, if their chronicles are accurate, dates back over seventeen hundred years, and were hence the overlords of the seventeen Kings of Capimpu.† Her Highness was seated on a dais about eight inches above the ground. This was covered with golden carpets and silken cloths, with rich cushions of purple velvet embroidered with gold and seed pearls. Six women, richly clothed, were kneeling on the dais, some presenting betel while the others with handsome fans in their hands were keeping away the importunate flies.

In another part of the Hall stood twenty old, venerable men wearing long robes of purple Damask. Two of them approached me and gave me a seat on a second and smaller dais, smaller and lower than the Royal dais. This was covered with a good carpet of the ordinary kind and had two velvet cushions on it.

As soon as I was seated I professed, with the usual expressions of submissive gratitude, my thanks for the interest Her Highness was taking in the Christians. In reply she said that ever since she came into touch with the Portuguese in Pegu she had been much attached to the Christians, adding that she had there, on several occasions, attended the *Varela* of the Christian *Quiay* and had seen the image of our Blessed Mary, of whom the priests had told her many wonderful tales. She had also learned the 'Ave Maria', which she had often repeated. But since the death of her Lord and husband and other misfortunes which befell her at the revolt of the Burmese Brama tyrant, including the murder of her sons and the destruction and ruin of her home, she had forgotten it.

She was quite incapable of carrying on the conversation owing to the tears which, in spite of her efforts to restrain them, she could not keep back, nor hide the grief caused by

*Refers to Phra-Chao (King) Sawlu (Shan name) of Sarnau (Siam).
†Capimpu is probably Kamphaeng Phet, which is half-way between Chiang Mai and Ayutthaya.

44

these memories of unhappy days. She uttered a deep sigh and was removed into the inner apartment in a state of collapse.

I was thus left in a state of uncertainty as to whether I should retire at once or await her permission to do so. At this juncture some of the old men present in the hall came up to me, and one of them said, 'Father, do not be dismayed because the Mistress of our heads has left without first taking leave of you. Indeed all we can do on recalling such great misfortunes, is to render the tribute of human weakness.'

At this moment a woman of rank came up, accompanied by two others of lower status, as it seemed to me. She apologized to me on behalf of Her Highness, saying it pained her much not to have been able to take leave of me more cheerfully, but she was confident that God would find her opportunities for advancing my good and that of the Christians.

I replied to this message with thanks and expressed my concern for Her Highness's grief. I trusted she would pray to the true God and His most sainted Mother Mary, as she would then obtain much consolation.

The attendant then left and I also, in company with the band of old men, and some ushers who carried silver wands in their hands. They accompanied me to the outer door. Some time passed without my finding an opportunity to speak to the King on the matter.

Meanwhile the widowed Queen sent a man to come and see me, presenting me with a fine gift, comprising hens, chickens, rice, *ghi*, and many kinds of fruits. Besides these eatables there were two pieces of muslin of the finest, each piece ninety yards long and seven palms wide, worked with flowers in gold, silver, and many coloured silks. They were very beautiful and rich, and I appreciated them immensely both for themselves and because they were so well suited for the adornment and embellishment of an altar.

I at once had them made up into three pairs of curtains with canopies decorated with fringes of the finest gold, for three Churches. They furnished an adornment which would have held its own in any great festival, in any cathedral in Europe.

At that time I also received a message that I should go to the palace next day, as the King was to appear in a gallery in order to inspect two baby elephants which some hunters had brought to him from the hills of Pre [Prome]. A *Tamaxā* or festival would take place and I should be able to see the King and talk with him, as she had already spoken to him about me and described my visit. Though she had said nothing about my business, as it seemed to her best to enter on it in the simplest possible way, she had nevertheless influenced him to show me favour and grace at my interview, and hence I should not let the chance slip. She added that I might be assured that she would love me as a son.

I replied to her message and presents as was most suitable, sending the porters away more satisfied by my acts than with my words, for the methods used there in such cases are not those employed in Europe.

Next day, at a suitable hour, I went to the palace taking with me some mechanical toys, which were rather curious than valuable. These were intended for the small sons of His Highness, who were to be with their father since it was a *tamaxā* day. Bestowing them in his presence would assist me in attaining my object. I reached a room of the palace in which some noblemen were already present. I awaited the arrival of the King and his two sons. I then went up to him with the usual salutation, and he smilingly asked me if I had come to see the Tamaxā de los Atis, which in our language means 'the Show of elephants'. I said my only object in coming was to see His Majesty, as to visit him was a greater *Tamaxā* to me than any other, especially when I saw him looking so well, a gift from the hand of the one true God. He answered me, 'Father, you say truly, for from His powerful hand all good comes to us. Let us go and see those Atis (elephants), whom He has created.' So I followed him to a gallery, where he seated himself at a spot in it which had been prepared for the purpose. Somewhat lower down the Noblemen of the Court were seated, I being among them.

The King's youngest son was being carried in the arms of a man, who was close by me. I took a small box out of my pocket, which was ornamented in black and gold with some designs in mother-of-pearl. Inside was a tiny figure of a dog, white and downy, very much like a real dog; it used to raise itself and move its paws about. It had been made by Chinamen, who can compete with all the most skilled nations of Europe in ingenuity. When I showed this toy to the young *Infante* he at once came to me, and sitting close by showed great delight at seeing this little toy dog which moved its paws about. I put the box into his hands and he at once went off, overjoyed, to his father, who met him with the elder son and accepted it, delighted at his son's pleasure. The elder son and first-born had just arrived. The Royal parent now began to play with them both, setting aside for the time being all royal dignity. He made many jokes about the toy dog. The elder boy now wished to take it in his hands and it was given to him, at which the younger became annoyed, wishing to recover it from his brother. He resisted relinquishing it, and began to cry and scream, till it was necessary, in order to pacify him, to take it away from the elder brother's hands. At this he in his turn became upset and unhappy, and came up to me asking me if I would give him another toy dog. At the same time I took out of my sleeve a curious case containing two knives with crystal handles, cunningly ornamented in gold and studded with tiny rubies. The sheath was made of green velvet, mounted with gold plates, these being also studded with similar small rubies. It had been designed and made in Ceylon and was more showy than costly.

The Prince was so pleased with this that he at once placed it in his *camarabando*, that is a waist-cloth or band, worn in place of a belt; these vary in accordance with the quality and wealth of the wearer. In these belts, to the right, they carry knives or crizes, a kind of short sword corresponding to our dagger or poniard. The Prince was carrying a *cris* in his belt, with a gold hilt set with pearls, which were of no great size, except one at the top of the handle that was of medium size. The sheath was of gold set with some good sapphires. He took this out of his belt and gave it to me, putting the case of knives in its place, an act which was applauded by all present as most generous, and especially by his father. The Prince then went off and drawing out these knives from his belt offered them on the palms of his hands to his father, kneeling before him. The Magh King on seeing them said, 'Prince, you gave the Father one *cris* after getting two daggers from him'. He then turned to the small boy who was playing with his dog, and calling him by name said, 'You gave the Father nothing, so I will do so for you'. He then turned to me and said. 'Father, you have afforded me one great *tamaxā* to-day, let us now go and see the other.'

He then turned to go and see the little elephants who came out into the square, the King noting those which appeared likely to turn out best. A quantity of sugar-cane was brought and thrown to them, which they ate with much fuss, especially near a reservoir of water, where they douched not only each other but many of the spectators with their flexible little trunks. When these animals had been shut up again I was asked if we had them in Portugal....

Lt.-Col. C. Eckford Luard, assisted by Father H. Hosten, *Travels of Fray Sebastien Manrique, 1629–1643*, a translation of the *Itinerario de las Missiones Orientales*, first published by Francisco Caballo in Rome, 1649; The Hakluyt Society, Oxford, 1927, Vol. I, pp. 193–201.

7
An Audience with King Bodaw-hpaya

CAPTAIN MICHAEL SYMES

It is thought that Michael Symes was born in 1753. Although he was said to have entered the army and gone out to India at about the age of thirty-four, he put himself on record as having served there 'from an early age'. Soon after he had been made a Captain, there was in 1795 a serious situation on the India–Arakan border: some Burmese troops in hot pursuit of Arakanese rebels entered British territory and refused to leave until the rebel leaders had been handed over to them. The Governor-General of India sent Symes as an envoy to King Bodaw-hpaya to reopen diplomatic relations between the East India Company and the Court of Ava after a lapse of thirty-three years, to attempt to defuse the border tension, and to further British trade. The Burmese capital at this time was Amarapura. There, Symes was deliberately kept waiting for a long time but his patience was rewarded when he was eventually allowed into the royal presence. By the time he left Amarapura, he had spent more than three months there but had been moderately successful, having arranged for the establishment of a British Residency in Rangoon.

A few years later he got married while on leave in England. By now a lieutenant colonel, he returned to India only to find that, because the officer appointed as Resident at Rangoon had soured the diplomatic relations he had initiated, Symes had to go to Burma again and attempt to patch things up. This second embassy met a frosty reception and achieved very little. Symes returned to England with his regiment in 1806, and served in it gallantly in Spain, in the first stages of the Peninsular War. But the hardships of the campaign broke his health, and he died at sea on the way home to England in 1809.

In this passage we see Symes, accompanied by two of his colleagues Buchanan and Wood, in the first audience at Amarapura, in 1795. It is significant that Bodaw-hpaya, who is used to dealing only with other kings, does not actually address Symes—whom he naturally sees as just an envoy of the governor-general of a mere trading company. 'John Company', on the other hand, saw itself as an imperial power.

O N the 30th of September, the day appointed by his Birman majesty to receive the English gentlemen in the character of an imperial deputation, we crossed the lake at ten o'clock in the morning, attended by our customary suite, and accompanied by Baba-Sheen and several Birman officers. We entered the fort, as usual, by the western gate, when, instead of passing, as on former occasions, along the north side of the enclosure of the palace, to reach the street leading down to the Lotoo,* we now proceeded round by the south, and in this new direction observed many more houses of distinguished structure than by the other route. In our way we passed through a short street, entirely composed of saddlers and harness-makers shops. On alighting, we were conducted into the rhoom, to wait there until the Engy Teekien† should arrive, which he did precisely at the hour of twelve. Several Chobwas,‡ who were to be introduced on this day, had taken their seats in the rhoom before we entered. Each of them held a piece of silk or cotton cloth in his lap, designed, according to the established etiquette, as a propitiatory offering to his majesty; and on the cloth was placed a saucer, containing a small quantity of unboiled rice, which it seems is an indispensable part of the ceremony. The

*The Hlutdaw, the building used by the council of principal ministers.
†Crown prince or heir apparent
†Sawbas: Shan princes.

Birman custom differs in this particular from the usage of Hindostan. A person, on his presentation at the imperial court of Delhi, offers to the sovereign an odd number of the gold coin commonly called Mohurs, an even number being considered as inauspicious; but the court of Ummerapoora, with a more delicate refinement, never permits an offering in money, but requires from a foreigner something of the produce of his country, and from a subject some article of manufacture. The donation of rice is not, as in India, when presented by Brahmins to the incarnations of Vishnu, meant as an acknowledgment of divine attributes, but is merely designed as a recognition of the power of the monarch, and an acknowledgment of the property of the soil being vested in him; a truth which is expressively declared, by offering him its most useful production. During our continuance in the rhoom, tea was served to us; and when we advanced to the outer gate, we were not obliged to put off our shoes, but were permitted to wear them until we had reached the inner enclosure that separates the court of the Lotoo from that of the royal palace, within which not any nobleman of the court is allowed to go with his feet covered. There is a double partition wall dividing the two courts, with an intervening space of ten or twelve feet, through which a gallery leads, that is appropriated exclusively to the use of the king when he chooses to preside in person in the Lotoo.

On entering the gate, we perceived the royal saloon of ceremony in front of us, and the court assembled in all the parade of pomp and decoration. It was an open hall, supported by colonnades of pillars twenty in length, and only four in depth. We were conducted into it by a flight of steps, and, advancing, took our places next the space opposite to the throne, which is always left vacant, as being in full view of his majesty. In our entrance, the basement of the throne, as at the Lotoo, was alone visible, which we judged to be about five feet high. Folding doors screened the seat from our view. The throne, called Yazapalay, was richly gilded and carved; on each side a small gallery, enclosed by a gilt balustrade extended a few feet to the right and left, containing four umbrellas of state; and on two tables, at the foot of the throne, were placed several large vessels of gold, of various forms, and for different purposes. Immediately over the

'The Audience Hall and Reception of the Envoy', from Henry Yule, *Narrative of the Mission to the Court of Ava in 1855*, Smith, Elder, London, 1858.

throne, a splendid piasath* rose in seven stages above the roofs of the building, crowned by a tee or umbrella, from which a spiral rod was elevated above the whole.

We had been seated little more than a quarter of an hour, when the folding doors that concealed the seat opened with a loud noise, and discovered his majesty ascending a flight of steps that led up to the throne from the inner apartment. He advanced but slowly, and seemed not to possess a free use of his limbs, being obliged to support himself with his hands on the balustrade. I was informed, however, that this appearance of weakness did not proceed from any bodily infirmity, but from the weight of the regal habiliments in which he was clad; and if what we were told was true, that he carried on his dress fifteen viss,† upwards of fifty pounds avoirdupois of gold, his difficulty of ascent was not surprising. On reaching the top he stood for a minute, as though to take breath, and then sat down on an embroidered cushion with his legs inverted. His crown was a high conical cap, richly studded with precious stones. His fingers were covered with rings, and in his dress he bore the appearance of a man cased in golden armour, whilst a gilded, or probably a golden wing on each shoulder, did not add much lightness to his figure. His looks denoted him to be between fifty and sixty years old, of a strong make, in stature rather beneath the middle height, with hard features and of a dark complexion; yet the expression of his countenance was not unpleasing, and seemed, I thought, to indicate an intelligent and inquiring mind.

On the first appearance of his majesty, all the courtiers bent their bodies, and held their hands joined in an attitude of supplication. Nothing farther was required of us, than to lean a little forward, and to turn in our legs as much as we could—not any act being so unpolite, or contrary to etiquette, as to present the soles of the feet towards the face of a dignified person. Four Bramins, dressed in white caps and gowns, chanted the usual prayer at the foot of the throne. A Nakhaan‡ then advanced into the vacant space before the

*Pyatthat: a spire of seven successively smaller roofs.
†A measure, still used in Burma, equal to about 1.5 kilograms.
‡An official whose main duty was to channel information between king and council.

king, and recited in a musical cadence the name of each person who was to be introduced on that day, and of whose present, in the character of a suppliant, he entreated his majesty's acceptance. My offering consisted of two pieces of Benares gold brocade. Doctor Buchanan and Mr Wood each presented one. When our names were mentioned, we were separately desired to take a few grains of rice in our hands, and, joining them, to bow to the king as low as we conveniently could, with which we immediately complied. When this ceremony was finished, the king uttered a few indistinct words, to convey, as I was informed, an order for investing some persons present with the insignia of a certain degree of nobility. The imperial mandate was instantly proclaimed aloud by heralds in the court. His majesty remained only a few minutes longer, and during that time looked at us attentively, but did not honour us with any verbal notice, or speak at all, except to give the order before mentioned. When he rose to depart, he manifested the same signs of infirmity as on his entrance. After he had withdrawn, the folding doors were closed, and the court broke up.

In descending, we took notice of two pieces of cannon, apparently nine pounders, which were placed in the court, on either side of the stairs, to defend the entrance of the palace. Sheds protected them from the weather, and they were gilded all over. A royal carriage also was in waiting, of curious workmanship, and ornamented with a royal spire; there was a pair of horses harnessed to it, whose trappings glistened in the sun.

We returned as usual to the Rhoom, where I understood that the letter from the king to the Governor-general of India was to be presented to me, together with some other documents that comprehended the objects of the embassy. Soon after the members of the royal family had ascended their elephants, the expected letter was brought from the Lotoo on a tray, borne by a Nakhaan, enclosed in a case of wood japanned and covered with a scarlet cloth. The mode of offering it, was not, I conceived, quite so ceremonious as the occasion seemed to require; and the officer who was charged with the delivery indicated a reluctance to say that it was a letter from the king to the Governor-general of India. This circumstance produced some difficulty, as, without being distinctly informed to whom the letter was directed, I declined accepting it. At length the interpreter, finding I would not receive it on other terms, delivered it in a suitable manner, with a declaration that it was a reply from his Birman majesty to the letter of the British Governor-general of India, and that a copy of a royal mandate was annexed to it, granting to the English nation certain valuable immunities and privileges of trade.

Whilst we were in the outer court, or that in which the Lotoo is situated, we had an opportunity of viewing the immense piece of ordnance found in the fortress of Arracan when captured by the Engy Teekien, which was afterwards conveyed by water to adorn the capital of the conqueror, where it is now preserved as a trophy, and is highly honoured, being gilded, and covered by a roof of a dignified order. It is formed of brass, rudely manufactured; the length is thirty feet, the diameter at the muzzle two and a half, and the calibre measured ten inches. It is mounted on a low truck carriage supported by six wheels. Near it lay a long rammer and sponge staff, and we perceived several shot made of hewn stone fitted to the calibre. It is remarkable, that most of the spoils which had been brought from Arracan were made of brass. The image of Gaudma [Gautama Buddha], the lions, the demons, and the gun, all transported from thence, are composed of that metal.

The discussion, on the ceremony of delivering the letter being ended, we returned home....

An Account of an Embassy to the Kingdom of Ava in the Year 1795, etc., Constable, Edinburgh, 1827, Vol. II, pp. 164–8.

8
A Relaxed Audience with Ba-gyi-daw and His Queen

HENRY GOUGER

Henry Gouger was born in 1799 or thereabouts. By 1822, he was living in Bengal where, as a private merchant, he was producing raw silk in competition with the East India Company, an organization that until recently had exercised a trade monopoly. He fell ill and at the suggestion of a friend went to Burma where, since 'Manchester cottons' were now edging local fabrics out of the eastern markets, he thought he might combine convalescence with business. He had read both the first optimistic report of Michael Symes and the contradictory one by Hiram Cox, the Resident at Rangoon who had undone much of Symes's good work.

After staying a month in Rangoon (where at the King's godown the Customs officers claimed a tenth of his stock), he went upstream to Amarapura and found the new king, Ba-gyi-daw, preparing a new capital city on the old site of Ava. Having read and heard about the procrastination and snubs experienced by Symes and Cox, Gouger was delighted to find that no such obstacles were put in his way. This was largely because he was not the representative of an overbearing foreign power but a private trader. But it may also have been because Gouger was more willing to accept local customs and attitudes rather than cling arrogantly to his own—see for example his remarks about footwear. Here we see his first euphoric reactions to the ease with which he obtains an audience and the informality with which he is treated.

Unfortunately for him, the British gave him no warning of their declaration of war in 1824. He was thrown into the dreaded Let-ma-yun *('Hand-not-flinch') prison along with other expatriates including the notable American missionary Adoniram Judson, and a resident British renegade called Rodgers whom he meets at the Court in this episode. All three survived their incarceration, but after the war Rodgers chose to stay with his Burmese family in Upper Burma, where he died a little later. As a result of the war, Arakan and Tenasserim became British territory.*

Gouger himself claimed compensation from the British government and, because of his knowledge of the Burmese language and culture, was first put in charge of the police at Rangoon during the temporary British occupation of Lower Burma, and then made Master Attendant for the port of Mergui in Tenasserim. Having returned to England, he published an account of his experiences in Burma in 1860 but died while a second edition was being prepared.

Here we see his first delighted reactions to the ease with which he is able to settle in and obtain an audience, and to the informality with which the royal couple treat him.

THE epoch of my arrival at Amerapoorah was rather an unfortunate one; for the King, who had succeeded to the Throne of his grandfather only three years, with the usual caprice of Burmese monarchs, had determined to abandon his stately Palace, and to build a new one on the site of the ancient city of Ava, five miles lower down the river. This city had met a similar fate in a former reign, and was, until the late order to restore it, a deserted heap of ruins. The removal of the palace means, in Burmah, the removal of the entire population of the Capital. The nobles did not care about it, as they were repaid for the little inconvenience it caused them, by filling their pockets from the corrupt distribution of the building sites of the new city, and the frequent litigation it gave rise to. To the people it was the source of ruinous loss and discomfort, to which none but an unfeeling despotism would have dared to subject them. It was melancholy to see them breaking up their old habitations, and seeking new ones at great cost and labour. This senseless custom of changing the Royal residence is by no means uncommon. I have since read, that when this present wayward King was a few years later deposed by his younger brother, a similar freak possessed the brain of the usurper, who, in his turn, gave up his brother's newly-built city and palace at Ava to the owls and the bats, for the whim of again restoring the seat of government to this now half-demolised town. Such is Despotism!

With the exception of a few of the principal streets where the houses boasted of tiled roofs, Amerapoorah was constructed entirely of teak wood, bamboos, and thatch. For a town built of such fragile materials, it must have presented a respectable appearance before the work of demolition commenced. The houses, according to the usual plan of their domestic architecture, were supported on strong poles of teak timber, the floor fronting the street being laid two or three feet from the ground, forming a kind of enclosed verandah, which served for the shops of the traders. At the back of this, a staircase or a short ladder leads to the dwelling-rooms, which from their increased height of floor, leave an enclosed room below, used as a store, or for various purposes; but where this is not required, a free passage is left under the whole building. This plan of building is peculiarly well suited to a country liable, like Amerapoorah, to frequent

'Amarapura, Looking East', from Henry Yule, *Narrative of the Mission to the Court of Ava in 1855*, Smith, Elder, London, 1858.

shocks of Earthquake. One of these occurred while I was there, but, though it was rather a severe one, no damage was done; the houses merely rocked backwards and forwards without injury, and it seemed to cause very little alarm to the inhabitants. I have since read that a remarkably severe shock occurred in 1839, which converted many substantial pagodas into heaps of ruins, and caused great damage to the new Palace then building at Amerapoorah, though the severest shock could do little injury to houses such as I have described. The duration of this earthquake, or rather of this series of earthquakes, was most remarkable. A respectable witness of them says, after describing the terrific violence of the first shock, 'For four or five days we had nothing but earthquakes, every fifteen or thirty minutes, and, *for six months after*, scarcely a day passed without one'. He estimates that 300 or 400 persons were killed in the first shock.

The main streets were wide and cheerful, dotted here and there with noble tamarind trees, affording an agreeable shade, though the natives hold it to be unhealthy to live under the shelter of these trees. The town was surrounded by a high brick wall with battlements, and a wide ditch; this was nearly half a mile from the river, which,—above an island that has formed in the stream opposite the town, appears to be a mile broad. A large proportion of the population lived between the wall and the river, and it was in this suburb, on the river side, that I hired a house.

The day after my arrival, my property and effects were carried up from the boats without having sustained any damage by weather, or loss by pilfering. No Royal or municipal dues were demanded; no troublesome official appeared to obstruct the course of business; my boats' crews were discharged quite satisfied with their treatment, and I found myself comfortably established in my new quarters, with less vexatious annoyance than I should have encountered in any town in Europe. All this was gratifying.

The news that a white foreigner had arrived, with a prodigious amount of goods for sale, spread like wildfire through the town, and the state of chaos into which everything was thrown by the unhappy exodus did not prevent a crowd of traders from flocking around my interpreter, urging him at once to open his stores. Cheering as this symptom was, he thought a little delay would only tend to sharpen their appetite: besides, it was imperative that I should first bow before the Golden Feet, to present my offerings and solicit the Royal protection. I therefore sent Shwai-ee to inquire of one of the Attwenwoons,* whether I might have that honour on the following day. He returned with a gracious answer.

After breakfast the next morning, I mounted one of their beautiful little ponies, and, accompanied by Shwai-ee, set forth on my Royal visit with alacrity, as to a holiday treat. I had first to go to the court of the Attwenwoons, called the *Bya-dyke*, dismount at the gate, and take off my shoes before I entered the building. And here I cannot help stopping a moment, to exclaim against the folly of my countrymen generally, in raising a senseless clamour against a custom so truly agreeable in a tropical climate. I found the comfort of it so great, that from that day forth I never wore our detestable foot-gear of stockings and boots so long as I remained in the country. The cool light sandal of the native, slipped on and off with facility, was quite a luxury after the foot became trained to the use of the strap that binds it to the sole. The entering a house barefooted, or walking abroad in sandals, carries with it an idea of degradation to the European, which is quite foreign to the mind of the Burman. They did not object to my retaining the stockings, nor the hat, but I did not wish either of them.

Our Envoys have always complained of vexatious delays before they could secure a reception at Court. Nothing of the kind was experienced by the foreigner who had no state dignity to uphold. As for myself, I found far less difficulty in gaining an audience of his Majesty than I should have had in getting an interview with our Secretary of State in Downing Street; a few questions were asked at the *Bya-dyke*, and in less than an hour I was in the presence of the King.

For some astrological reason, His Majesty had vacated his gorgeous Palace, and was inhabiting a temporary one near to it, constructed of bamboo and thatch. Of course no attempt had been made to decorate such a building. The apartments were large, and the Royal style of raising roof upon roof had been attended to, a huge bunch of straw crowning the whole, as the gilded *tee* or umbrella did the finished building; but it was so slightly put together that the floors creaked and

*Atwin-wuns: ministers in charge of palace administration.

bent uncomfortably under our weight as we walked over them.

My ideas of the Court of His Majesty of Burmah were derived from the descriptions of our former Envoys. I left my house, expecting to gain a momentary glance at a personage dressed up like a heathen idol, before whom all people were bowing in profound adoration—whose glory was too great to permit him to unbend, and to whom I should not be suffered to address a word in person. My imagination was filled with the idea that I was merely to go through a needful ceremony which I might not be permitted to repeat, and it was with the sensation of one who had to witness a curious and splendid show rather than to secure any tangible and permanent advantage, that I appeared before the Palace gates. From what I had read, I could not disconnect the King's human nature from the pageantry and exclusiveness with which it pleased his Court to invest it.

Filled with these misconceptions, judge of my surprise, when, on entering a spacious apartment used as an Audience Hall, the floor creaking in a most uncourtly manner at each step, I beheld at the end of it a young man, about thirty years old, with a pleasant, good-humoured countenance, seated cross-legged on a gilded arm-chair of European make, manifesting no sign or symbol of state other than the chair he sat in, which rested on a stage very slightly raised from the floor. This was His Majesty! His costume did not vary from that of his courtiers, except that the silk cloth worn round the loins was a bright scarlet check, a colour confined to the use of the Royal family. This, and a light jacket tied with strings in front, made of white muslin, with a handkerchief of the same material twisted round the head to confine the hair, completed the costume of both the King and his people. There were probably forty or fifty persons assembled before him on the floor, in a posture half sitting, half kneeling, their bodies bent forward, their eyes fixed on the ground, and their hands clasped as in an attitude of respect, with some of whom His Majesty was apparently conversing on rather familiar terms.

The presents intended for His Majesty were borne in gilded trays by some of the attendants in the Royal household, and, being numerous, they formed rather an imposing procession. They consisted of a large, richly-cut crystal dish, selections from the best portions of my British manufactures, and twelve stands of capital muskets and bayonets, which were, no doubt, used against us with effect in the war which followed. These last attracted the greatest notice, and were examined with attention. These offerings were carried forward and placed in front of his Majesty for his inspection, while I followed, bending forward as I walked, and took my seat on the floor in a spot pointed out to me in advance of the assembled company, imitating, as well as I was able, the attitude of those whom I saw near me. My interpreter, Shwai-ee, was crouching behind me.

The disease of Court favour is very contagious. I caught it at once; though it cannot be denied there is a mixture of fear in the gratification one feels at being in favour with an uncontrolled Despot. I could not but reflect that the man sitting before me, cross-legged, on that arm-chair, was indeed an object to be feared, and by no means to be trifled with, though at the present moment clothed with smiles. How soon might this calm surface be lashed into fury by an unguarded word or an untoward circumstance! It is at such a time, when the lives of human beings are mere toys in his estimation, that the unbridled power of an irresponsible Despot shines forth in its true and hateful colours, and to such sudden changes and paroxysms this smiling Monarch was far from being a stranger. Well might those who sought his favour, crouch in his presence! At the present moment, however, kindness and good-humour were in the ascendant.

After some inquiries about my country, and the objects I had in view in coming to Ava, His Majesty addressed a few words to some one in the ranks behind me, which, to my no small astonishment, elicited an address to me in clear, good English accent—'Are you, sir, an Englishman?' Robinson Crusoe's surprise at the celebrated footprint in the uninhabited island could hardly have surpassed mine, for I thought myself 500 miles away from any of my own race. I turned my head to the quarter where the voice came from, and shall never forget the whimsical figure the speaker presented to my view. He was a large, strongly-built man, slightly bent by age, attired after the fashion of the natives, already described—a long, ample silk cloth round the waist, a loose muslin jacket, tied with strings in front, covered his body, but did not conceal the white skin beneath, barelegged of course, and his long grey hair twisted into a knot at the crown, where it was confined by a strip of white muslin. His long grey beard was so thinned, according to the native fashion, that that portion only which appertained to the middle part of the chin was preserved, and this being of a texture stiff as horsehair wagged backwards and forwards in a most ludicrous manner whenever he attempted to speak. He spoke Burmese fluently, and might well have passed for a native, had not his fair complexion, his light-blue eyes, and prominent nose, of such shape and colour as I have never seen except among my own respected countrymen, unmistakably attested his origin. He was addressed as 'Yadza' (the nearest approach the Burmese language admits to 'Rodgers'), and I now recollected that when in Rangoon I had heard of such a person residing at Amerapoorah, who had formerly held the office of Collector of the Port, now filled by Mr Lanciego. His history is a melancholy one, and I will give it hereafter as I heard it from his own lips. The King was highly amused at hearing a conversation in the English language for the first time, and encouraged us to continue it, though I fear some of the free remarks his aged servant was imprudent enough to make, would not have gone unpunished if they had been understood.

The King was extremely affable, permitting me to take many little liberties which would not have been tolerated for a moment in his own subjects. Finding, from my awkward and undignified twistings, that I could not accomplish the native feat of sitting on one half of my body only, he desired that I should be at my ease, when, to the horror of all present, I proceeded to change my posture to a cross-legged seat, such as a tailor uses on his shop-board. I was not rebuked for this, nor when I sat upright, nor when I had the audacity to stare His Majesty in the face. It was evident he was pleased at the idea of my settling at the capital, by the protection he promised, in a manner that left no doubt it was intended. After liberty had been given to present my offerings to the chief Queen, and to come to the Palace as often as I liked, I was allowed to withdraw, backing out, as I saw others do, on all-fours for a few yards before rising.

I had now to be presented to a more powerful person in the State even than His Majesty. The chief Queen had been raised to the Throne from the humble condition of chief gaoler's daughter. Although some years older than the King, and far from possessing any personal charms, she had, by the judicious use of her influence, and a certain determination of character, obtained complete control over the mind of her easy husband. By corrupt means she had acquired immense wealth—her intrigues had filled most of the important offices in the Kingdom with her creatures, and through the instrumentality of her only brother, a fit agent for the purpose, she was enabled to carry on a large traffic in bribery and extortion. As avarice, backed by unlimited power, naturally leads to cruelty, this venal pair were as unscrupulous and vindictive as they were avaricious. They were equally feared and detested by the people.

On our first acquaintance her Majesty was pleased to be unusually gracious. I was ushered into her reception-room without much ceremony, the presents which I had prepared being borne in front as before. She was seated on a square cushion laid upon the floor. Several persons were crouching before her, apparently engaged on business, while a few female attendants behind had charge of her betel-box, golden cup, fan, &c. She did me the honour to order a rush mat to be spread for me on the floor, which was considered to be a mark of great condescension. Unlike the King she examined the presents carefully, and was so much enamoured of the fine muslins and prints of Manchester and Glasgow that, on being told that I had a large quantity of them for sale, she expressed a wish that I should send forward several packages and repeat my visit on the morrow, when a great many of the ladies of the Palace would like to buy them. Here, indeed, was a piece of good luck I had little expected! Her Majesty could not have made a proposition more exactly suited to my taste. No one was there to taunt me with becoming the Court Haberdasher,—or even if they did, or ten times worse, such an opportunity for a day's amusement would not have been allowed to pass neglected. I gladly promised obedience.

Her Majesty then condescended to present me, as a mark of her especial favour, with a pawn from her own box. It was a leaf enclosing a combination of substances at which my stomach revolted,—areca-nut, tobacco, terra japonica [cutch], lime, and spices, and I know not what besides. What was I to do? I could not chew all this nastiness to a pulp, as was evidently required of me, so with great deliberation I put it into my waistcoat-pocket. A burst of laughter followed from the young ladies behind at what they supposed to be my ignorance; another peal, when I told them I should keep it for ever as a mark of Her Majesty's distinguished favour. The present of a pawn in its crude state is not much amiss, but the exhibition of it in a different shape quite sickened me. Her Majesty, after some chewing of one of these delicacies, took it from her mouth and handed it over to a pretty girl behind her, who, esteeming herself highly honoured by the gift—*horribile dictu!*—popped the nasty morsel into her mouth, and completed its mastication. How fortunate an escape that her Majesty did not so far honour me! I have witnessed a more unceremonious transfer of this delicious quid than even the one related, but I spare my reader the disgusting detail.

Among my presents to the Queen was a handsome box of musical glasses, and while I was explaining to her the method of using them, His Majesty unexpectedly entered the apartment. He asked me if I could play upon them. I answered that I would attempt to do so (for I had amused myself with them in my voyage up the river), but that it would be necessary to provide me with a cup of water for the purpose. A large cup of water was brought. His Majesty seized it from the attendant *in transitu*, and dashed it with great force over the ranges of cups, deluging the musician, and sprinkling the great Lady besides, as she was seated not far off. As His Majesty laughed heartily at this Royal practical joke, it was of course expected that the company should join in the merriment, and we all did so. After putting my glasses in order again, I had the honour to entertain them with 'God save the King', performed in very tolerable style for an amateur, in a place where it certainly had never been heard before.

It is not, however, altogether prudent for a man to parade his accomplishments at the Court of His Majesty of Ava. I saw there a band of adroit but unfortunate jugglers, who had crossed from Madras, on speculation, to exhibit their feats before the King. They were so successful that he issued his Royal command that they should be kept at his Court, on an allowance of a basket of rice to each person monthly. I was told that they had suffered this detention for two years, and were still not allowed to depart.

On returning home, and thinking over the events of the day, I confess I was very much bewildered. All my preconceived notions of the dignity and exclusiveness of this great Monarch had been suddenly blown to the winds. It is true that when a private merchant only had to be presented, some descent from the formality of state might reasonably be expected,—but that I should have been laughing and joking with the King and Queen, and that I should have been invited to what was pretty sure to be a repetition of it tomorow on a larger scale, seemed almost incredible. My interpreter, Burman though he was, seemed equally astonished. In the mean time this footing of intimacy with Crowned Heads was far from disagreeable to think on, and I looked forward with pleasing anticipations of amusement in repeating my visit to the Palace on the morrow.

A Personal Narrative of Two Years' Imprisonment in Burmah, 2nd edn., John Murray, London, 1862, pp. 25–37.

9
A Yankee at the Court of King Mindon

FRANK VINCENT

Frank Vincent, whose father was a wealthy merchant, was born in Brooklyn in 1848. At the age of eighteen he entered Yale College but completed only one year of studies before falling seriously ill. Four years later he had recovered sufficiently to set out on a series of travels that took him through the Far East, South-East Asia, India, Scandinavia, Central and South America, and Africa.

He described these travels in many books and articles, but his best-known work was The Land of the White Elephant, part of which deals with his trip to Mandalay. Here, with his kingdom now reduced to less than half its size by British encroachment, King Mindon was looking out for friendly nations that might help him to counterbalance British influence. The French were proving to be willing in this respect; perhaps the Americans might too. In this extract,

Vincent tells us how, having arranged an audience with Mindon through a rich Chinese intermediary called Seng-Ko, he finds the king somewhat too welcoming for comfort.

AFTER waiting five or ten minutes we were summoned to a small pillared portico, open on two sides. At our backs there was a golden door leading to another chamber, and before us was a large green baize curtain, extending from the ceiling to the floor of another room which was some few feet above us. In the centre of this screen was an opening about ten feet square; here a red velvet cushion and a pair of silver-mounted binoculars were laid upon the floor, where there was an elegantly carpeted staircase connecting the two chambers. The roof was supported by immense pillars, grouped around the bases of two of which were the royal umbrellas and other insignia. No one save the King is allowed to possess a white umbrella, and princes of the blood are allowed to have two umbrellas (gilt, with poles ten or fifteen feet in length attached) carried above them by their servants when they walk or ride in public—ministers but one. There were about half a dozen princes in the 'Audience Chamber', among them the heir-apparent, an intelligent as well as handsome young man, plainly dressed, *excepting* a pair of immense cluster diamond ear-rings. Our party—for there were several others whom we found waiting—was disposed in the following order: The princes sat upon the right, then came the *Yaw-Ahtween-Woon*,[*] then another minister, then myself, next Mr Seng-Ko, then two ex-ministers of the former King; adjoining them were two Portuguese Roman Catholic missionaries, and then two commercial gentlemen upon the extreme left; besides these, in the rear, were some dozen or more clerks, who were paying their respects to His Majesty upon the receipt of new appointments, each offering a large basket of fruit in support of his loyal feelings. Our presents were displayed before us, placed on little wooden stands about a foot in height. The natives were all prostrating themselves flat upon their stomachs, with their noses nearly touching the carpets and their eyes cast down in a most abject and servile manner.

[*] A minister empowered to collect goods, services, and funds from the town of Yaw.

66

In a few moments we heard two or three muffled booms—taps on a large tom-tom probably—and then all of us becoming at once silent, the King appeared, and quietly and slowly laid himself down, reclining against the velvet cushion and only partially facing the audience. At the same time one of the queens entered and placed a golden spittoon, betel-box, *chatty** (with water), and cup on the floor before him. The King is a short, stout, pleasant, though, like many of his ministers, an exceeding crafty-looking gentleman, fifty-four years of age. His hair was thin and was tied in the usual Burmese knot; the head was high at the crown, showing 'self-esteem', large, and the eyes were closely set, indicating cunning (if we are to believe phrenology and physiognomy); the neck was thick, expressive of vitality and physical power, and the face close shaven, excepting a thin black moustache. His dress was very plain and simple, consisting merely of a white *engie*, a white linen jacket, and a silk *putso*, a cloth worn around the hips and thighs; there were no ornaments in the ears, though their lobes contained holes nearly an inch in diameter, which did not improve the expression of his countenance very materially. His Majesty first took up his opera glass, though we were not more than twenty feet distant, and surveyed us in a very grave and leisurely manner, ending with a flourish of the glass, as if to say, 'Now, then, for business.' The royal secretary read aloud our names, business, and the list of the presents which were placed before us; this was done in a loud, drawling style, and concluded with a sort of supplicating moan.

His Majesty then began the conversation through the Minister and my Chinese friend as interpreters. After the usual questions concerning my age, business, residence, and travels, the King said he wished me to convey to my Government the sentiment that 'he had a great partiality for Americans, and wished them to come over and colonise in his dominions'. But a word preliminary: it seems that I had the honour to be the first American presented at the Court of Ava (excepting a mechanical engineer, who was in His Majesty's employ ten or twelve years ago), and that the King in his astuteness graciously thought me a *spy*, or at least that I was visiting Burma for political purposes, and consequently had

*A large spherical earthenware water jar.

'The King', from Henry Yule, *Narrative of the Mission to the Court of Ava in 1855*, Smith, Elder, London, 1858.

some influence with as well as instructions from the Government at home. It was in vain that I protested being a simple traveller, visiting different countries for the purpose of studying their geography, climate, productions; the people—their manners and customs, government, religion, laws, language, literature, industries, and commerce—and all for the improvement of mind and health of body, and that I had travelled about twelve thousand miles more especially to pay my respects to the King of Ava, and to see the wonderful white elephant, about which I had heard and read so much in my own country; but to no purpose, for it was quite evident His Majesty thought politics were surely my main object and end. Promising to make his wishes known to the proper authorities at home did not seem to be alone sufficient for his purposes, for he said he would keep me in Mandalay while I wrote, and until an answer came from America. At this I demurred of course, when His Majesty said if I would remain he would give me a house, living, and *as many Burmese wives as I wished* (a rather tempting offer, for the women of the upper classes are both pretty and modest), and, furthermore, he would 'make my fortune'. I was fast becoming very much interested, and slightly excited as well. His Majesty wished to make also a commercial treaty with America, and my services would be indispensable. Thus were alluring nets spread for my feet and enticing temptations presented to me. Still I was not then prepared to enter the King's service; the idea was too new and novel, the change—from republican America and steam ploughs to monarchical Burma and white elephants—too great. 'I must have time to consider His Majesty's gracious offers,' said I to the interpreter. 'You will never have a better chance,' was returned from the King. Seeing me still reluctant, the King condescendingly offered to 'make me a great man'—to give me high rank among his own nobles and princes. To this I answered my duty was first to my parents, and next to my own country, and that I would return to the latter and consult with the former, and then, *if they were willing*, I would be most happy to accept his magnificent and unusually gracious terms. He replied, 'It might then be too late'; and there the matter dropped, and the conversation was changed to other topics, though the King was evidently not a little vexed at my obstinacy, and doubtless thought me mad or certainly very foolish not to accept such generous proposals. One of the missionaries then presented some petitions, which were referred to the proper minister; some State business was transacted; a present of Rs. 100 was brought me ('to use for my travelling expenses or to purchase a memento of my presentation at the Court of "His Golden-Footed Majesty"'), and then the audience was terminated by the King suddenly rising and abruptly retiring from the room.

One of his queens or concubines (he has four of the former and about a hundred of the latter) who, though out of sight, had been fanning the King with a gorgeous fan of peacock's feathers during the audience, now took a peep at us, of course exhibiting herself at the same time, and such a beautiful creature I have rarely looked upon before and perchance never shall see again. She was one of the veritable 'houris of Paradise', an oriental pearl of indescribable loveliness and symmetry. I will not attempt a description; but the King's liberal offers came at once to mind, and I felt what a great sacrifice it would be to return to my native land, and refuse—nay, almost spurn—rank, wealth, and beauty under the peacock banner and golden umbrella of His Majesty of Ava.

The 'audience' lasted over an hour. The King seemed to have very respectable ideas of America and a high appreciation of the (usually conceded) enterprise and industry of her people; perhaps he wished Americans to settle in Burma as a sort of political offset to the English, whose power—now owning two-thirds of ancient Burma—is naturally very great, but I think his main idea was simply to obtain from the United States a commercial treaty advantageous to himself. His Majesty's use of the binoculars, which he invariably employs in *all* audiences, is not altogether pleasant; but the manner in which he would scan our countenances while replying to some of his *commanding* speeches was most amusing. His voice is soft and low, and he speaks in a very deliberate manner, taking ample time to arrange his thoughts before giving them utterance.

The present King is a son of the famous Tharawaddi; his brother—the eldest legitimate son—assumed the government in 1845, but, proving a tyrant, was deposed and succeeded by King Mounglon in 1853. In 1857 he removed the capital from Amarapoora to Mandalay. The King, little thinking that he would ever attain the crown, had in early youth taken the vows of a *pongyee*, or Budhist priest, and lived secluded in a monastery until his accession. Like his predecessors his reign has not been without its troubles. In 1866 a rebellion broke out headed by two of the King's sons, the Mengon and Mengondyne princes, having for its object the dethronement of their father. The attempt failed, and the former is a refugee in the Shan States, while the latter resides under British protection in Bengal. As regards the events of the King's rule much might be said of blame and something also of praise. The Government is a despotism; among many others we notice the royal title of 'Lord of the Power of Life and Death'. The *Holt-daw* (Council of State), composed of the four principal ministers of State, are the executive officers of the Government; they also try all appeal cases, forming a high court for that purpose, and receiving ten per cent. of the property in suit, are said to derive very handsome incomes from this source alone. The tyranny and weight of the King's rule is most felt at, or in the immediate vicinity of, the capital, the remote districts being almost independent, and paying but little more heed to the ruling monarch than to swear allegiance whenever visited by his officers. And so limited in extent of territory is the real power of the King that the people dwelling upon the borders of Yunan are said to acknowledge the sovereignty of the local rulers of the Emperor of China as well as those of the King of Ava, and so enjoy privileges from both Governments. At present there is a royal monopoly of the *paddy* (rice) and cotton and other leading products—marble, amber, gold, copper, coal, and gems above a certain size (all over Rs. 100 in value). The King dare not leave his palace for fear of foul play, and he has consequently never seen his own war canoes or steamers, nor has he ever visited his new palace built near the river.

The Land of the White Elephant: Sights and Scenes in South-Eastern Asia, Harper Brothers, New York, 1874; reprinted 1988 by Oxford University Press in association with The Siam Society, Bangkok, pp. 54–62.

10
A Private Interview with King Thibaw

SHWAY YOE

Shway Yoe was the pseudonym that the young James George Scott was using when in 1882 his celebrated study of Burman culture was published. He was the son of a Scottish minister who died when James was only ten, and the young man's university studies were cut short for financial reasons. At the age of twenty-four he went first to Malaya as a newspaper correspondent and then to Burma, where he taught in St John's College, Rangoon. He also wrote articles for publication locally as well as in Britain. (His pen-name literally means 'golden-honest' but is also the name of a traditional character who dances along with musical processions.) While on leave in London, Scott studied law and on a second leave passed his examinations for the Bar. It was during this second absence that Upper Burma was annexed to bring the whole country under British rule in January 1886. He returned to Burma a few months later to join the Burma Commission whose task was to administer the territory. He served in this capacity (largely in the Shan States) until his retirement in 1910, by which time he had been knighted for his services to Burma. He died at home in England in 1935 at the age of eighty-four.

He had remained active, writing books about the country, but it is his first and most famous book, published when he was only thirty, that remains essential reading for anyone wishing to understand Burmese culture. Here is his account, written in 1880, of how he and some other foreigners (kalā) obtained an informal audience with the young King Thibaw and of what then took place. The British in Lower Burma despised Thibaw as an ineffectual, cruel, and wanton despot, a fact which explains the faintly sneering tone of Scott's account.

TIME was, when to get an interview with the Arbiter of Existence was as difficult a matter as to see the Grand Lama, or the Sherif ul Islam of Mecca. When the servants of 'the Foreign Woman', Her Most Gracious Majesty Queen Victoria, protested in 1879 against the new sovereign's summary settlement of domestic matters, Thibaw swore a royal oath by the sacred hairs of Gautama, by the Lord, the Law and the Assembly, the three precious things, that he would never look on a white man again. For a year the vow was religiously kept, and ambitious 'globe-trotters' and prying special correspondents were kept at a distance, and had not even the satisfaction of being admitted within the outer gate of the nandaw [palace]. In time, however, the royal coffers got low, and it was thought foolish not to make use of the barbarian merchants, seeking for monopolies and grants of forest land, and able and willing to pay enormous sums for such concessions. His majesty's ministers therefore speedily found means of relieving the great King of Righteousness from his solemn oath. The first principle of the Buddhist faith is charity. How, then, could the Lord of the Rising Sun gain more merit and advance some miles on the noble Eightfold Path better than by conquering his just personal antipathies and allowing awe-stricken foreigners to grovel before the splendour of his effulgence and worship at his Golden Feet! When once they had experienced that supreme delight, his majesty's ministers might be trusted to see that the wealth of the merchants was made to subserve the royal interests. And so it came to pass that Thibaw first received a few speculators and their friends, and has ended by granting an audience to any European that can get a minister to speak for him. And so the Golden Hairs are forgotten, and the three precious things calmly flouted. Still the royal barbarian is not comfortable at these interviews. He was too curious to be dignified. He had not the fund of conversation that his father had, and he was impatient apparently of being looked at, as strangers in remote parts of China and wild beasts in zoological gardens may be supposed to be.

Securing an interview is not always an easy matter, unless you are a great capitalist, desirous of a grant somewhere. If you merely wish to see his majesty, the process is somewhat difficult. You probably apply first of all to the Chevalier Andreino, Italian Consul in Mandalay, and master of cere-monies and mysterious 'doing duty' man at the Burmese Court. He may get you the desired audience, but more prob-ably refers you to one of the higher ministers. Almost cer-tainly these officials will say that it is impossible for you to see the king. His majesty is too busy, 'working hard all day at affairs of state'; and they gaze stolidly upon you. You regret the circumstance extremely, make the minister a present of a few hundred rupees, and continue to deplore your bad luck. Then he brightens up suddenly, recollects that on such and such a day his majesty is possibly free. He will find out and do his best for you.

Next day you are told that an interview will be granted, that the king of kings graciously permits you to come and place your head under his gilded feet. If you are a wise man and have been warned by considerate friends, you will now commence to practise sitting on your feet. It is as well to rehearse the process frequently beforehand, for they must be tucked away so that his majesty cannot see them; and if you do not find the most agreeable way of effecting the conceal-ment, your audience will be chiefly memorable to you for frightful agony, a vast amount of internal 'popular language', and vows of vengeance against the ministers, who seem to have an irritating faculty of grinning all down their backs.

The journey to the palace is not a pleasant preparation. It is too hot to ride, and accordingly you decide to go in the apotheosis of a dog-kennel on wheels, which does duty for a carriage in Mandalay. There is not room for much more than one Englishman in the vehicle, and the only way you can get in is by scrambling over the backs of the bullocks. I shall never forget my first experience of a Mandalay carriage. After an exciting ten minutes spent in trying to circumvent a kicking bullock, I at length got in and sat down on the floor— there are no seats—to gaze out at the round hole by which I had got in. The rest of the party followed, each man in a kennel of his own. The beasts set off at a swinging trot over roads of the early depraved order, and in a couple of minutes we were all regretting that we did not brave the sun and ride, or even walk. However, the drivers disregard our entreaties, and hustle up the cattle all the more energetically. We pass over the moat, and through the enormous wooden gateway into the walled town. We enter by the a-mingala gate, the south-western, the only one through which corpses are allowed to be taken from the city. It is almost invariably used by Englishmen as being nearest to the Residency and the river, but no upper-class Burman will pass through it if he possibly can avoid doing so. After five minutes' more jolting

'Burmese Public Carriage, Mandalay', from Noel F. Singer, *Burmah*, Kiscadale, Gartmore, 1993.

we arrive at the outer stockade of the palace, and get out of our conveyances with some alacrity and a lot of bruises. Immediately inside the gate is a guard-house, with a cluster of the royal soldiery, who, as we come up, squat down on the ground and hold their Enfields in front of them at the third motion of the present, looking like frogs on a Christmas card.

We cross a wide open space, pass through the 'Red Postern', and turn to the left, for it is to be a private reception, and we do not ascend the steps to the Hall of Audience. We pass a gallop which Thibaw has laid down for his ponies, and enter the Royal Gardens. They are not much to speak of. Laid out in squares, with raised paths, deep brickwork canals running in every direction, grottoes and 'fads' of all sorts in every available place, they are rather tiresome, and we prefer to talk to a remarkable gentleman who meets us here. This is the Pangyet Wun, or governor of the glass manufactories—rather a mysterious title, seeing that there are no such works in the royal city. But names mean anything or nothing in Mandalay. The Pangyet Wun is the familiar example of Western flippancy triumphing over Eastern conceit and forgotten good manners. He speaks the English of the primer overlaid with the language of the young subaltern and the seafaring man on Atlantic steamers of the inferior class.

As we shake hands with him he smiles demurely, and says he regrets he cannot offer us 'a liquor'. 'Wine or spirits, you know, are not drunk in the palace', and an apparition suggestive of a barbarian wink flits across his face. We have not long to talk with him, however. Everything, he says, is ready, and we make for a side-door into the palace, or rather into one of the numerous audience chambers connected with the nandaw, each having a name of its own, and being used according to his majesty's whim. We are to be received in the Hmaw-gaw, 'the Crystal Palace', so called from the decoration of its walls, resplendent with bits of mirror and coloured glass. We have to put off our shoes before stepping into the palace, and do so not without dire misgivings, for in times gone by we had been to see King Mindôn, and have lively recollections of the nails in the floor. A Burman, they say, never likes to finish anything, and therefore does not drive home the nails in the planking of his house. People more versed in the ways of the nandaw assert that this is not the true reason, and declare that it is an ingenious method of making the presumptuous Kalā* approach the neighbourhood of the Lord of Land and Sea in respectful fashion, with his eyes humbly lowered. It certainly is very effective in that way. You cannot gaze about you with any degree of freedom when you have a lurking suspicion that the next step will drive a nail into the ball of your big toe. Consequently every one used to go in with meekly downcast face, and respect to the sovereign was thus triumphantly enforced. But Thibaw disdains such petty ways of compelling outward respect. Has he not made the English Resident run away? Or perhaps it is the European experience of the Pangyet Wun that we have to thank. At any rate, the corridors and passages are covered with thick soft carpets, three or four deep, and we walk along in comfort, if with a somewhat undressed feeling.

It is not far to the Hmaw-gaw. We find the chamber almost empty. A thick carpet, woven in one piece, covers the floor, and the far side is raised a couple of feet above the rest of the room. On this dais stands a couch. The Pangyet Wun tells us to sit down and not to speak. We obey, and stare at the couch and a door behind it. Again we have misgivings. Mindôn Min used to keep visitors waiting a trifle of an hour or so, till they got so cramped that they had to be hoisted on to their legs. But it is not so with his son. He comes almost immediately, jerking himself suddenly in at the door, as if somebody had stuck a pin into him behind, walks hurriedly to the couch, kicking off his slippers on the way, and throws himself upon it, with his elbows sunk in the crimson and gold cushions. He looks straight at us for about thirty seconds, and then falls to examining his finger-nails and the carpet. He is embarrassed; his father was embarrassing. The pious potentate used to scrutinise his visitors (at a distance of twenty feet or so) through a field-glass, and people who were not overawed used to grin, which required explanation. King Thibaw comes alone, except that there is a page with cheroots. The gigantic gold spittoon and betel-nut box and other salivating and chewing paraphernalia, which were deposited before his late lamented father, are wanting. He knocks off the ash of his green cheroot on the carpet and presently lets it go out. Meanwhile the thandawsin, the royal herald, has

*Foreigners, especially Indians and Westerners.

commenced chanting our names, business, and the list of our presents. This is done in a high-pitched recitative, and takes a long time, for all the names, styles, and titles of his majesty are declaimed for a matter of quarter of an hour, each sentence ending with a longdrawn payā-a-ah.*

At last it is over, and Thibaw asks if we are well. We announce that we are, and the interpreter, who throughout sees fit to translate bald monosyllables into obsequious, not to say grovelling periods, says that by his majesty's merciful permission we are in the enjoyment of perfect health. Thibaw then demands our business. The interpreter replies that we have come to view the glories of his majesty's mighty kingdom, and to lay our heads under his golden feet. This is a lengthy formality, for an epitome of the titles comes in with every answer. Thibaw looks very ill at ease, and has an occasional glance at us out of the tail of his eye. Having inquired after the well-being of the Queen, the Viceroy, the Chief Commissioner of British Burma, and his dear brothers in Calcutta, who, he hopes, are being well treated, as befits their rank, it seems as if there was going to be a sudden end to the audience, to avert which we wildly grasp at the idea of saying that we had taken tickets in the royal lotteries, but had not been successful in the drawing. His majesty twirls his cheroot over his shoulder, which is a sign that he wants a light, and says he is very sorry, but hopes we will try again. We announce that we are going to make another attempt, and add, in the desperate hope of getting his majesty into a controversy, that lotteries are considered a very bad thing for the people in Europe. The interpreter gazes for three quarters of a second reproachfully at us and says, that by reason of his majesty's great might, glory, and clemency, we are encouraged to make a fresh venture, and that we are lost in wonder at the wisdom which has fallen upon such a method of increasing the revenue, a system which had never occurred to the unilluminated minds of barbarian financiers. Burmese is a language with which some of us are acquainted, and which affords unusual facilities for the relief of the irritated mind, but while we are hesitating as to whether we shall break through Court etiquette and address the great Lord of

*A term of respect used when addressing or referring to a royal person or object of religious veneration.

77

Righteousness mouth to mouth, Thibaw graciously remarks that he is glad to hear that the wisdom of his ministers has increased the knowledge of political economy in the world, and adds that he is unacquainted with any trade which for an outlay of two rupees will bring in a return of ten thousand. Having announced that he will give orders to his ministers and officials to show us every respect while we remain under the shadow of his throne, he suddenly gets up and vanishes as rapidly as he appeared. The Pangyet Wun calls out, 'Get on your legs, gentlemen, "long chairs" are better than this sort of thing,' and we obey with great alacrity, and are regaled outside with brandy and water of considerable potency, poured out of a teapot into teacups.

The Burman: His Life and Notions, Macmillan, London, 1882; 3rd edn., 1910, pp. 459–65.

11
Burma's Last King and Queen Go into Exile

SIR HERBERT THIRKELL WHITE

Because of certain massacres that King Thibaw had ordered, he was regarded by the British as a sadistic tyrant, and his wife Su-hpaya-lat was generally depicted as a scheming harridan. Seizing the opportunity of a dispute between Thibaw's Court and the Bombay Burmah Trading Corporation, Lord Randolph Churchill in London sent to Mandalay an ultimatum that was in effect a declaration of war. Sending a heavily armed flotilla of steamships up the Irrawaddy, the British took Mandalay in November 1885. It had been decided that King Thibaw and his queen should immediately be deported to India.

The steamship Thooreah *('The Sun') carried them down to Rangoon, where a junior administrator called Herbert White had been told to meet the vessel. White's account of this sad moment in Burma's history is short but worth quoting because it goes some way towards correcting the somewhat exaggerated reputations of the royal couple. White himself went on to com-*

*plete thirty years of service in Burma, reaching the position of
Lieutenant-Governor. Sir Herbert was writing in 1913, when
the couple were still living in India. Thibaw died three years
later, never having been allowed to return to his country; his
widow was then permitted to go to Rangoon and live the rest of
her life quietly in a modest house.*

AS the junior officer in the Secretariat, I was told off to
board the *Thooreah* on her arrival. I was thus the first
officer in Rangoon to see the ex-King and his Queens.
King Thebaw was in appearance a Burman of very ordinary
type. He looked neither dissipated nor cruel; nor did he show
any emotion or feeling of his melancholy position. His somewhat heavy features were unmistakably those of the House of
Alaungpǎyá.* Both he and his elder sister (who died not long
ago) closely resembled the familiar picture of Mindón Min.
Queen Sūpǎyá-lāt's features were more finely marked than is
usual with Burmese ladies. She bore no appearance of special depravity, but she certainly looked a little shrew. The legend of Sūpǎyá-lāt is that she was a monster of cruelty and
wickedness, and that she was mainly responsible for all acts
of State during her husband's reign. From all that I heard in
Mandalay, where I had many sources of information, for the
most part unfriendly to the ex-Queen, I believe that both her
wickedness and her influence have been much exaggerated.
She seems to have been of a jealous temper, and to have
checked any inclination on the part of her husband to follow
the footsteps of Mindón Min. Doubtless it went hard with any
maid who attracted the King's attention. On one of the
golden doors of the palace used to be shown bloodstains,
marks of a little hand, signs of the tragic end of a Princess
who had incurred the Queen's wrath. (I am aware of the
learned explanation of these marks, but the legend is far
more interesting.) Beyond this there is no credible evidence
of her cruelty, nor is it well established that she ruled the
State. Clearly she wielded some influence; but apart from the
story of her speech to the Kinwun Mingyi,† the most arrogant
action imputed to her was that she used to have her meals

---

*Alaung-hpaya was the first king in a dynasty that ended with the reigns of
Mindon and his son Thibaw.
†This is the title of an influential minister who served Mindon, then Thibaw.

'The Burmah Expedition: Departure of King Theebaw From Mandalay', *Illustrated London News*, 6 February 1886.

before the King. Of course, this was very unusual and unseemly for a Burmese woman of any class. It hardly shows that she was paramount in the direction of the kingdom. The royal exiles were transferred to the R.I.M.S. *Clive*, and, after remaining for a few days in Rangoon, were taken to Madras. They were finally transferred to Ratnagiri in the Bombay Presidency, where King Thebaw and Sūpâyá-lāt still live. The poor little second Queen, of whom nothing, good or bad, has ever been heard, died last year.

A Civil Servant in Burma, Edward Arnold, London, 1913, pp. 108–9.

Royal and Holy Buildings

12
Pagodas

SHWAY YOE

We have already met Shway Yoe, alias J. G. Scott (see Passage 10 above). The foremost authority on Burma of his time, Scott's work is still highly valued by scholars. Resident in Burma for most of his life, he had ample opportunity to travel about the country and to study its innumerable shrines. In the following extract, he introduces Western readers to what are usually called 'pagodas', though travellers more familiar with Burma will call them zedi. *The Burmese distinguish four kinds of* zedi *according to whether the objects placed in the interior chamber are relics of Gautama Buddha, or the eight articles used by a* hpongyi *(monk), or images of the Buddha, or Buddhist scriptures. The word 'temples' is perhaps best reserved for those sacred buildings that enclose spaces for the use of monks and devotees of the Great Teacher, although we should remember that such buildings are not dedicated to the worship of a god.*

Scott tells how the building of a pagoda brings great kuthó *(merit) to the* hpaya-taga, *or 'pagoda-giver', and introduces us to pagodas other than the great Shwe Dagon, which is described in a later passage.*

SOME one with a greater regard for alliteration than the truth once said that the principal productions of Burma were pagodas, pôngyis,* and pariah dogs. As a superficial impression this is neat, and therefore it will continue to be

---

*A *hpon-gyi*, spelt in various ways, is a monk.

quoted by forcible feebles to the end of their days, in Bayswater or Ealing. It certainly is marvellous how many pagodas there are in the country, far exceeding the number of those raised in the sacred island of Ceylon, or by the Thibetans and Chinese, pious Buddhists, though they have fallen into sad doctrinal heresies. A Burman does not notice the multitude of the religious edifices in his country till he leaves it and finds how far more sparing other nations are in their places of worship. The poorest village has its neatly kept shrine, with the remains of others mouldering away round about it. No hill is so steep and rocky, or so covered with jungle, as to prevent the glittering gold or snow-white spire rising up to guard the place from ghouls and sprites, and remind the surrounding people of the Saviour Lord, the teacher of Nirvana and the Law. There is good reason for this multiplication of fanes. No work of merit is so richly paid as the building of a pagoda. The Payā-taga is regarded as a saint on earth, and when he dies he obtains the last release; for him there are no more deaths. The man who sets up a row of water-pots on a dusty road does well; he who raises a ta-gôn-daing, or sacred post, who builds a rest-house, presents an image or a bell, or founds a monastery, gains much kutho and ensures a happy transincorporation when he passes away; but the Payā-taga is finally freed from the three calamities, his kan[*] is complete, the merits outweight the demerits, and he attains the holy rest. That, at any rate, is the comforting belief, cherished by the most reprobate. Little wonder then that, with such a glorious reward in store for him, the pious man hoards his wealth for such an object, and that pagodas are so plentiful in the land. It avails little to repair a previous dedication, unless it be one of the great world shrines at Rangoon, Pegu, Prome, or Mandalay. In the case of ordinary pagodas the merit of the repair goes practically entirely to the original founder. Hence that puzzle to Europeans, the building of a bright new place of worship close to one which a very little care would save from crumbling away into a simple tumulus.

* * *

[*]Fate, destiny.

The Shwe Dagôn Payā is by far the most widely celebrated of the great Buddhist shrines, but there are others which, if not so venerated in other lands, still enjoy an even greater local reputation for sanctity, and attract pilgrims from all parts of Burma and the dependent hills, with now and again a band of pious worshippers from distant countries. Chief among these is the Shwe Hmaw-daw at Pegu, which commands Talaing worship before even the shrine of 'the slanted beam' on the Theinguttara hill. The pond close by it was covered with lotus blossoms immediately on the construction of the shapely spire and the great Tha-gyā Min, and countless Byammās* and Nat-déwas* assisted at the enshrinement of the relics. As with many other fanes, the king granted to the pagoda, and set apart from secular uses for ever, the whole space round it on which the shadow of the original pile fell between sunset and sunrise. Several hundred families were dedicated to its service, and in 1881 large sums were raised throughout all the low country for the manufacture of a new hti and the gilding of the whole surface, while many wondrous signs in the neighbourhood attested the sacred character of the undertaking. Similarly the Shwe San-daw at Prome, with its multitude of bells on the cramped hill-top, enjoys a special reputation on account of the prophecy there spoken by Shin Gautama himself, and the connection of the payā [pagoda] with the national hero-king, Dwut-tabaung, as recorded in the sacred books. In proof of this there exists to the present day, and may be seen at the foot of the hill, a huge stone with an inscription which none but the pure-minded can read, and few even of them understand. In other places examples of this duganan kyeganan, a kind of cypher-writing, or cryptograph, as it appears to the unenfranchised, exists, and usually records in mystic phraseology and inverted orthography the alms presented to the pagoda. Many of the lists of donations are, however, graven in a less cramped kyauk-sa, or 'stone writing', the givers having probably had a weak hankering after earthly fame. Thus a goodly marble slab with a long list of names may be seen at the Shwe Hmaw-daw, and a tablet near the Mya Thalôn, the Temple of the Emerald Bed (of the Buddha), at Ma-gwe in Upper Burma records how Min Din and Min La-go had in the

*Heavenly beings.

year 2399 of religion covered the whole payà with yellow cloth, repaired it thoroughly, and had it painted red and gold. An exact account is given of the amount of materials used and the money paid to workmen, and the inscription ends up with a prayer that the family of the donors might be gratified with the birth of a son. Near it is a magic stone with the figure of a hare, surrounded by stars, deeply graven in it to represent the moon, and a peacock to represent the sun.

A frequent adjunct of many pagodas is the Shwe Zet-daw, the imprint of the Lord Buddha's foot. It is too nearly square to command a painter's or sculptor's praise, and the toes are all of the same length, as may be seen in the example carried off by Captain Marryat, the novelist, in the first Burmese war, and now preserved in the British Museum. The sole is divided into a hundred and eight squares (taya shi' kwet), and on them are many lekkhana, representations of monasteries, pyathats, tigers, kalawaiks,* henthas,* parrots, seipputi fish, and the like, to signify that all things were under the feet of the Great Master. The number of beads on the rosary corresponds with the number of squares on the Shwe Zet-daw. The most famous example is at the pagoda of that name east of Mandalay, the great resort of the Shans, and another well-known one is opposite Magwe, inland from Minbu, where the mud volcanoes are, 'the boiling vats of the nagās'. But there are many specimens all over the country, not a few with the figure of a nagā, or sea monster, reared over them.

Most famous among the small pagodas is the Kyaik-hti-yo, insignificant in size, but unique from its position. The hill on which it stands takes its name from the payà, and is over three thousand five hundred feet in height. On its summit are numbers of granitoid boulders, many of them balanced in a most extraordinary way, and all the more striking surmounted by little shrines. The Kyaik-hti-yo stands on a huge boulder, which itself rests on a projecting rock, separated from the rest of the hill by a chasm, fathomless to the eye, and reaching, so say the villagers, far below the depth of the hill. The boulder stands on the extreme verge of the bare rock, and hangs over it as if a gust of wind or a few extra pounds added would make it topple over and crash down

*Mythical creatures.

the dizzy height far away into the green valley below. To this shrine people from all parts of the country, but more especially the Talaings,* come in the month of February, and cast jewellery and precious stones into the yawning rift, and, clambering up the rock by the aid of a bamboo ladder, cover the payá with flowers and small lighted candles, making it look like a new nebulous constellation from the far-off plains. Inquirers are told with the utmost confidence that the pagoda is five thousand years old. It certainly has been there time out of mind, and the boulder has solely been kept in its place by the hair buried under the shrine, and given to a hermit by the great Budh himself when he returned from Tawa-deintha, the second heaven of the Nat-déwas, on the occasion of his preaching the Law to his mother. Near it is a spring which always flows freely with crystalline water, unless there is evil talk among the assembled people or if the sexes are not separated. A complete Thin-bông-gyi, the alphabet, is graven on the rock. The view from the pagoda is superb; bounded on the east by the blue Martaban hills, fading away into the dim peaks of Siam, and extending southwards over tangled jungle and yellow paddy lands to the bright waves of the Gulf of Martaban, while to the west the jewelled speck of the pagoda at Pegu almost leads one to imagine the stately bulk of the sacred Shwe Dagôn beyond.

There are many such shrines on the abrupt limestone hills in the Maulmein district, where the devotee has to clamber up bare rock faces, and scramble through treacherous débris, occasionally swinging over perilous deeps on the precarious footing of a rough bamboo ladder; his offerings tied to his back, and his heart between his teeth. And yet women are found to make the ascent, especially at the Zwè-kabin, the precipitous 'Duke of York's nose', some forty miles up the Sittang river from Maulmein, where the Englishman is lost in amazement as to how they ever got the bricks and ironwork up the rocks to construct the pagoda and the hti. Yet thousands of people scramble up at the time of the annual feast, and the pagoda is as well adorned with offerings as any in the flat lands down by the sea, where a rise of a few feet in the ocean would put hundreds of square miles under water.

*The Mon, a people of Burma and Thailand.

Every district pagoda has its special feast and all are well attended, for even though the locality may be thinly populated there are always to be found visitors from other places round about; partly as a kind of neighbourly courtesy, partly because there is always some fun in the shape of a travelling troupe, or a marionette play, at a pagoda feast, and chiefly, there can be no denying, from a feeling of genuine piety and a real desire to acquire merit. Pagoda feasts enable a Burman to see the world, as far as it can be seen in his native land. Without the periodical festivals he would only stop chewing betel in the wattled bothy* where he was born to go out and smoke a cheroot round his patch of paddy land, and speculate on the time when the Rangoon or Bassein broker would come up to buy his crop from him. Most of the district Burmans would never see the Englishman and his doings were it not for the annual pilgrimage to Rangoon to worship at the Shwe Dagôn. During the rest of the year, unless he lives in the headquarters of an assistant commissionership, all he sees of the British occupation is a stray visit from a young official on shooting, or the chance appearance of an inspector of police in search of a criminal.

Similarly very few Burmans, except those attracted by business to the capital, would ever visit Mandalay were it not for the great 'Arakan pagoda'. The Mahā Myat Muni Payā is rendered especially sacred by the sitting image of Shin Gautama there preserved, and is on this account regarded by Upper Burmans as not inferior in sanctity to the Shwe Dagôn itself. The huge brass image, twelve feet in height, was brought over the hills from Akyab [Sittwe] in the year 1784 (1146 BE). According to the inscription, the king drew this Arakan Gautama to the shrine by the charm of his piety, but the historical books speak only of rough force of arms. However that may be, it is a mystery how the huge masses of metal—the figure was cast in three sections—were brought over the steep, pathless mountain sides. The inscription flatters the king, and the monks ascribe the feat to supernatural help, as they do the faultless joining together of the pieces. The image was set up, so says the legend, during the lifetime of the Great Master. The utmost skill and most persistent energy had failed in fitting the parts together, and the feelings of the pious

*Humble, wooden dwelling.

were fearfully lacerated by the cracking of the head in their futile struggles. But the Buddha, perceiving from afar what was going on, and ever full of pity, came himself to the spot, and, embracing the image seven times, so joined together the fragments that the most sceptical eye cannot detect the points of junction, while the head was restored to its pristine smoothness. So like was the image, and so sublime the effulgence which shone around during the manifestation, that the reverently gazing crowd could not determine which was the model and which the Master. The resemblance has no doubt faded away with the wickedness of later times, for unlike most Burmese images, the Payā Gyi has most gross and repulsive features. Inspired by the divine embrace the figure spoke, but afterwards received the Teacher's command never again to open its lips till Arimadéya* should come to reveal the new Law. The shrine in which it stands is one of the most splendid in the country. The image itself is covered by a great seven-roofed pya-that [spire] with goodly pillars, the ceiling gorgeous with mosaics. Long colonnades, supported on 252 massive pillars, all richly gilt and carved, with frescoed roofs and sides, lead up to it, and daily from the royal palace used to come sumptuous offerings in stately procession, marshalled by one of the ministers and shaded by the white umbrella, the emblem of sovereignty and the prerogative of the Arbiter of Existence. On its first arrival a hundred and twenty families of Arakanese were assigned as slaves of the payā, and the number was frequently afterwards added to. In a long gallery there is an enormous number of inscriptions, gathered from all parts of the country, many on gilt slabs of marble, a still greater number on sandstone. All day long circles of constantly renewed worshippers chant aloud the praises of the Buddha, and the air is heavy with the effluvia of candles and the odours from thousands of smouldering incense-sticks. Within the precincts of the pagoda is a large tank, tenanted by sacred turtle, who wax huge on the rice and cakes thrown them by the multitudes of pilgrims. Probably not even at the Shwe Dagôn Payā is more enthusiastic devotion shown than at the Payā Gyi in Mandalay. It is regarded with special reverence by the Shans.

*The next Buddha after Gautama.

Near the royal city, about nine miles up the river, on the right bank, is a huge monster of a pagoda, built on a low green bluff, running out from the barren, pagoda-sprinkled Sagaing hills. The groundwork of the great misshapen Mengôn Payā covers a square of 450 feet and its height is 165 feet, about one-third of the elevation intended for it when completed; but Mintaya Gyee, the crack-brained monarch who founded it, ran short of funds, and the building was stopped. Nature was jealous of the miniature mountain—the largest mass of brickwork in the world—and an earthquake in 1838 rent the gigantic cube with fantastic fissures from top to bottom, and cast down great masses of masonry, tons upon tons in weight, and yet not sufficient to destroy the main structure, massive and imperishable as Time itself. There it stands, unharmed alike by rain-floods and blistering suns, and laughing even at earthquakes. According to Burmese custom, Bodaw Payā* built a model for the guidance of the workmen. This is called the Pôndaw Payā, and is fifteen feet high. This consists of a bell-shaped dome surmounted by a *sikkhâra*, a pointed spire, and resting on a square plinth of solid brickwork. It is a hybrid between the Shwezigôn and Ananda pagodas of Pagān, and has all the requirements of a place of worship, circuit walls, staircases, ornamented arches, and leogryphs.

Perhaps it was this proud stability which induced King Mindôn Min to attempt an even greater work. He planned a huge shrine to be raised east of Mandalay, under the shadow of the Shan hills. The Yankin-taung Payā was to be larger than the Mengôn monster, and it was to be built of stone. A fair-sized hill was hewn into blocks to furnish material. Canals several miles long were dug to convey the stones, and huge lighters were built upon them. The whole kingdom was called upon to furnish men to labour a few months at a time on the pious work. Architects, monks, foreigners, were called upon to offer suggestions and make plans. A French engineer, who declared that, with 5000 men working every day, it would require eighty-four years to complete the original design, came near being crucified on the spot. After four years' labour the basement, some four feet high, was

*Burmese king who reigned from 1782 to 1819.

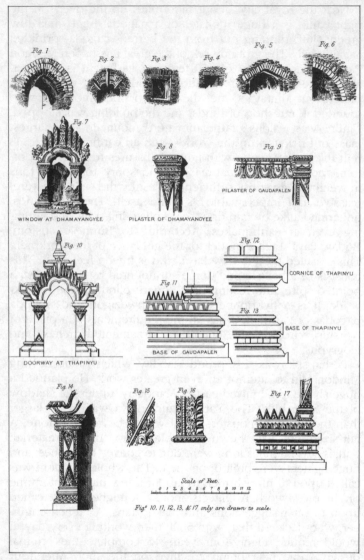

'Architectural Details of Remains at Pagan', from Henry Yule, *Narrative of the Mission to the Court of Ava in 1855*, Smith, Elder, London, 1858.

completed, and then the Convener of the Fifth Great Synod returned to the village of Nats.* Theebaw Min, who succeeded him, was the last man likely to finish the work, and there lie the mountains of squared stones and the heaps of rubble for the centre. The canals have silted up and the lighters foundered with their unloaded cargoes, and instead of a monument, King Mindôn has simply left a ghastly chaos. What kan King Mintaya Gyee must have had to get so far as he did!

The whole neighbourhood of Mandalay, Amarapoora, and Ava is rich with splendid fanes; but a detailed account of them would only weary the reader, as the visiting of them tires out the non-religious observer. Nevertheless some must at least be adverted to. There is the Ku-thu-daw, the 'Royal Merit House', the richly-gilt shrine built by King Theebaw's uncle, the 'War Prince', one of the most compact and tastefully adorned of pagodas, with beautifully carved gilt gates, the main spire being surrounded by a triple square of shrines, each shrine containing a marble slab engraved with a chapter of the Bitaghat† on the back and front. The text of the three volumes of the Buddhist Scripture was carefully collated by the most learned Sadaws‡ in the royal city, and is considered the best extant.

Especially interesting also is the Atumashi, the incomparable payā, the great, oblong, lofty-terraced chapel monastery of Mindôn Min, outwardly plain white, but within splendid with a gorgeously decorated shrine, purple and scarlet, and gold hangings, and velvet carpets. Here were preserved the gold spittoon, betel-box, kalawaik,§ and other paraphernalia of its founder. Unhappily it was burnt in 1892.

Down the river there are hundreds of others of every variety and degree of decoration. There is the Naga Yôn Payā, the whole building wrought into the form of a dragon; the huge round-domed Kaung-hmu-daw, and the 'king's victory pagoda' at Sagaing, the 'golden cock-scratching', on the other side, commemorating a favourite legend of the boundless

---

*That is to say, he died.
†Buddhist scriptures.
‡Or Hsayadaws: senior monks.
§A state barge in the shape of a mythical creature.

charity of the Budh. There are glistening white pinnacles, or flashing gold spires, far up the Sagaing hills, with thousands of steps wending wearily up over the steep, rough hill-side, and gazing up to them from the Amarapoora side are great massy temples, frowning over the river with all the stern solidity of a knightly hold. Each has its legend, some tale of bloodshed or piety, some event in Burmese history, or birth-story of the Buddha.

Most renowned, however, for its pagodas is Pagán, in many respects the most remarkable religious city in the world. Jerusalem, Rome, Kieff, Benares, none of them can boast the multitude of temples, and the lavishness of design and ornament that make marvellous the deserted capital on the Irrawaddy. Deserted it practically is, for the few flimsy huts that stand by the river are inhabited only by pagoda slaves and men condemned to perpetual beggary. For eight miles along the river-bank and extending to a depth of two miles inland, the whole space is thickly studded with pagodas of all sizes and shapes, and the very ground is so thickly covered with crumbling remnants of vanished shrines, that according to the popular saying you cannot move foot or hand without touching a sacred thing. Some of the zedis are all but perfect. Restored by the pious, they stand out glistening snow-white, only to render more striking the hoary, weather-beaten ruins of their less-cared-for neighbours. Here the bell-shaped, solid pyramid of Lower Burma is rarely seen. The religious structures fully merit the word temple as understood in ordinary language.

The Burman: His Life and Notions, Macmillan, London, 1882; 3rd edn., 1910, pp. 153–73.

13
The Biggest Pile of Bricks in the World

HIRAM COX

The above title is the rather unkind phrase often used when describing the remains of a massive unfinished pagoda at Mingun, not far from Mandalay.

Following the favourable reports submitted by Michael Symes (see Passage 7 above), the Governor-General of India sent out Captain Hiram Cox in 1796 to be Resident in Rangoon. His brief was to improve diplomatic relations between the East India Company and the Court of Ava while at the same time keeping an eye on the commercial aspirations of the French. But Cox, though very capable as a military engineer, was no diplomat. He had ideas above his station, claiming ambassadorial status and causing conflicts over protocol, and finally set out upriver determined to seek redress for some perceived slight.

On arriving at the capital, Amarapura, he found that King Bodaw-hpaya had shifted to a temporary 'capital' on an island, from which vantage-point he could oversee the construction of a huge pagoda on the right bank of the Irrawaddy. With a height of 152 metres on a base of 42 square metres, it was to be the largest pagoda in the world; but after seven years' work there was only the huge brick base to see. Built into it was the square chamber for the treasures dedicated by the king, including not only such things as models of pagodas and monasteries in silver and gold but also an incongruous novelty, a soda-water machine. Cox, himself lodged on an island nearby, was taken to see the work in progress. In this passage we see how as an engineer he views both the construction and the builders with a supercilious eye. The year is 1797.

Cox was kept waiting for seven months before obtaining an audience, at which he caused embarrassment and offence. On returning to Rangoon, he was recalled to Calcutta and put in charge of a refugee settlement scheme for the tens of thousands of Arakanese who had fled into India to escape forced conscription into Bodaw-hpaya's army. During this work, Cox fell ill and died leaving behind him a settlement which came to be named, and is still called, Cox's Bazar. He was only thirty-nine.

FEBRUARY 12. At seven A.M. the rayhoon* came to my bungalow, and informed me that the mayhoon* had sent two war-boats, to convey me and my suite to the main, to visit the new pagoda. After breakfast we set out on our excursion, myself with a part of my suite in one boat, Mr Burnett with the interpreter, &c., in a second, and the rayhoon in his own boat. In a few minutes we crossed the narrow channel which divides my island from the main, and landed on a sandy beach, and walked up to the pagoda, which is but a small distance from the landing-place, as the foot of the hill on which it is erected is washed by the river in the rains. On our way we were met by the third whoon* of the palace (accidentally); he stopped and inquired kindly after my health, and said he wished to be better acquainted with me; that his majesty had appointed him to go with the army to Vizalley [Vesali] that he meant to return by the way of Calcutta, and would be obliged to me for letters of recommendation and introduction. I told him I should be happy to render him any service in my power. We then parted, he proceeding to his own house, and we towards the looto or public court of the whoonghees. The rayhoon requested I would pull off my hat in passing the looto, as the whoonghees were there, a compliment which I begged leave to decline paying, as being inconsistent with my public situation. When we came a-breast of the looto (an open shed with a raised platform about four feet from the ground, and thatched), the rayhoon desired us to stop a little. The second whoonghee who is also generalissimo of his majesty's forces, was sitting in the looto in his undress. He sent for Mr Moncourtuse and desired him to tell me, he hoped I would excuse a little delay, as he had sent to know his majesty's pleasure as to what he wished I should be shewn: he added that I was a lucky man, that my conduct had given such satisfaction to every one, that his majesty regarded me as one of his own children. During this conversation, I was standing about fifteen yards from the looto, remarking the royal boats near the bank; in a few minutes the rayhoon joined me, and desired I would return to the steps ascending to the pagoda from the river front. These steps consist of three flights, about thirty feet broad at the lowest step, and twenty at the highest; of ordinary

*Various types of minister.

94

brickwork masonry, with a low parapet wall on each side, and led to the first terrace about fifteen feet above the ordinary level of the river in the rains. The revetement of the river-face of this terrace was of stones wrought to an equal surface on their exterior superfices; but rough and irregular on their interior, laid in common mortar made of stone pounded, or lime and sand. At the lowest step we were requested to take off our shoes, which we immediately did: all our servants were allowed to attend us, and I was allowed to take my Hindoostanee punkah.* We were not at any time desired to take off our hats. Immediately within the verge of the first terrace, on either side of the steps, are erecting two colossal figures of lions, or rather sphinxes, in positions rather couchant than rampant. They are of brick masonry, and seated on pedestals of the same materials: the surface of the pedestals are about two cubits above the level of the terrace, and the height of the figures from the surface of the table to the crown of their heads is fifty-eight cubits; making altogether sixty Burmhan cubits of nineteen inches each, or ninety-five English feet. The body and limbs are of proportionate magnitude, according to the Burmhan ideas of sculpture; the eyes and teeth are of alabaster, the eye-ball, which we had an opportunity of measuring, was thirteen feet in circumference. The northernmost figure is finished to the plastering and ornamental parts, the sockets for the eye-balls are left vacant, and to place the eye-balls in them will require some exertions of mechanical ingenuity, which I should like to see. There are six terraces rising above each other, their parapet walls equidistant, and revetements of the faces of each of good brick masonry, with stone spouts ornamented with sculptured alligators' heads, to carry off the water. Above these is a seventh terrace, on which is the plinth of the pagoda, and the eighth terrace is formed by the upper surface of the plinth. The seven lower terraces have not been wholly formed by art, but advantage taken of a little mount, the sides of which have been cut down, and then reveted with masonry; the levels of the terraces so far, being left of the common soil, a sandy loam mixed with shingly stones. Upon the seventh terrace rises the exposed part of the base or plinth of the intended structure; the foundation of which is sunk of solid masonry still

*A servant paid to fan his master.

lower; how much I have not been able to ascertain. Within the plinth a hollow chamber is left, forming a quadrangle whose extent is sixty-one feet six inches, its depth eleven feet, and the walls being twelve feet eleven inches thick, make the exterior surface a square of eighty-seven feet four inches. The interior of this chamber is plastered with white chunam [lime], and decorated with painted borders and pannelled compartments, with trees and flower-pots in them. There are also rows of columns twenty-nine inches square, and pilasters, to support the leaden beams and terrace with which the whole is to be covered when the dedicated treasures are deposited there; with a number of quadrangular compartments, large and small, from ten feet to four feet five inches square to contain them; the smaller ones being lined with plates of lead three-fourths of an inch thick. The innermost quadrangles are intended for the preservation of the treasures dedicated by his majesty, while the span around them is devoted to the oblations of his courtiers. Opposite each of the smaller compartments, whose depth is equal to that of the larger ones, and which appeared like so many wells, was placed on small Bengal carpets, little hollow temples, three feet square, with pyramidal roofs ornamented in the Burmhan style; the interior frame being of painted wood covered with thin plates of silver, alloyed to about fifty per cent. standard; in height from the base to the pinnacle seven feet, the eves ornamented with strings of red coral, about six beads in each, terminated with heart-shaped pieces of common window-glass. Round the solid part of the building and upon the terrace, were arranged piles of leaden beams, about five inches square, and of sufficient length to cover the respective chambers, with plates of lead of the same length fourteen inches broad, and three-fourths of an inch thick for the coverings; and besides these, a number of slates of a schistous granite were arranged in readiness to cover the whole. We were told that there was another set of chambers of the same dimensions and structure, charged with treasure below these: how true this is I cannot pretend to determine. The invention of lining the chambers with lead for the preservation of the treasures, is an honour claimed by his present majesty, who has great skill in these matters. That the design has a divine sanction we had ocular demonstration, three piles of leaden plates gilt with gold-leaf being shewn us, which had been brought and arranged where we saw them at night by angels. Our conductors assured us that the building was surrounded at night by watchful guards, so that no human agents could have transported such weighty materials unobserved: it is, therefore, justly considered and believed as a miracle of divine favour. All this I was particularly desired to note down in my pocket-book which I did on the spot, and added to it an observation of my own, that a good deal of melted wax, such as is used by the Burmhans for candles, had been dropt on the slabs; I, therefore, suppose the night must have been dark, and that the angels worked by candle-light. From the level of this terrace, a conical spire of solid masonry is intended to be erected, the weight of which I am afraid will prove too great for the leaden beams; but it would be a dangerous piece of impertinence for a stranger to offer any advice on these sacred matters, otherwise I could easily secure the safety of the superstructure, by shewing them how to turn arches over the hollow chambers. From the summit of this terrace is commanded a very extensive and pleasant view of the meanderings of the Erawuddy, the valley it winds through, and the adjacent mountains; but my attention was too much occupied by the building, and the crowds of both sexes that flocked to gaze at us, to examine distant objects.

Journal of a Residence in the Burmhan Empire and More Particularly at the Court of Amarapoorah, John Warren and G. & W. B. Whittaker, London, 1821; reprinted by Gregg International, Farnborough, 1971, pp. 102–9.

14
Amarapura's Golden Monasteries

MICHAEL SYMES

We have already met Symes (see Passage 7 above) on his first mission to Amarapura. During that same visit, although he was not particularly welcome as an envoy of the East India Company, he was shown the usual courtesies as a visitor. These included a tour of the city's monasteries (kyaung, here spelt 'kioum') in which he and his party were accompanied by the head of the monks, the hsayadaw *(here* 'Seredaw'*). Symes was counted as a well-read and cultured man but, like most Western visitors of his day, was sufficiently ignorant or prejudiced to regard his Buddhist hosts as mere wretched idolaters. But he was clearly astonished at the size and splendid ornamentation of the monastery buildings.*

It is September 1795. Symes and his party, lodged on the south side of a seasonal lake, have escaped the ravages of a dysentery outbreak that has decimated the Chinese community, and are about to cross the lake and begin their tour of Amarapura's beautiful kioum.

O N the day appointed for our visit to the Seredaw, we took boat at seven in the morning, and, attended by our usual retinue, crossed the lake. One of the surviving Chinese also accompanied us. Baba-Sheen, the Shawbunder [harbour-master] of Rangoon, and some Birman officers, met us on the opposite bank, where our elephants were waiting. When we approached the causeway or bridge, instead of crossing it, we turned to the left, and proceeded close to the ditch, parallel with the west face of the fort, till we came to the north-west angle. At this place the river approaches so near to the walls as to render a continuation of the ditch impracticable. We then went along the north side, passing on our left a handsome kioum crowned with a gilded piasath or spire, which we were told had been erected by Meedaw Praw, the venerable lady whom we had visited. On arriving at the north-east corner, we observed at some distance on the plain another religious edifice of distinguished splendour, dignified by the title of Kioumdogee, or royal convent, where, we were informed, the Seredaw or chief priest intended to receive us, and not at his usual residence, which was at a kioum about two miles farther. The articles I designed to present to him having been sent forward to his customary abode, we were obliged to wait in an adjoining house until they could be brought back. Being prepared, we were conducted into a spacious court surrounded by a high brick wall, in the centre of which stood the kioum, an edifice not less extraordinary from the style of its architecture, than magnificent from its ornaments, and from the gold that was profusely bestowed on every part. It was composed entirely of wood, and the roofs, rising one above another in five distinct stories, diminished in size as they advanced in height, each roof being surrounded by a cornice curiously carved and richly gilded. The body of the building, elevated twelve feet from the ground, was supported on large timbers driven into the earth after the manner of piles, of which there were probably 150 to sustain the immense weight of the super-structure. On ascending the stairs, we were not less pleased than surprised at the splendid appearance which the inside displayed. A gilded balustrade, fantastically carved into various shapes and figures, encompassed the outside of the platform. Within this there was a wide gallery that comprehended the entire circuit of the building, in which many devotees were stretched prostrate on the floor. An inner railing opened into a noble hall, supported by colonnades of lofty pillars; the centre row was at least fifty feet high, and gilded from the summit to within four feet of the base, which was lackered red. In the middle of the hall there was a gilded partition of open latticed work, fifteen or twenty feet high, which divided it into two parts, from north to south. The space between the pillars varied from twelve to sixteen feet, and the number, including those that supported the galleries, appeared to be not fewer than one hundred, which, as they approached the extremities, diminished in height; the outermost row not exceeding fifteen feet. The bottom of these was cased with sheet lead, as a defence against the weather. A marble image of Gaudma, gilded, and sitting on a golden throne, was placed in the centre of the partition; and in front of the idol, leaning against one of the pillars, we beheld the Sercdaw sitting on a satin carpet. He was encompassed by a circle of Rhahaans [monks], from whom he could be no otherwise distinguished, than by his preserving an erect position; whilst the others bent their bodies in an attitude of respect, with their hands joined in a supplicating manner. On entering the hall, the Birmans and the Chinese who accompanied us pros-trated themselves before the figure of Gaudma, after which they kneeled down, and made their reverence to the Seredaw, touching the ground with their foreheads, whilst we took our seats on fine mats that were spread at a little distance from him. He received us with much politeness, and in his looks and demeanour affected more liveliness and complaisance than any of the fraternity I had hitherto seen. His appearance denoted him to be about forty years of age; not meagre and austere as they generally are, but fat and jocular. I presented to him my offering, which consisted of a piece of yellow cloth, the sacerdotal colour; some sandal wood, and a few wax-candles covered with gold leaf. He asked several questions respecting England, such as how long the voyage usually was from thence to India. Being told this, he observed, that we were an extraordinary people to wander so far from home. I noticed the magnificence of the kioum: he replied, that such sublunary matters did not attract his attention; he was on earth but as a hermit. I desired his prayers; he said they were daily offered up for the happiness of all mankind, but that he would recommend us to the particular protection of Gaudma. He made some observations on our appearance, which I did not understand, and he even smiled; a relaxation very unusual in a Rhahaan. We retired without ceremony, and, mounting our elephants, proceeded along a wide road leading to the northward, which soon brought us to an extensive plain, that seemed to stretch in an uninterrupted level to the foot of a range of mountains ten or twelve miles distant. The soil was a poor clay, and the pasturage indifferent. We saw at a distance some fields of grain, and understood that capacious reservoirs had been constructed with great labour and expense, by order of the king, in the vicinity of the mountains, which enabled the inhabitants of the low countries to water the grounds, and render the earth productive in a season of drought. Several kioums and villages were scattered over the plain; but when we had advanced about two miles, religious edifices increased, beyond our power to calculate the number. The first that we entered was called Knebang Kioum, or the Kioum of Immortality, from the centre of which rose a royal piasath, to the height of a hundred and fifty feet; the roofs were of the customary complicated structure, one above another. This was the place where the embalmed bodies of deceased Seredaws are laid in state. The building rested on a terrace of brick, and was not elevated on pillars, as kioums and dwelling-houses usually are. The hall was very handsome, about seventy feet square, surrounded by a wide gallery. The roof was sustained by thirty-six gilded pillars, the central forty feet in height. Mats were spread in different parts for the repose of the Rhahaans, and on each was placed a hard pillow. There was also a tray containing books on the duties of Rhahaans, on religion, and the forms of religious worship.

Having rested here for a short time, we next visited the kioum, which was the ordinary residence of the Seredaw. This building far exceeded, in size and splendour, any that we had before seen, and is perhaps the most magnificent of its kind in the universe. It is constructed entirely of wood, and resembles, in the style of its structure and ornaments, that in which we had an interview with the Seredaw, but was much more spacious and lofty. The numerous rows of pillars, some of them sixty feet high, all of which were covered with burnished gilding, had a wonderfully splendid effect. It would be difficult to convey, either in language or by pencil, an adequate description of this extraordinary edifice. The profuse expenditure of gilding on parts exposed to the weather, as well as in the inside, cannot fail to impress a stranger with astonishment at the richness of the decoration, although he may not approve of the taste with which it is disposed. I could not have formed in my imagination a display more strikingly magnificent. This kioum was also divided by a partition, which separated it in the middle from north to south. There was a small room on one side, made of gilded boards, which we were told was the bedchamber of the Seredaw. Mats were spread on the outside for the attendant Rhahaans. The figure of Gaudma was made of copper, and an European girandole of cut-glass stood before his throne.

Leaving this building, we passed through many courts crowded with smaller temples and kioums. Several gigantic images of Rakuss, the Hindoo demon, half beast half human, made of brass, were showed to us, as composing a part of the spoils of Arracan. From these we were conducted to a magnificent temple which is erecting for the image of Gaudma, that was brought from the same country. The idol is made of polished brass, about ten feet high, and sitting in the usual posture, on a pedestal within an arched recess. The walls are gilded, and adorned with bits of different coloured mirrors, disposed with much taste. Peculiar sanctity is ascribed to this image; and devotees resort from every part of the empire, to adore the Arracan Gaudma, which is not exposed at all hours to the view of the vulgar. The doors of the recess are only opened when persons of particular consequence

'Carved Work of one of the Royal Monasteries', from Henry Yule, *Narrative of the Mission to the Court of Ava in 1855*, Smith, Elder, London, 1858.

come to visit it, or at stated times, to indulge the populace. As we approached, a crowd of people thronged after us with tumultuous enthusiasm, striving for admittance to offer up a prayer to this brazen representative of the divinity. We soon turned from these wretched fanatics, and the object of their stupid adoration, to view the noble piasath, or royal spire, that crowned the building, and attracted much more of our attention and respect, than an image, from which even the statuary could claim no praise. The spire rose in seven separate stages above the roof of the kioum; and the gold leaf, which had recently been applied, glistening in the sunbeams, reflected a brilliant lustre. This temple, with its auxiliary buildings, which are yet in an unfinished state, will, when completed, be the most elegant in the empire, though perhaps not so spacious as that which is the present residence of the Seredaw. From hence we were conducted to what is called the Chounda, or place for the reception and repose of strangers who come from a distance to offer up their devotions. It communicates on the north side with the great temple, and is also a very beautiful specimen of Birman architecture. It comprehends five long galleries, separated by colonnades, each consisting of thirty-four pillars, or two hundred and four altogether. The two central rows were about twenty-five feet high, but the external ones do not exceed fourteen. They were painted of a deep crimson ground, enlivened by festoons of gold leaf encircling them in a very fanciful and pleasing manner, and in a style much more conformable to European taste than an unvaried surface of gold. The ceiling likewise was embellished with a profusion of carved work, executed with great labour and minuteness. Measuring by our steps, we judged the length to be five hundred and seventy-six feet, and the breadth of each distinct gallery about twelve—the central rather wider than those on either side. A low railing extended along the outer pillars, to prevent improper persons and dogs from defiling the place. It is built upon a terrace of brick, elevated three feet from the ground; and the floor is made of Chunam, or fine stucco, composed of lime, pounded steatites and oil, the cohesion of which forms a hard and smooth surface, that shines like marble. Our conductor informed us that this edifice had been lately erected at the sole expense of the senior Woongee. It certainly reflects credit on the projector, and is an ornament to the country.

The heat of the day, which had now attained its greatest force, and our having been in constant exercise from seven in the morning till two o'clock in the afternoon, rendered a place of repose extremely acceptable; and here we not only rested ourselves, but likewise found a plentiful collation prepared for us. Our conductors, aware that the attention of strangers could not fail to be engaged for some hours by such a multitude of new and striking objects, thought it would be more prudent for us to wait under the shade of this hospitable roof till the afternoon, than expose ourselves unnecessarily to a burning sun. We had brought with us, at the instance of our friends, wine, bread and butter, and cold fowl, to which the Shawbunder had added a tureen of excellent vermicelli soup, and a tolerable good pillaw. We sat down to our repast about two o'clock, and after it was finished, continued to recline upon our mats until evening, fanned by a cool and refreshing breeze from the west, whilst we conversed, and contemplated the scene around. The crowd of people, whom the novelty of our appearance had collected, were neither intrusive nor troublesome. On such an occasion, in most other countries of the East, it is probable that, from the prejudices of bigotry, we should not have been suffered to depart without receiving some insult, or remarking some indication of contempt; but here, notwithstanding we entered their most sanctified recesses, we were every where treated with uniform civility. The presence of those who accompanied us had doubtless some influence in commanding the awe of the multitude; and if their respect was owing to this motive, it speaks highly for the state of their police; but I am inclined also to give them credit for a disposition naturally kind and benevolent.

An Account of an Embassy to the Kingdom of Ava in the Year 1795, Constable, Edinburgh, 1827, Vol. II, pp. 135–42.

15
Intruders in Mandalay Palace

GRATTAN GEARY

As a result of the Third Burmese War in 1885, the whole of Upper Burma was now in British hands though there was widespread resistance throughout the countryside as well as banditry, or 'dacoity'. Of the occupying force most were Indian troops under British officers, the campaign having been headed militarily by General Prendergast and politically by Colonel Sladen. In administrative charge of the whole country was the Chief Commissioner, Mr Bernard. As we saw in Passage 11, on the capture of their capital city King Thibaw and his Queen Su-hpaya-lat were immediately removed from Mandalay palace and sent into exile.

One of the first visitors on the scene was a lively and perceptive journalist, Grattan Geary, the editor of The Bombay Gazette. *He had lost no time in getting to Mandalay, yet it had still taken him a fortnight to travel by train from Bombay to Calcutta, by ship to Rangoon, by rail to Pyé (Prome) and by river steamer to the Burman capital. This final part of the journey, up 'The Road to Mandalay', had itself taken a whole week. Since it was the usual route from Rangoon, what most travellers saw first on arrival was just the 'bund' that prevented severe flooding of the town, then some disappointingly drab suburbs, and finally the walled city within which stood the palace and associated buildings. Close behind the city was Mandalay Hill, and behind this in the distance rose the Shan plateau.*

In the following passage Geary manages, in describing the scene, to convey how strange it was to see a British army of occupation in such incongruous surroundings.

MANDALAY itself can scarcely be seen by those who approach it from the river. The bank is some thirty feet higher than the river at its present level. The city proper, enclosed by walls, is about a mile and a half inland, and though the intervening space has been utilised, the houses are little better than huts, constructed of bamboos and matting. A wide roadway leads from the landing-place to the city, but it is not macadamised or cared for, and ruts and holes render the drive in a bullock cart precarious and unpleasant. Scarcely a horse is to be seen in the whole city, and the same may be said of all Burma. The climate is unfavourable to horses, and their place is supplied by the hardy little animals, coming principally from the Shan hills, which are known in India as Pegu ponies. They are very scarce, however, now in Upper Burma; they are dear, and of indifferent quality.

The city is surrounded by a high well-built brick wall forming a square, each side of which is one mile long. An earthen embankment, nearly thirty feet broad, and twenty-two feet in height, supports the wall and gives access to its crenelated top. A deep and wide ditch in advance of the wall is crossed by wooden bridges. The fortification is that of Mongol cities of the middle ages, and takes no note whatever of the necessities of modern defence. Twelve gates, three on each side, give admittance, and the streets are laid out from gate to gate, parallel to the walls. The roadways are eighty feet wide, and trees are planted along the sides, a little too close to the line of the houses. When they are macadamised they will make fine streets. The houses are for the most part constructed of teak or of bamboo. They are very frail and ephemeral.

The religious edifices, monasteries for the most part, are well designed, covered with curious carving, and architecturally effective. They redeem the general aspect of the city from meanness. Under the old régime the scavenging was given up wholly to the care of a ferocious looking breed of black pigs, and packs of quarrelsome dogs, who performed their task indifferently well, but were themselves an intolerable nuisance. Mr Bernard, the Chief Commissioner, has organised, amongst the unemployed coolies, gangs of sweepers, and of road-makers, who are effecting already a considerable improvement. The pigs and dogs are gradually disappearing from the main thoroughfares. A new roadway has also been commenced to give employment to starving men and women who might have been driven by hunger to join the dacoits. The main streets will be metalled. The number of houses is estimated at 12,000, and the population at 100,000, a large proportion of whom were supported by the palace, either by largesses or by employment. It is said that 20,000 were dependent for subsistence on the Court.

The Royal Palace occupies the centre of the city, and is enclosed by a strong teak stockade, twenty feet in height, and by two brick walls, the first a hundred feet inside the stockade, and the second two hundred feet, all three being, like the city walls, in straight lines, as if the purpose was to minimise the difficulties in the way of an assailant. The British military authorities have lost no time in cutting through the long lines at intervals, and erecting block houses which will command the front of the stockade. The eastern gate was reserved for the King, but now it is thrown open. Looking towards the Pavilion of Audience from this gate, the royal

'The Palace, Mandalay', from Frank Vincent, *The Land of the White Elephant*, Harper, New York, 1874.

throne, raised on a dais, is seen amidst the gilded pillars and under the canopied roof. This Hall of Audience is the finest structure of all that go to make up the totality of the palace. A beautiful pinnacle of wonderful lightness and grace surmounts it. Corrugated iron has been turned to ornamental use in filling in the light timber framework which soars up to bear the resplendent golden umbrella that crowns the whole. The fluting of the corrugated iron harmonises very successfully with the bold and aspiring lines of the structure. Iron wire ropes of great tenuity run from the ground to the slender spire, and give it a certain amount of support; they, too, harmonise with the general flow of the lines upwards and seem to be a necessary and artistic detail of the general design. The golden umbrella was viewed with covetous eyes by the Prize Committee; if made of solid gold, it would pay handsomely for the trouble of getting it down. But there is a belief, which is possibly well founded, that the golden umbrella, which was constructed for the Pavilion of Audience and shown to King Mindo-Min and the Court, was not put up, the model, which had been made in gilt metal, being quietly substituted, no one being much the wiser. It is whispered that certain royal coffins, occupying the coquettish little tombs seen at intervals amongst the other gilt and carved buildings inside the royal precincts, are of gold. But the Prize Committee would not dream of rifling tombs even for gold coffins; and to prevent unauthorised desecration, effectual precautions have been taken.

The Palace consists of a series of pavilions and other buildings, differing in size and detail, but all composed of teak, elaborately carved, and painted red when not covered with gilding. The application of gold is on so liberal a scale that the eye gets tired of it, and the Indian red of the bases of the pillars is a welcome relief. The ingenuity of the designer and the skill of the workmen give variety and interest to every varying detail. There is no monotony, and no straining after the grandiose. Some of the buildings, if reproduced in gold and silver work, would make exquisite caskets for the boudoir of a queen. The prison in which the survivors of the massacres were confined was a wooden structure, painted red, close to other buildings from which it shut out the breeze. Partly on this account, and partly because of the sinister associations of the place, the present occupiers of the

Palace have caused the prison house to be rased to the ground, and it now exists only in the memory of the ranees and princesses who were so long immured in it.

The King's Summer House, in which Theebaw used to spend the evenings and the nights in the hot weather, is a bright little kiosk of silver and looking-glass, in a small ornamental piece of water surrounded by a large number of alcoves. In each of these latter was a highly decorated couch intended for the Phoongyes, who visited His Majesty and received largesses at his hands. In each alcove was a handsome glass chandelier. A roystering company of Madras Sappers rushed round, and smashed every lamp, for the enjoyment of seeing the showers of glass fall to the ground. This seems to have been the worst if not the only act of wanton destruction committed within the precincts of the palace. The remoteness of the enclosure around the summer pavilion enabled the mischief-makers to commit this act of vandalism. The royal gardens have enjoyed a great reputation, but they appear to have been much neglected of late. Winding walks, the rockeries, little lakes, and a gilded bridge, with a small canal and a pleasure boat, form its chief features. The restricted area available within the palace enclosure rendered it impossible to make a garden of any size. When I first visited the palace, the most conspicuous objects were perhaps two highly-gilt cannon, with their carriages, flanking the entrance to the pavilion of audience. A number of smaller gilded guns and carriages were in an adjacent part of the grounds. These were removed and put on board the transport Along Pyah and sent to Rangoon. They will doubtless ornament the Maidan at Calcutta. Besides these resplendent cannon, which were obviously meant for show, there were several guns carefully mounted on elaborately contrived platforms enabling them to point in any direction. The singular thing was that their muzzles, wherever they pointed, were within a few feet of the palace walls around, so that unless to clear out the Royal apartments and bring down the palace, they were absolutely useless. In the Arsenal, which was included, like the Mint, amongst the appurtenances of the palace, there was a considerable number of Remington and Martini–Henry rifles. The latter were of Burmese manufacture, and were very well made. Had the Burmese been able to obtain English gunpowder, these weapons would have been as formidable as our own. But the Burmese gunpowder is deficient in energy, being afflicted with a curious apathy, which delays its explosion. I have seen a lighted match thrown on a plate filled with Burmese powder, and it only blew up after some of the grains had ignited. A quantity of the dahs,* laid down by the King's soldiers who were disarmed on the surrender of Mandalay, were found to be made of soft iron which bent double under moderate pressure. Many of the scabbards were made of tin. The war department of Burma was as incapable as that of foreign affairs.

The Palace was the centre of the city life, as well as of the Burmese administrative system. The Hlootdaw or Supreme Council assembles in a building contiguous to the Hall of Audience, but just outside the inner of the three walls enclosing the palace and grounds. Like the Audience Hall it is open in front and at the side, the members of the Council sitting virtually in the open air, and under the public eye. They sit there still *coram populo*, each of them wearing a white fillet around the head, much as Cæsar wore his laurels. It was in the midst of his colleagues in this Council Hall that the Tyndah was summoned to receive from the Chief Commissioner the information that he was to be simultaneously removed from the Government and deported from the capital under the circumstances which I shall presently relate.

Some thirty or forty yards from the Council House a tall campanile stands isolated, bearing a water-clock, and what is of more importance, a great bell on which the four watches of the day are beaten, giving the time to the city. The cessation of the booming of this bell is always taken to signify that the government machinery has given way, and general consternation takes the place of Burmese confidence in the political situation. On the day of the surrender of Theebaw, the bell-ringers disappeared, and the ominous silence added greatly to the terrors of the situation, and contributed to the disorders which ensued during the night. It was the first care of Colonel Sladen on reconstructing the Hlootdaw to cause the bell to be sounded, and the moral effect was very marked; the citizens understood that the Government had been set going again, and the shops were re-opened and business resumed. The official bell-ringers for a few days per-

*Knives, cutlasses, etc.

formed the traditional prostrations towards the palace on descending from the campanile; but then probably thinking that neither Mr Bernard nor Colonel Sladen, who were now the chief occupants of the august building, cared much for that mark of homage, they omitted the prostrations, and treated the ringing of the bell as a mere matter of business.

On Christmas morning I was present when divine service was performed in the Hall of Audience for the soldiers by the Reverend Mr Beattie. The chaplain stood in front of the throne, the militant congregation facing him. The sun streamed into the pavilion, and lighted up the gilded pillars, and the empty throne. The scene was brilliant and suggestive. The words 'Give peace in our time, O Lord!' rang out with a strange dramatic effect in the midst of such surroundings.

The roads within the Palace precincts are broad and well kept; Mr Bernard has improvised a public works department to make and metal roads in Mandalay, with a view to the employment of the starving people. No time has been lost; roads are being already widened and levelled, and between two and three thousand men and women are in receipt of four annas a day. They are employed on piece work, as when paid by the day they did only one anna's worth of work. The industrious, women mainly, earn six and even eight annas* a day. They are paid every evening, not having anything else to live upon. If the earthwork of the Mandalay–Toungoo railway, which is in contemplation, be put in hand, and the villagers given employment on it, there will be a great diminution in the number of dacoits. There is something like a complete cessation of dacoiting now in the city; the couple of dacoits shot in the mornings or the half-dozen flogged, have, as a rule, been given over by the villagers to the military. Dacoity prevails in the surrounding plain, and at times there are regular engagements during the night, the villagers defending themselves, or attacking their neighbours, with more or less success.

The Chief Commissioner, who is ubiquitous, invited me to join him in the ascent of the picturesque Mandalay Hill, which stands in a commanding position to the north of the city. The heliograph station was at work on the summit, keeping up communication with military posts at considerable

---

*Eight annas is equivalent to half a rupee.

distances. Some fine pagodas complete the hill, and in one fane there is a colossal statue of Buddha, some forty feet high, which is remarkable as having, contrary to usage, the arm extended as if in expostulation or command. From the summit of the hill there is a magnificent panoramic view, the great river swelling here into a lake and shut in by islands, the wooded hills on both banks dipping in some places almost into the water. A large earthen embankment to the northward protects the city from inundation when the river overflows. The sun setting above the low western hills on the opposite side of the river, sets the sky in a glow of gold and crimson which is reflected upon the river, and the city, and the pinnacles of the palace. The plain is narrowed to the eastward by the gray and inhospitable Shan mountains, which extend east and north towards Tongking and China. The narrow and tortuous valleys of the Sittang and the Salwein pierce this great mountain region from the south-east, but from the Mandalay side it is practically inaccessible. The military guard in charge of the heliograph tell us that every night there is firing in the villages, dacoity being prevalent.

Burma after the Conquest, Sampson Low, Marston, Searle, & Rivington, London, 1886, pp. 86–97.

16
The Incomparable Pagoda

W. R. WINSTON

With the annexation of Upper Burma to the British Empire on 1 January 1886 came the need for the 'pacification' of a territory about the size of France, so large numbers of troops were sent by steamer up 'the road to Mandalay'. The Christian churches, perceiving a need to 'uplift the nations' (W. R. Winston's own words), sent missionaries upstream soon afterwards. The Rev. Winston, a Wesleyan Methodist minister, left Calcutta a year after the annexation, spent a few days in Rangoon, proceeded by rail to Pyé (Prome) and then took an Irrawaddy Flotilla Company steamer to Mandalay. The city was so full of troops that its monasteries and pagodas had to be used for the accommodation of soldiers and clergy alike.

One of these buildings was the Atu-ma-shi Hpaya, the 'like-of-which-there-is-not' pagoda. As we have already learnt (see Passage 11) this edifice was soon to perish in one of Mandalay's frequent city fires. This pagoda was atypical in that from a distance it resembled a squat pyramid, its white-washed stucco brilliant in the sunlight. Beneath its seven receding terraces was a lofty golden hall supported by thirty-six pillars, some of them about 21 metres high. Some observers thought the exterior ugly, but the interior was generally agreed to be magnificent. It was built by King Mindon in honour of his father, whose throne was placed next to the huge Buddha image in the hall. Winston also describes the nearby Kuthodaw, built to Mindon's specifications to mark the Buddhist Synod that he had convened in 1871.

T HE first thing to attend to after we had looked round a little was to find a place to lodge. This matter was soon settled by our army chaplain taking us to the quarters which had been assigned to him by the military authorities. This lodging was novel, for it consisted of one of the buildings belonging to a large Buddhist monastery, substantially built of teak, and with the usual highly quaint, ornamental and fantastic-looking roof, richly decorated with most elaborate carving all over, and tapering at one end into the form of a spire. There were many other buildings of a similar kind around us, some of them really grand and imposing. Within a very short distance of us, in buildings of a similar kind, which are quite different from the ordinary Burmese houses, the whole of the 2nd Battalion of the Hampshire Regiment, several hundreds strong, were lodged. It was said by the chief Buddhist authorities about the time of the annexation that there were close upon six thousand monks in Mandalay, but there are monastery buildings to accommodate many times that number. In addition to all the monks, the entire British force of English troops, Native Indian Sepoy troops, and military police in Mandalay, altogether several thousands strong,

'The Atu-ma-shi', from Noel F. Singer, *Burmah*, Kiscadale, Gartmore, 1993.

were lodged in monastery buildings, and still there was plenty of room to spare.

Mandalay has been well styled the Vatican of Buddhism. So numerous are the religious buildings they seem almost endless, and it is evident that no small portion of the resources of the country must have gone in these works of merit. Within a day or two of our arrival, when we began to look about, we found that we were in close proximity to many remarkably fine religious buildings, and many startling contrasts were brought into view by the exigencies of the times. Close by the quarters of the Hampshire Regiment was a pagoda of fantastic shape. Being a brick building, and not liable to catch fire, it had been put in use as the armourer's shop, and there the regimental blacksmith was at work with his anvil and tools, his portable fireplace and bellows, and close beside him, as he worked, was the beautiful marble image of Buddha for which the pagoda was erected.

The regimental canteen, from whence proceeded of an evening the loud laughter of the soldiers in their cups, and the singing of many a long-drawn-out song in the true English vernacular, was originally a building consecrated to Buddhist meditation, asceticism and prayer. The regimental guard-room—and in those days they had to keep good watch and ward, for the country was in a state of great disturbance—was a Burmese zayat or resting-place, built by the piety of some one for the benefit of frequenters of these holy places, who little imagined that his zayat would ever be used as a place of detention for drunken and refractory British soldiers.

But the great sight of the place is the 'Incomparable Pagoda', as the Burmans proudly style it, situated close by the guard-room, and directly facing the beautiful monastery building then used as the officers' mess. This remarkable structure is a huge pile of building raised upon vast masonry pillars. It measures fully 300 feet in length, is proportionately broad, and rises in the form of a pyramid to such a height as to be visible several miles off. Its sumptuously carved and gilded teak-wood doors, forty-four in number, are quite a sight to see in themselves, as is also the magnificent decorative plaster work all around and over the building, and rising to its very summit. At that time, in the absence of churches and chapels, for want of a better place with sufficient space for hundreds to assemble together, the Hampshire Regiment used to have 'church parade' in the vast expanse amongst the pillars at the basement of the Incomparable Pagoda. It was a cool, airy, comfortable place, and open on all sides to the breeze, so that it answered very well in such a hot climate.

There also many other meetings were held in those days of 'Field Service', when we had all to be satisfied with such accommodation as we could get. It was there our prayer-meetings and class-meetings were held for the soldiers, and there, amidst that wilderness of pillars, under that vast heathen shrine, we had the joy of directing anxious penitents to the Saviour, and there, too, we held, in company with Major Yates of the Royal Artillery, the first temperance meeting ever held in Mandalay.

Leaving this Bethel of ours at the basement of the Incomparable Pagoda, and ascending by one of the fine broad flights of steps, the visitor comes to the wooden platform of the pagoda, and on being ushered in by the polite old abbot or presiding monk, he sees a very fine, spacious building, very lofty, with many images of Buddha, sheltered under great white canopies, besides some curiosities of European manufacture, such as mirrors of vast size, and gigantic coloured glass chandeliers, that must have been imported at immense cost.

But *the* sight of the place is the hall which contains the marvellous wood carvings in relief, all of Burmese workmanship, representing most clearly all manner of sacred histories and incidents, the whole of this elaborate and ingenious work being overlaid with gold leaf. Truly Mandalay is a wonderful place for religious buildings.

Close beside the Incomparable Pagoda are to be seen the Ku-tho-daw or Royal Merit pagodas, forming a unique and truly wonderful piece of work. They consist of a triple square of sets of little white pagodas, each of which is amply large enough to form a shrine for one large slab of Burmese marble, which stands up in the middle, like a cemetery headstone, enshrined each in its own neat, bell-shaped pagoda building. Each slab of marble is covered completely with a most accurately executed inscription in the Pali language, in letters about three-eighths of an inch in length. I have never counted these pagodas, but I am told by those who have that there are 730 of them in all. They are arranged in perfect symmetry, forming three squares one within another, each square being surrounded by a wall with handsomely carved gates. In the centre of the innermost square is a large pagoda, and ascending the steps of that the spectator can obtain a good view of the whole, extending over many acres of ground. The whole space between the rows of pagodas is carefully paved with bricks. Every part of the work has been most thoroughly carried out, utterly regardless of expense, and everything is of the best. There is no crowding, but ample space is given everywhere. Is there to be found anywhere or in any religion a more striking, impressive and unique example of thoughtful devotion and loving care of those writings supposed to contain the sacred truth? These 730 pagodas contain 730 tables of stone covered with inscriptions, and it is considered to be the best edition extant of the text of the three Pitakahs, and the three Pitakahs are the scriptures of Buddhism, acknowledged as authoritative wherever Buddhism is the people's faith.

Close by the Ku-tho-daw we found another marvel. In a tall brick building is an immense marble sitting figure of Buddha, 25 feet high, scores of tons in weight, and thought to be perhaps the largest monolith in the world.

Four Years in Upper Burma, C. H. Kelly, London, 1892, pp. 15–18.

17
The Pinnacles of Sagaing

V. C. SCOTT O'CONNOR

Sagaing stands a short distance downstream from Mandalay, opposite the old capital cities of Ava and Amarapura. For two short periods Sagaing too had been a capital, but its main significance has long been religious rather than secular, its hills being smothered with monasteries and pagodas.

V. C. Scott O'Connor was a British colonial officer of long standing who travelled all over the country during the period from 1891–5. He began a second tour of duty in 1899 and produced in 1904 an affectionate picture of Burma in his book The Silken East. *The following passage comes from a book published three years later, one which is far more useful as a guidebook. O'Connor used it also as a chance to convey a great deal of historical information, perhaps because—as he says in his Preface—'Since returning to England I am more than ever impressed with the wonderful indifference of the British public to all that lies outside of England.'*

In reading the following extract, one can sense O'Connor trying to make the reader see in the mind's eye the shapes and colours of Sagaing.

SAGAING, founded six hundred years ago, upon the extinction of Pagán, is one of the many past capitals of Burma, and if it has no great place in history, it retains, for it can never lose, the glory of its site. It is built on the west bank of the river, in the elbow of a curve made by it after leaving Ava. The great stream here narrows to a thousand yards, between cliffs which the architectural instinct of the people has crowned with flights of white pagodas. There are few richer landscapes in the world; and whether the spectator comes upon it suddenly through the secluded ruins of Amarapura on the further shore, or looks down upon it with deliberate intent from one of the neighbouring eminences, it is of unfailing beauty.

The town is built on a level plain which spreads away from the south-western territory of the Sagaing hills. A great embankment along the river face to the old fort protects it now from the main floods of the Irrawaddy; but of old the town was apt to be inundated by the waters which almost encircle it. In the early summer the river shrinks, leaving wide tracts of sand uncovered; leaving also between the sand and the embankment wall, a sloping terrace that is green with close turf in the dryest season. Trees are a gracious feature of Sagaing, and one may walk through the town at noonday entirely screened from the sun's rays by the great tamarinds which are its legacy from the past.

Of the once royal capital few secular traces now remain. But the old walled enclosure, an irregular square, can still be

Sagaing, photograph by Gerry Abbott.

easily traced, and its walls will remain to bear testimony to its past for many centuries to come. Raised high above the intermediate hollows, they have now been converted into excellent highroads, along which the wayfarers pass, and smart new people drive in painted gigs.

It is in its pagodas that the past of Sagaing really survives; and these are built for the most part on the spurs and pinnacles and in the shady hollows of the hills which reach away north of the town. The Kaung-hmu-daw, a solid stupa of antique design, is a great and notable exception. Its vast bulk towers up over the level plain near the new railway town of Ywa-taung. It was built in 1636 to commemorate the restoration of Ava as the capital of the Empire. The Aung-mye-law-ka Pagoda, built entirely of stone, was erected by King Bo-daw-paya, after the model of the Shwé-zigon at Pagàn, on the site of the residence allotted to him before he came to the throne. It has five pairs of leogryphs, and was considered by successive Burmese kings to be a good model to copy. The Tupayōn is a pagoda of very rare type in Burma, and of peculiar architectural interest as marking a certain phase in the development of these structures. The Shwé-mok-taw Pagoda, according to tradition, was originally built by Asoka in the third century BC, since when it has had many outer shells added to it. Some way to the west of the old walls there stands a remarkable colossus of Buddha, two and a half centuries old, a figure of white and gold, lifted high on a terraced platform under a pillared roof of imposing design. A paved court enclosed within a ruined wall spreads below it, and here of a summer evening, as the sky behind its contour flames with the glory of the passing sunset, one is apt to come upon such a spectacle as this; consider it, for it is typical of the land. A solitary worshipper kneels in the wide court before the image exalted above him. His hands are folded and held up in supplication. There is no sound in the great precincts, save that of the wind, and of his voice as it chaunts the aphorisms of his faith. The effect of the spectacle is enhanced, and lifted up to something strangely majestic, by the atmosphere, dry, prismatic, mystical—glorious with all the effulgence of the closing day. One does not come upon sights like this out of Burma. There is some unconscious under-current of great qualities in the Burman personality that alone makes them possible.

By far the most interesting part of Sagaing lies in the hilly country above it, where austere monks live; and every peak bears testimony to the piety of bygone kings and people. The hills are skirted in the early summer, before the river has begun to rise, by a low sloping shore, along which a horseman can ride to the great bell of Mingun. The soil under foot varies from smooth turf to broken rock, with long intervals of silver sand. Cliffs rise up above it on one side, clothed with cactus and aloes, and on the other there spreads the purple river. It is easy to believe at times that one is riding by the sea. There are bays at intervals, and openings of miniature valleys wooded with the most splendid trees. In such shelters hamlets and monasteries repose, and near the village of Wachet there is a colony of nuns.

At Wachet, also, there is a monastery, notable for its size and architecture. It combines, with some success, the antique wooden architecture with the modern masonry style now coming into vogue. The main building is entirely of wood, carved and gabled, and finished to the last point of its ascending roofs and gilded spire. Its deep Vandyke colour makes a rich contrast with the pale purple of the barren hills behind. It is built on a great platform of masonry, surrounded by a handsome wall, and is supported, where the natural slope makes this necessary, by buttresses and terraces. The terraces are roofed over, and make long corridors parallel to the river. Flights of stairs ascend through these from the river's bank to the lofty platform above. The walls and the balustrades are plain but well wrought, and no attempt has been made here to rival in mortar the delicate and complex character of carved wood. The monastery courts and open terraces have been planted with vines and Bougainvillias, which grow luxuriantly over light pergolas of cane. The familiar sight of the grape vine, its curling tendrils, its clusters of hanging fruit, its delicate light and shade, is peculiarly refreshing here to one who has not looked upon it before in Burma. The broad river flowing below these monastery walls extends at flood time nearly ten miles to the opposite shore.

As I came upon the village of Wachet for the first time, the peace of evening was spreading itself abroad. From the village lanes the red cattle were streaming down to the river to drink, the young men mounted on their backs. Women and girls were splashing and laughing in its waters. Down the noble stream, boatloads of travellers were being borne, some on long journeys, others only to Sagaing to a common festival. Their swift passage alone spoke to the eye of the river's movement. Along the sandy tracts, half overgrown with yellow-cupped flowers, the passing carts raised up small clouds of golden dust. Here and there a traveller took his way, his sandals in his hand. Yellow-robed monks went by, grave and reverend, with no thoughts of haste. The novices lounged in the monastery courts, beside the open balustrades, lazily observant of the passing world. From the shelter of their doll-like houses, nuns in salmon-pink garments, a little richer in tone from the reflected sunset, made their careful way with water-pots to the river. The old-world life was afoot, and the scene before me was culled from the very heart of Burma.

All the road to Wachet and beyond is lined with pagodas, some of which reach by lion-guarded stairs to the river, while others crown the pinnacles of the hills. One of the most beautiful is the Lekyun-Manaung, embosomed in great trees at the mouth of a little valley which opens on the river not more than a mile from the steamer-landing at Sagaing. It is of tulip shape, merging through narrowing rings to a point. The tulip rests on an octagonal base, within which there is enshrined a figure of Gautama surrounded by rows of curious beings cut in brown marble with long queues of hair. The porches of entrance are royal doors of the flamboyant design peculiar to the palace. There was of old a handsome wall around the court of the pagoda, decorated with figures of ogres in semi-relief. Its pattern may be gauged from one or two panels which still survive. But for the most part the plaster in which these figures are moulded has crumbled away, and the wall is in ruins. The two white leogryphs that face the river are in perfect preservation. Their heavy jaws and pointed fangs were meant to inspire fear; but they are become the home of pigeons which nest over the hollows of their tongues.

Near this interesting pagoda, there is a smaller one whose dome is a lotus flower half open and surmounted at the four corners by sphinxes. The flower upbears the small spire, which is surmounted by a canopy of bells. A little farther off, on low spurs of the hill-side, are two pagodas of the Kaung-hmu-daw pattern. The second of these is beautifully formed, and it raises the conviction that the tale of the countryside concerning the shape of the Kaung-hmu-daw is true. On a nearer view, the delicate dome of the edifice resolves itself into a polygon, faintly fluted. It rises from a narrowing base of three concentric tiers, each of which is inlaid with masonry panels of fine design and workmanship. Little notice has hitherto been taken of the pagodas of Sagaing; but they will be found instructive in any study of pagoda architecture; and it is noticeable that most of the masonry, and especially the plaster decoration, compares well with that of Pagān, and is much superior to modern work of the same kind.

Stairs lead up to the pagoda from the river, guarded by small lions with marble eyes. Immediately above it there is a brick Thein or Hall of Ordination for monks, notable for its frescoes. These have suffered from the lapse of time, yet enough remains to make a picture of lively, even of historic, interest. It consists of the red crenellated walls and battlements of a royal city, with the familiar Bahosin or Clock Tower and the Reliquary that were a feature of Amarapura and of Ava as they are of Mandalay. There are trees in flower, mangoes and palms; there are crows upon the palace roof, and sentries with guns upon the ramparts; and there are gateways like those of Mandalay. Next there is a large scene depicting in a very spirited manner an attack on the palace. In the centre there are the many-roofed royal buildings, within which the king is shown seated, his ministers in yellow *gaung-baungs* [kerchief] making obeisance before him. About them all there is a palisaded enclosure, filled with sentries carrying *dahs*, ministers in flowing robes and court hats, and, most interesting of all, two Europeans with muskets, in the high gaiters and cocked hats of a hundred years ago. Without this palisade the red crenellated walls of the city are manned by the defenders, unmistakably Burmese, under the command of a chief with a red umbrella; while cannon and muskets at the embrasures and loopholes vomit their fire. Outside of all are the assailants; some in the agonies of death, others galloping, all armed with muskets and swords, and pressing the attack, led at one end by a European. At the far top corner of the picture, another European with a red queue is depicted galloping up. Lances with pennons, elephants with castles on their backs, a stray tiger, boats on the river with savages dancing upon them in ecstasies, complete the list of details. It is with a curious sensation that one comes thus unexpectedly upon the cocked-hatted European—Englishman perhaps—of a century ago, here in a monkish hall of ordination amidst the lonely and barren hills, frequented now only by strict anchorites who have left the world.

Mandalay and Other Cities of the Past in Burma, Hutchinson, London, 1907, pp. 170–84.

18
A Canoeist in Pagán

MAJOR R. RAVEN-HART

Downstream from Sagaing but on the left bank of the Irrawaddy stands Pagán, once the international capital of Theravada Buddhism. For perhaps four centuries the city had grown in splendour until Kublai Khan sent an army, led by his grandson, to teach the Burmese king, Nara-thiha-paté, a lesson for slaughtering an ambassadorial party sent by the emperor himself. In 1287 the glorious city was sacked. Today many of its pagodas and temples, spread over 40 or so square kilometres of the Irrawaddy plain, still stand despite the ravages of weathering and of earth tremors.

Major R. Raven-Hart was a retired British army officer of a mildly eccentric nature whose pastime was canoeing down the world's great rivers. He had already paddled down the Mississippi and the Nile when in the cool season of 1937–8 he arrived in Burma. He travelled north by steamer and train to Myitkyina where he made himself a canoe, hired a Kachin lad called Nyo as companion and translator, and set off downriver. The bluff Major was an energetic, no-nonsense sort of person: he disliked British residents who would look askance at the way he fraternized with 'the natives' and who dismissed much Burmese decorative art as 'tawdry'. But he was also sensitive and full of curiosity, as the following extract shows.

When the Major and Nyo beached the canoe, Raven-Hart realized that it would take weeks to see Pagán properly, so numerous and widespread were its pagodas. . . .

123

I decided to see the principal ones thoroughly and let the others slide: I suppose that it is unnecessary to add that in Rangoon later people who really knew Pagan bemoaned that I had missed the 'really important' ones, those farthest from the river.

As in duty bound we went first to the Ananda, the only pagoda still in use at Pagan and the only one at which 'Foot Wearing is Prohibited', to quote the notice. It is a nuisance, but not worth the fuss that many British residents make about it.

Strictly speaking, the Ananda, like several other 'pagodas' at Pagan and the Arakan at Mandalay, is not a pagoda at all but a temple. The true pagoda is like the Shwezigon, a vaguely bell-shaped edifice with a spire, built solid over relics or earlier pagodas or both: in many Buddhist countries such relics are exposed at the greater festivals for the edification of the pilgrims—the idea of walling them up in Burma seems to have been to prevent this, from a fear that reverence might degenerate into idolatry. Architecturally the idea can be very satisfactory: the trouble is that, at popular pagodas, the pilgrims naturally desire to have somewhere handy some images to be revered, and so shrines are added. The awful example is the Shwe Dagon in Rangoon, where the fussy shrines completely hide the beauty of the pagoda proper: only from the air or from far off is it impressive.

But the Ananda is entirely different. It is a frozen fountain, an aspiring uprush of brickwork, almost feminine in its grace, terraced back step by step to a mitre-pyramid and a gilded spire, with four ground-level shafts driven into the heart of it from the four points o the compass; and, at the end of each shaft, a standing figure of one of the Buddhas of this Cycle. Light comes from terrace-windows on to the head and shoulders of each thirty-foot statue, the rest of the figure being lit dimly from below by the little candles of worshippers. The shaft-passages are high, with pointed roofs, and smaller passages cross-connect them and bring in light: there is no feeling of entering into some mystic Holy of Holies—one feels rather that the entrance-halls have emanated from the statues, are the expression of their welcome to pilgrims and of the out-sending of blessings to the world. The one criticism that can be made is that the statues are too high for the arches in front of them, cut off and cramped by these until you are close to them, a great pity.

That open-airness is for me the most striking feature of Burmese religious architecture. Never is there any mystic gloom, any successive passage from courtyard to antechamber to nave and nave to choir and choir to sanctuary, screens and arches and grilles to be passed until at last you reach the holiest place: instead, in most cases even from the street you look right through into the face of the Lord Buddha, and nothing bars you from approach.

The vestibules, those straight corridors, had here children selling candles, and little two-inch vases with real flowers, and larger ones of tin with artificial ones (oh, I'm sorry, they were not tawdry although paper flowers 'always are'), and packets of gold-leaf to help to regild the spire, and books. Nyo bought a guide-book to the pagodas: the fact that there is enough sale for such a book to be sold, passably printed in Burmese and with pictures, for fourpence, goes further I think to indicate the high level of literacy in Burma than pages of statistics would do.

At the little free museum, again, there was a Burmese guide-book only, and the labels were in Burmese: I deplored that there was not also an English one, and that Nyo had to translate, but it does seem to show that the Burman visits his own antiquities intelligently, not leaving them to foreigners.

There was one beggar only in those vestibules, a woman chanting a litany; and one fortune-teller, busy with a villager as we passed. 'All nonsense *and* rubbish,' said Nyo severely: I felt snubbed, having half intended to consult him myself. There were, thank Heaven, no deformities begging such as pester one at mosques and Hindu temples and Italian churches.

It is difficult, and for me at any rate embarrassing, to look at archaeological details when worshippers are present: I could almost envy people who can serenely push them aside and clamber on altars to study details through magnifying-glasses— it must be jolly to have a skin that thick. For this reason I saw less of the little panels of sculptured scenes from the life of the last Buddha than I should have done: besides, they looked Indian, and I have not yet learned to like or appreciate Indian sculpture. Some I saw had good moments: the monkey offering honey to the Lord, for instance, and His entirely unstereotyped attitude and expression—He is quite frankly grinning at the reverent beast.

After the Ananda we wandered around, in part with a friendly couple, man and wife down from Myedaw for the festival, very amused that we knew 'their' stranded steamer. It was hot and dusty walking, between hedges of cactus and euphobia, on wiry turf: convolvulus on a cactus hedge made a contrast so strong as to be painful—it looked like the ideal Early Victorian marriage; with the weaker partner quite successfully getting the best of it, you notice.

Our eventual goal was the distant Damayangyi. I struggled in vain not to see it as a gloomy, dungeon-like pile: knowing the character of the man who built it, the man who started by murdering his father, and killed right and left until he was a lonely tyrant, I felt that it was merely this which oppressed me. But Nyo felt it too: he stood by the entrance wall and looked at it—'Do you want me?' he said. 'I wait here.'

It is oppressive; but the brickwork is superb. Brick here does impossibilities, and does them precisely, crisply. There is little plaster left to-day to conceal minor imperfections: the whole was intended to be plastered over, so that such imperfections might have been tolerated—but there are none. Everywhere brick fits to brick as if in a mosaic of precious stone.

When I returned the old watchman, employed to see that tourists or archaeologists do not damage the building, was chatting to Nyo.

'He says the King used to come every day to see the work. If he could put in a needle between one brick and another brick he put the needle under the finger-nails of the workman, he says; and if he could put in a knife he put the knife into the workman, here; and if he could put in a sword he cut off the workman's head.'

It is not impossible, it fits the character of the builder; but it is not enough to explain the perfect work, there must have been in addition here a love of craftsmanship for its own sake. Even the wall on which Nyo had been sitting to wait for me is as perfectly built as the pagoda itself—the watchman pointed this out with pride.

'Nobody knows building like that now, he says': already in 1795 Symes also was told that this was a lost art. He, incidentally, did not like Pagan, using of it phrases like 'inelegant mass', 'mouldering temples', 'clumsy appearance'. The criticisms tell more about Symes himself than about the pagodas.

From there we wandered back to the Ananda, and looked at the stalls, unfortunately only just opening up. It was officially already the second day of the festival: it reminded me of the second month of the Paris exhibition that summer. They seemed preparing to sell everything from cane floor-mats to tin cooking-pots made on the spot, and from clothing to furniture. Some of this last was unpacked, jolly stuff with carved and gilded wood, and glass jewels let in, intended specially for monasteries and shrines: the effect ought to have been gaudy, horrible—I made a despairing attempt to see it as such, but remained unconvinced, and rather wishing I had any excuse to buy some of it. The matting-built theatre was ready, near the stalls, a huge affair: Nyo said that this festival was one of the largest in all Burma. (I *was* a fool....) Small children were giving a performance all by themselves on the low stage, quite unabashed by our entrance: the sunlight through the matting-chinks sifted across the pillars in a geo-metrical pattern, soothing, hypnotic, which seemed to remove the posturing midgets to centuries ago.

A street of half-built stalls led us thence to the city gate: the slots for the portcullis are as clear-cut to-day as when it was built, a thousand years ago and more. Small children were saluting the festival-decorated shrines of the *nats* [spirits] that guard the gate, brother and sister.

Everyone knows their story in Burma. Nga Tinde, the brother, was the village blacksmith at Tagaung (yes, the Tagaung I liked so much that I want you to go there). His strength scared the king: 'he commanded his ministers, say-ing, "This man will rob me of my prosperity. Seize him and do away with him." So Nga Tinde, fearing to lose his life, ran away a far journey and lived in the deep jungle. And the king was afraid; so he took the young sister and raised her to be queen. Long after the king said to her, "Thy brother is a mighty man. Send for him straightaway, and I will make him the governor of a town."'

Nga Tinde came. 'But the king had him seized by guile and bound to a yellow jasmine tree, and he made a great pile of fuel and coal and caused the bellows to be blown. And the queen descended into the fire, saying, "Because of me, alas, my brother hath died!" Men say that the king clutched the queen's topknot and rescued only her head and face, but her body was burnt.'

And the spirits dwelt in that *saga* tree: 'and any man, horse, buffalo or cow that entered so much as the shade of that tree, died. And they dug up the tree from the root, and floated it in the river Irrawaddy. Thus it reached Pagan; and they carved from it images of the spirits, brother and sister, and kept them on Mount Popa. And the king, ministers and people visited them once a year.'

They are known as the *Mahagiri nats*, the brother being the one in whose honour the coconut is hung up in houses: they became the oracles of the kingdom, consulted at the yearly royal visit....

The best of the pagodas came on our way home, the Thatbinnyu. This, like the Ananda, is a temple and not a pagoda proper; but it is entirely different from the Ananda in conception.

There, in that graceful composition, the eye is led up gradually from base to spire, each terrace a little smaller than the last: here, in the Thatbinnyu, there is a low, flat, two-storey base, and above it a sudden drop in area to a disproportion-

View of Pagan, photograph by Gerry Abbott.

ately high, heavy, square tower, which then tapers by step-terraces to spire and 'umbrella'. It looked all wrong: the base was squashed, puny, the tower overpowering. It worried me, I felt I wanted to complain to someone about it—and then I saw that in the tower, right in the centre of it but fully visible to the east through an enormous archway, sits the Lord Buddha.

The result is indescribably effective: it is as if the base were human, insignificant, antlike, crushed by the magnificence of the statue and its setting. It is a work of genius, of genius able to disregard all the laws of proportion for a symbolical meaning.

(It is, incidentally, also a very practical design, the two lowest storeys having served as the monastery, the tower as the temple, the upper storeys of this as a library, and the solid part from there up protecting relics just as does the whole edifice in the pagoda proper. There was a battle here in the First Burmese War: thank Heaven it was not a war of bombing-planes and heavy artillery!)

Nyo spent the evening in the village: I had a solitary (and excellent) supper, and sat on the verandah to watch the sunset, lampless because of swarms of flying things, including that annoying insect which 'flies backwards'—alights, that is, behind the place where he takes off. Instead of books I had the Gawdawpalin pagoda, just across the road from me, a white temple-pyramid against the blue sky at first, and then later red-flushed against green; and next morning it unbelievably echoed the sunrise, creamy on one side like the higher dawn-touched clouds, ash-grey on its shaded flank like the lower ones; and with a little unplastered brick ruin beside it to pick up the redness from the sky.

After breakfast I left Nyo at the bungalow (I can walk faster with my long legs than he can, hampered by sandals) and revisited the Damayangyi: after sleeping on the memory of it I had begun to doubt if the brickwork was really so good as I had thought. It was, and better; and on my way back I came across a minor item, previously unnoticed, the Thandawgya image-shrine, a further revelation of the way they juggled with brickwork. Here the Buddha-figure, the traditional seated one, is of brick only, the plaster having broken away; but it is not a mere formless core, to be made presentable by the plaster. Instead, the whole face is moulded in brick, even lips and eyes: I doubt if one-sixteenth of an inch of plaster would have been needed to complete it. It is interesting also in that it was the private chapel of the palace occupied by the last of the Pagan kings: it is hard to remember that Pagan was not merely a collection of pagodas, but a royal city, capital of an empire.

Keeping Nyo waiting I climbed the Gawdawpalin: I hate climbing but it was irresistible; and the view was worth it, giving some idea of the extent and number of the ruins. From up there it was hard to believe them of human origin: it was more like a dissected plateau, or a moon landscape.

This pagoda is again a temple, with images of the Buddha on the ground level like Ananda, and others on the first terrace-level. The construction is like that of the Thatbinnyu, a tower on a two-storied base: the difference is that here the tower is smaller than the base, lighter, more in keeping with normal canons—and far less striking. The tower diminishes by more terraces to the spire: I climbed to the base of this, as far as one can get, up startlingly steep little arched stairways, black against incandescent terraces, the risers very high and the treads very narrow. Coming down was much worse, with a long way visible for a skid right to the ground if you missed a step: If I had had to come down before I went up I shouldn't have gone up at all.

This pagoda is covered with coarse modern plaster, and spoilt in detail. Only here and there does one find bits of the old sculptured plaster, and get some idea of what the pagodas must have looked like; and they had coloured tiles as well, now disappeared.

I was in no hurry to leave: it was well after eleven before we got away, and we were nevertheless in Chouk before four. The steamers loop far over to the right bank: we found a channel on the left, among sandbanks and rocks, by no means currentless. Pagan showed up gloriously as we left it and its forest of pagodas....

Canoe to Mandalay, Frederick Muller, London, 1939, pp. 166–76.

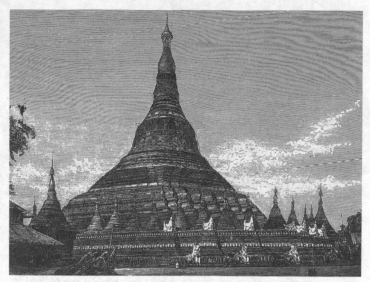

'Great *Shoay Dagon*, or Golden Pagoda (Rangoon)', from Frank Vincent, *The Land of the White Elephant*, Harper, New York, 1874.

19
An Artist Views the Shwe Dagon

ROBERT TALBOT KELLY

The Shwe Dagon Hpaya is probably the most revered Buddhist edifice in the world. According to ancient lore, relics of four Buddhas—the last of these being the Gaudama Buddha—lie enshrined inside the base of the great zedi. It is said that over this chamber was placed a series of pagodas made successively of gold, silver, tin, copper, lead, marble, iron, and brick, until the structure was about 9 metres high. Around this zedi the village of Dagon grew as people came from afar to make their devotions. It is known that in 1362 a king increased its height to 20 metres and that Shinsawbu, Queen of Pegú, added to it until it acquired approximately its present shape, and that she donated her own weight in gold for its gilding. In 1755 King Alaung-hpaya, having captured Dagon from its Mon inhabitants, renamed the town Yangon ('end of strife'). When King Hsin-byu-shin of Ava crowned the pagoda with a new hti

131

in 1774, the structure reached its present height. In 1871, the year of the Buddhist synod, King Mindon replaced that jewelled 'umbrella' with a splendid new one.

Such is the effect of the pagoda's gilding and gold plating that the orientalist Edwin Arnold called it a 'pyramid of fire' and Somerset Maugham likened it to 'a sudden hope in the dark night of the soul'. Such is its elevation that, even on a distant ship working its way upstream, what Rudyard Kipling saw was 'a golden mystery (that) upheaved itself on the horizon—a beautiful winking wonder that blazed in the sun'. By the end of the nineteenth century, Upper Burma having been annexed and 'pacified', a steady stream of tourists (called 'globe-trotters' in their day) came to see the beautiful sights of Burma, and not a few of these were photographers and artists.

Robert Talbot Kelly was a minor painter who was forty-three years old when he spent seven months travelling widely in Burma in the year 1904. As he travelled he produced watercolour paintings of scenes that caught his eye. In the following description the attention to shape, light, shade, and colour might almost constitute notes for a painting.

AS the roads in the suburbs are well wooded and pleasant for promenading, here and in Cantonment Gardens, as well as the public parks, the Burmese lady, gay in coloured silks, is fond of walking with her no less daintily clad children. In the neighbourhood are many Burmese villages with their quaintly carved 'kyaungs' [monasteries] and 'zeyats' [rest-house]; but above all you are in close proximity to that wonderful building, the central and most sacred shrine of Buddhism, not only in Rangoon but throughout the country, the great Shwe Dagon Pagoda.

Here at last you find the Burman in his purity, and amid surroundings which are entirely complimentary, and much of my time in Rangoon was spent upon its platform, charmed but bewildered.

I find it increasingly difficult to give any adequate idea of this marvellous building, which Edwin Arnold fitly describes as a 'pyramid of fire'. It is simply wonderful, and impossible of description. As, however, this, the greatest of all Burmese pagodas, is but a glorified example of the rest, I must make the almost impossible attempt to describe it.

First let me say that there are two principal forms of temple in Burma—the 'thein' or square-built temple, which is often surmounted by cupolas and pinnacles, as we will presently see among the ruins of Pagan; and the 'zedi' form, as here.

Viewed from a little distance, the Shwe Dagon is a graceful bell-shaped form rising above the trees which clothe the mound on which it is built, the apex being surmounted by a 'ti' or umbrella, a graceful finial of wrought-iron overlaid with gold and studded with precious stones. From it depend little bells and cymbals which tinkle prettily as they swing in the breeze. The whole of this dome is gilt, a large portion being covered with plates of solid gold, and it may be imagined how glorious is the whole effect as it blazes under an Indian sun. A rather effective introduction of a single band of silver in one of its upper courses only adds to the richness of its appearance.

Four ascents, one from each cardinal point, lead to the platform from which the pagoda proper rises. Of these, that from the south is the most important. Formerly this entrance was perhaps the most striking architectural feature in the country. A broad flight of steps leads to a platform or terrace bounded by an ornamental wall; passing between two enormous leogryphs, a further flight of steps and shorter terrace lead to a doorway of Gothic form, richly embellished by figures of 'Nats' [spirits] and 'Beloos' [devils] in high relief, the arch being surmounted by a characteristic 'pyathat'.* Beyond rise in succession the carved roofs of various bazaars which mark the different levels of the hill, the whole perspective culminating in the glowing mass of the Shwe Dagon itself.

Quite recently (it was only finished in 1903) this terrace has, at enormous cost, been covered in by a 'tazaung' [pavilion], which, though handsome enough in itself, is in my opinion, an unforgivable act of vandalism, as it entirely obliterates a view of an interesting and picturesque procession of historic structures which was quite unique.

The interior of this covered ascent is full of interest both architectural and human. On either side are stalls for the sale of anything, from candles and artificial flowers for presentation at the shrines to jewellery and toys. In fact it is probably the best bazaar for 'odds and ends' in Rangoon; and as the

---

*Pyatthat: a spire of seven successively smaller roofs.

steps are steep, and crowded with gaily clothed passengers moving up and down through odd effects of light and shade, the whole forms, I think, one of the best pictures I saw in Burma.

Ascending the steps, you finally emerge from the half-light on to the sun-bathed platform (a huge circular space of many acres) which surrounds the base of the golden pile which towers 370 feet into the air.

Here again modern addition has somewhat marred the general effect of the building, the indiscriminate building of additional shrines upon this platform having almost hidden the plinth of the pagoda, so that the general sense of its proportion has been lost. Each of these shrines, however, is in itself so interesting, and so lavish in its decoration, that one is reconciled to their intrusion by a study of their own intrinsic merit.

Whether it be in their general design, elaborate carving, or glass mosaic, the number and size of the Buddhas in bronze or alabaster they enclose, their enormous bells and ornamental 'tis', every bit of these structures and their adjuncts is absolutely interesting and beyond my powers of description. The whole effect is one of golden splendour amidst which a throng, clad in all the most delicate tints of silk, move like scattered petals from a bouquet of roses.

Before the shrines are groups of devotees kneeling, or in the position of 'shikoh' [reverence], some with rosaries, others with flowers between their palms; they pray fervently, while lighted candles gleam before the niche from which a gilded Buddha smiles.

They appear very devout, and the hum of many voices joined in earnest supplication is impressive. Yet I am informed that the Buddhist prays 'to nobody and for nothing'! This may be so, and the Buddhist faith is one which few have been able to fathom; but the sight of these evidently sincere worshippers would seem to contradict this negative assertion, and at any rate presents a striking instance of that dependence the human heart must always instinctively feel when contemplating the omniscient and the unknown.

These shrines are not for Burmans only, however, Buddhists of all races are represented, and all are dressed in gala costume. On festivals the Indian Buddhists particularly are richly clad: in one group which I noticed, the women, who were closely veiled, in addition to their other ornaments wore shields of silver on their toes. Each race or tribe appears to affect a particular shrine, which no doubt accounts for the erection of so large a number, but I was glad to learn that any further building on the pagoda platform has now been prohibited.

On the outer circle of this platform are many other buildings—offices for the custodian and his assistants, a library and Chinese temple, sundry shrines and 'zeyats' for pilgrims, between which are stalls and booths for the sale of foodstuffs and votive offerings. Away in a corner, shaded by a pepul tree, are the graves of our officers who fell at the storming of the pagoda; and not far away, in a half-ruined and neglected shrine, is the most beautiful figure of Buddha I have seen, in which the face, admirably modelled, really combines in its smile something of human sympathy together with the eternal peace of heaven. On the platform are two particularly good Shan 'tis' beautifully wrought in perforated iron, also two others of stone, and a really fine 'tagundaing', or flag-staff, the pediment of which is in five stages, each embellished with carved representations of dragons, garuda birds, ghouls, ogres, and fairies, in the order given. Among the many curios safeguarded by the custodian is a silver model of the Sulay Pagoda in which is enclosed a tooth of Gaudama, a relic supposed to be genuine, while facing the principal shrine two life-sized figures of teak, a man and a woman, in all the bravery of gaudy paint and tinsel, are dancing to the accompaniment of two gramophones which bellow forth in a noisy rivalry the latest comic songs from the London music halls! It is all very incongruous but deeply interesting: everywhere is some object to claim attention or admiration, to excite sympathy or amusement, but what at first puzzled me most was the great number of *bells* in every corner of the temple. Some of these bells are of enormous size, canopied by a handsome 'pyathat'; others of less size are in the open, suspended by handsomely wrought slings and bosses of bronze between their coloured posts. Beside each bell is a deer's antler with which to strike it, and I was informed that it is the custom for Buddhists, after praying, to strike first the earth and then the bell in order to draw the attention of the 'Nats' of the nether and upper worlds to their act of piety! In all Burmese pagodas bells figure largely, and I think, without exception, each temple is also adorned by huge leogryphs as guardians of the entrance. The legend is that in the misty past a king's daughter was stolen by a forest 'Nat' and hidden in the woody fastnesses. All attempts at recovery failed, until one day a lioness rescued the princess and restored her to her father. Since then the lion, conventionalised in course of time into the leogryph, has been perpetuated as the symbol of protection and guardianship.

Ever fond of a joke, the Burman likes to point out in the case of the Shwe Dagon Pagoda that one of these guardian effigies has a *sharp* tongue, while that of the other is *blunt*; one, they say, is a female, the other a male, but as to which is which the visitor is left to decide!

Burma Painted and Described, rev. edn., Charles Black, London, 1933, pp. 10–15.

Some Burmese Beliefs

20
Nats: The Spirits of Heaven and Earth

SHWAY YOE

Among the peoples of Burma, animism historically preceded all the other religions that consecutively found a foothold among them—Hinduism, Buddhism, Islam, and Christianity. Of these religions, it was Buddhism that flourished most, though Islam is still well represented, especially in Arakan, and there are plenty of Baptist and Catholic congregations among the hill peoples, especially the Karen.

In the middle of the eleventh century the great king Anáwratha of Pagán (where the main cult had been the worship of the naga *or serpent) managed to bring a whole pantheon of spirits (*nats*) under the wing of Buddhism, no doubt hoping that, once subsumed, animism would fade away. But while Buddhism did indeed go from strength to strength, even the most devout Buddhist still maintains respect for various kinds of* nat.

For an overview of the spirit world that is still very much a part of the daily life of most Burmese people, we turn once again to the expert, 'Shway Yoe', who has already been introduced (see the introductions to Passages 10 and 12).

WHAT concerns us is the fact that 'nat' means in Burmese two distinct kinds of individuals. It may be applied to the inhabitants of the six inferior heavens, properly called déwas, who figure in Hindu mythology, and have thence been transferred to the Buddhist world system. Kings and virtuous people are rewarded with happiness in

'The Nga Mo Yeik *nat* of Rangoon', painting by
Noel F. Singer.

these six seats after a good life upon earth. The Tha-gya min,
the king of the nats, or déwas, comes down to earth at the
beginning of the Burman year, and remains here for three
days, and his subjects generally display great solicitude for
the pious state and welfare of mankind, but otherwise they
are matters of no concern to dwellers in the lupyi unless as
objects of envy. Perfectly distinct from these are the nats of
the house, the air, the water, the forest,—the spirits of nature,
fairies, elves, gnomes, kelpies, kobolds, pixies, whatever
other names they have received in other countries. Burmans
never have any confusion in their mind on the subject, such
as may occasionally occur to a foreigner. The genii and peris
of Eastern story, though doubtless springing from the Hindu
déwas, have no real analogy in Burmese literature, any more

than the idea of the *devil*—etymologically connected with the word dév-a or déwa—has anything to do with the joys of Tawadeintha and Tôtthita, the best-known heavens of nats of the superior order.

The worship of nats, of the spirits, then, has nothing to do with Buddhism, and is denounced by all the more earnest of the pyin-sin [monks] as being heretical and antagonistic to the teachings of the Lord Buddha. King Mindôn, who was a true defender of the faith, and possessed of a deeper knowledge of the Pali texts than many of the members of the Assembly of the Perfect,* fulminated an edict against the reverence paid to the nats, and ordered its discontinuance under severe penalties, but the worship was never really stopped, and can no more be stopped than refusing to dine thirteen at table, to walk under ladders, to cross knives, or to refrain from throwing spilt salt on other people's carpets.

The term spirit-*worship* hardly conveys a proper notion. Even the Karens and Kachins, who have no other form of belief, do not regard them otherwise than as malevolent beings who must be looked up to with fear, and propitiated by regular offerings. They do not want to have anything to do with the nats; all they seek is to be let alone. The bamboo pipes of spirit, the bones of sacrificial animals, the hatchets, swords, spears, bows and arrows that line the way to a Kachin village, are placed there not with the idea of attracting the spirits, but of preventing them from coming right among the houses in search of their requirements. If they want to drink, the rice spirit has been poured out, and the bamboo stoup is there in evidence of the libation; the blood-stained skulls of oxen, pigs, and the feathers of fowls show that there has been no stint of meat-offerings; should the nats wax quarrelsome, and wish to fight, there are the axes and dahs† with which to commence the fray. Only let them be grateful, and leave their trembling worshippers in peace and quietness. For the Karen all nature is filled with nats, every tree and stone and pool and breath of air has its spirit. The dead are only separated from the living by a thin white veil, through which, however, none but the gifted can see and venture to speak to them in words. So the Caffres [Kaffirs]

---

*Probably the Committee on Religious Affairs, established by King Mindon.
†Knives, cutlasses, etc.

leave an open space in their line of battle that there may be room for the spirits of dead heroes to join in the conflict and fight on their behalf.

The Burmans are naturally not so wholesale nor so demonstrative in their recognition of the existence of spirits. The yahans [monks] would not endure it, and Buddhism has at any rate a somewhat softening and reassuring power. Nevertheless evidences of the fact of the belief are universal and not to be mistaken, in all parts of the country, whether among the Government school educated youth, or among the bumpkins, who follow the plough, and crush the clods, and know the jungle better than anything else upon earth. At the extremity of every village, the Ywasôn, there is a nat-sin, a shrine for the nat or nats of the neighbourhood. This varies very much in size and character. Sometimes it is a mere bamboo cage, hung in a pipul or other tree, or slung on a post, a bird-cage kind of construction, with an image inside, and a little hole through which the superstitious can introduce their offerings, tiny water-pots, oil-lamps, and little morsels of food. Often, if the village is larger, the shrine is much more pretentious, assuming almost the size and appearance of a zayat, a large tectum or roof, gabled and supported with red posts, the platform ornamented, and with a dais at one end, on which a representation of the nat is placed at the feast time, which, in imitation of the pagoda festivals, occurs at a regular fixed season. At other times these images are kept stowed away in an adjoining chamber, built for the purpose. It is particularly irritating to an educated Burman to see these absurd figures, which remind one of nothing so much as the fetiches of the prognathous African. Two gaudily dressed puppets, masquerading with spire-like crown, and royal, sharp-pointed swords, represent the much-feared nats, Shwe Pyin-gyi and Shwe Pyin-ngè, the Nyi-daw, Naung-daw, the Royal Younger Brother and the Royal Elder Brother, who command much respect in the neighbourhood of Mandalay and in Upper Burma generally. A still more dreaded spirit is one whose representation figures in a shrine at Tagaung, one of the ancient capitals of the country, half-way between Mandalay and Bhamaw. He appears simply as a head on a post, four feet high or thereabouts. A spire-like crown rests on his head, his eyes protrude and goggle in semi-globular wrath, asinine ears and a Punch-like nose complete the likeness, for he has no mouth, and his body is that of a dragon. Every one avoids his temple as much as possible, but the inhabitants of the village bow in that direction before they venture to do anything, and passing boatmen kindle lamps and offer flowers, of which he is said to be particularly fond, and fruit, for the nat has an incorrigible habit of giving people the stomach-ache when he is offended, and death punishes the recalcitrant. 'Tagaung colic' is a recognised ailment with the Burmese faculty. The demon is said to have been one of the ancient kings of the place, who acquired his power from magical arts which he learned in Northern India. Three famous pagodas in the defile take their names from episodes in his life; and his two sons founded the dynasty of Prome. Oftenest of all, however, the nat-shrine contains no figure. It is occupied only by the viewless spirits of the air.

First in the list of personal spirits may be considered the kosaung nats, a kind of confusion of ideas between the proper spirit and the butterfly spirit, and representing as it were the genius of each individual, a kind of materialised conscience. They are twelve in number, six good and six bad, six male and six female, and regulate the life and doings of their *protégé* accordingly as the benevolent or the malevolent gain the upper hand.

Next to these comes the eing saung nat, very often called Min-magayi, the guardian nat of the house. For his comfort the tops of all the posts in the house are covered with a hood of white cotton cloth, for it is in this situation that he usually takes up his abode. In almost every house, at the end of the verandah in front, you will find a water-pot full of pareityé, water over which certain gathas, magic spells, or religious formulæ have been uttered by the astrologer, or the prior of the district. This water, which is replenished once a month, or oftener in cases of danger from disease, or when a member of the family is absent on a journey, is every now and then sprinkled about the house as a protection against bilus and spectres, ogres and tasés. When the water is consecrated in this nyaungye-o, which is of a special shape, something like an overgrown Indian spittoon, there are always a few twigs and leaves of the thabyé tree floating on the top. These are mostly taken out and hung round about the eaves, but occasionally left in the water. The inordinately superstitious sometimes keep a small thabyé bin (the sacred eugenia) growing in a pot in the house, so that its benign influence may keep harm away. Talaing houses may usually be known by the cocoa-nut hanging up at the south side of the building. This is covered with strips and tags of yellow or red cloth, and is offered to Min-magayi, whom they call the king of the nats. Of these spirits (called kaluk in their language) they say there are thirty-seven distinct varieties, but Min-magayi rules them all. These are the 'thirty-seven nats of Burma,' but whether they were borrowed by the Burmese from the Talaings or not seems at any rate doubtful. At the beginning of the wet season they always wrap up the cocoa-nut afresh, and when the rains are over make new offerings of money, glutinous rice, eggs, jaggari, and fruit, in order that the eing saung nat may keep away fever from the household. It must not be supposed that the nat guardian of the house has necessarily any affection for those who have built the place where he has taken up his abode. He probably regards them only with cold indifference, however generous they may be in their offerings, and were he not propitiated by these gifts he would almost certainly display his anger by doing the inhabitants some grievous injury. But then he dislikes his haunts being intruded upon, and if a stranger comes at an unwonted time—a burglar at midnight, for example—it is quite likely that the eing saung nat will attack him violently, scare him out of his wits, or give him the colic. Thus without any really estimable purpose in his mind, Min-magayi may be a considerable protection to his worshippers, just as an 'awful example' is useful to teetotallers.

Beyond this guardian, or demon of the house, there is the guardian nat of the village, the ywa saung nat, of whose shrine at the end of the town I have already made mention. None of the lower-class Talaings would ever think of eating a morsel without first holding up his platter in the air, and breathing a prayer to the village nat. They are particularly fond of putting up shrines to the nats under the le'pan [*Bombax malabaricum*] tree, from the wood of which coffins are frequently made. A feast must be held every three or four years in honour of this nat, at which the natkadaw, a woman called the nat's wife, dances. This is done in order that sickness may be kept away. Should an epidemic actually break out, a very elaborate ceremony is gone through. Probably first of all the figure of a spectre, or of a bilu, is painted on an ordinary earthenware water-pot, and this is solemnly smashed to pieces about sundown, with a heavy stick or a dah. As soon as it gets dark, the entire populace break out into yells, and make as much noise generally as they can compass, with the view of scaring away the evil spirit who has brought the disease. This is repeated on three several nights, and if it is not then effective the yahans are called in to give their assistance. The prior, with his following, repeat the Ten Precepts, chant the Payeit-gyi, and then one of the sermons of the Lord Buddha is declaimed, the same by the preaching of which he drove away the pestilence which was devastating the country of Wethali. If this last ceremony is not effectual the village is abandoned. The inhabitants leave the sick and the dying to their fate, and go off to the jungle, where each household camps out by itself for a time. Before they return again, the yellow-robed monks, in recognition of much alms, read the Law up and down the street between the houses. When they have gone back to the monastery, the nat's shrine is repaired, and abundant offerings deposited. Having thus made their peace with the representatives of both religions, the people return to their houses, light fires, cook rice for new offerings, and then enter upon their ordinary pursuits as if no interruption whatever had occurred.

The Burman: His Life and Notions, Macmillan, London, 1882; 3rd edn., 1910, pp. 232–7.

21
One Christian's View of Buddhism

A. W. WILLS

In the autumn of 1889 an elderly Englishman and his wife set out on a short visit to Burma. A. W. Wills and his wife travelled across Europe to Naples and boarded the P & O Company's ship Chusan, *bound for Calcutta. Here they transferred to a British India Steamship Company vessel, the* Bundara, *which arrived in Rangoon on 7 December. Wills had begun to write detailed notes during the trip, not for publication but simply for his children and grandchildren to read, and this narrative eventually filled four thick volumes. He considered that the account was in any case too personal for publication, but late in 1901 he began to rewrite it for the sake of his family and friends. Shortly after completing this task he died, but fortunately for us his widow decided to publish a limited edition, illustrated by the photographs that her husband had taken, developed, and printed himself. This task was entrusted to her son Leonard, and a beautifully produced book was the result.*

In this extract Wills explains simply, as if thinking of the young ones at home, the basic principles of Buddhism as he perceived them both in theory and in practice in Burma.

WHAT, then, are those principles? What is the essence of that faith which still has, perhaps, a more vital influence upon the character of a whole nation and upon the daily life of each individual in it, than any other?

It is immensely difficult for any European to enter into Oriental modes of thought, even if he has spent years in sympathetic contact with an Eastern nation; almost impossible for one who has not had this education; but the following are, as far as I have been able to realise them, the main outlines of that faith.

While the Christian believes that each human soul begins its existence with the birth of the body with which it is associated on this earth, the Buddhist holds that it is no new thing, but that it has existed in the past, in association with other bodies, for an indefinite period, and that it is destined to a further indefinite but not eternal existence, in connection with a series of other entities, after the death of the body in which it is enshrined for the time being.

'The beginning as well as the end is out of our ken', and a man's present condition, whether he be wise or foolish, pure or impure, generous or mean, depends upon the sum of the actions performed in the earlier stages of that existence, of which his present life is but one quickly passing phase. More than this, not only is a man's character during his present life absolutely in his own control, but just as 'if he is righteous and charitable, long-suffering and full of sympathy, it is because in his past existence he has cultivated these virtues', so also is the next stage in his existence dependent upon his career in the present one, whether he mould it for good or ill.

If for good, then he will in the next, start his life, so to speak, from a higher plane, and thus by patient continuance in well-doing he may at last attain to the Perfect Peace. If, on the other hand, he shape it for ill, he dooms himself to a long period of purgatorial expiation of his ill-doing, for, whether for good or for ill, man is ever the architect of his own destiny, not only for his present life, but for his next, and through these, more or less, for an indefinite succession of existences. Fidelity to the truth will not be rewarded by a nearer approach to the Perfect Peace with more unerring certainty, than will evil-doing be visited by a terrible retribution.

The sinner may, if he has deliberately chosen the evil way, be even reborn into the body of one of the lower animals or find himself condemned to linger in one of the 136 divisions of purgatory, where he may have to pass at least 500 years, each day of which equals fifty terrestrial years, after which purification by penal fires he may be once more reborn into a higher and better state.

Nine million one hundred and twenty-five thousand years would seem a disproportionate punishment for even three score years and ten of misconduct, but the very conception of so horrible a retribution emphasises the strength of the Buddhist's sense of immeasurable responsibility, resting upon every man born into the world, to live in accordance with the unchangeable laws of righteousness.

Thus, then, by the gradual extinction of all evil in the soul, is the Perfect Peace to be attained at last.

But wherein does evil consist, and what is the Perfect Peace which is only to be reached by so long and laborious endeavour? When we try to answer these questions we find ourselves face to face with conceptions so alien to our habitual modes of thought, and to the religious teachings with which we are alone familiar, that it is most difficult for us to enter into the mental condition which makes them seem entirely natural to the Buddhist. He holds that the one great evil is life itself, the personal existence of each man; for life and sorrow are inseparable, ever going hand in hand from the cradle to the grave; all life involves pain and suffering, all suffering is caused by the craving for things sensual, for pleasure, wealth, and personal existence and gratification. 'The world is unhappy because it is alive, because it does not see that what it should strive for is not life, not change and hurry and discontent and death, but peace—the Great Peace. There is the goal to which a man should strive.'

Therefore by long meditation and negation of self all desires are to be finally extinguished, and thus each man may arrive at one of the higher stages of being, through which he must successively pass till he reaches the consummation of his hopes in Nirvāna; a state in which he will float eternally in perfect repose and cessation from all personal consciousness, the state finally attained by Gautama, the Buddha or Perfected One.

When we enquire how a man is so to shape his life as, so far as is possible, to approach the perfect extinction of self, we find ourselves on more satisfactory ground, for we receive in answer those practical laws and precepts of personal piety, the general observance of which accounts for those traits of character which make the Burmese people so attractive, and which may well excite the admiration, as they deserve the emulation, of nations of more advanced 'civilisation'.

For this is how he must live:—He must crave for no riches, nor strive to be greater than his fellows; and to the question, 'How shall a man so think and so act, that he shall come at length unto the Great Peace?' the answer of Buddhism is:— 'Be honourable and just, truth-loving and averse to wrong.... Do good to others, not in order that they may do good to you, but because, by doing so, you do good to your own soul. Give alms and be charitable.... Be in love with all things, not only with your fellows, but with the whole world, with every creature that walks the earth, with the birds in the air, with the insects in the grass.... To make others just, you must yourself be just; to make others happy, you must yourself be happy first; to be loved, you must first love. Consider your own soul, to make it lovely.'

Yet 'honour and righteousness, truth and love', beautiful as they are, 'are only the beginning of the way; they are but the gate. In themselves they will never bring a man home to the Great Peace', but if he have perfected himself, as much as in him lies, in these virtues, then shall his eyes be opened to the worthlessness of 'the world, which is sorrow', and of all selfish desires, and his soul 'weary of the earth ... shall come into the haven where there are no more storms, where there is no more struggle, but where reigns unutterable peace', even the peace of Nirvāna, the state in which all personality is finally extinguished.

It will be seen how entirely this Buddhist teaching differs from that of Christianity, which encourages in its followers the hope that a life of faithful endeavour here, may lead, in the dim hereafter, to a personal and conscious reunion with the loved ones who have shared with them the joys and sorrows of this present existence.

The absolute and undoubting belief of every Burman and the practical effect of his faith upon his own daily life, and through the individual upon the character of the nation, is accounted for, as alone it could be, by the fact that every male becomes at some time in his life, for a longer or shorter period, an actual inmate of one of those monasteries which are found in every town and village throughout the length and breadth of the land, and there receives systematic teaching in the life of the Buddha and in the books of his law. But of this, more hereafter in its proper place.

There is no religion which is carried out in the daily life of those who profess it with entire consistency, no code of morality which is obeyed with perfect fidelity; nor are the Burmese wholly an exception, although probably among no race is there less divergence between precept and practice. In spite of the doctrine that life is but sorrow there are, perhaps, no people into whose homes the gift of children brings more happiness, none more habitually cheerful in youth and manhood, none who take more pleasure in music and dramatic performances, or more keen interest in some forms of sport; none who look forward more eagerly to the great festivals, at which all give themselves up to innocent amusement, and it is difficult to suppose that the groups of graceful girls whom one may meet any morning tripping along through the shadows of palm and bamboo, on their way to market or to the Pagoda, with their luxuriant black hair decked with flowers, and singing as they go, have a very profound conviction that this present life is but sorrow and misery.

But 'the heart is wiser than the head', and the precepts of the Teacher which inculcate loving-kindness to every living thing, doubtless exert a more powerful influence on these children of the Sun than his philosophic theories, and bring their natural reward in the brightness of the people.

Fish is one of the staple foods of the country and is sold openly in the bazaars, and next to rice, '*Gnapee*'—dried and salted fish—is its most important article of commerce, yet its use involves wholesale destruction of life, in flagrant disobedience of the Buddha's law. Perhaps it is, as Mr Fielding Hall has suggested, because a fish is a creature incapable of inspiring affection or of evoking those feelings of sympathy which are possible in regard to most of the higher animals, especially the domesticated ones, that the use of it as food is looked upon as a comparatively venial offence, although it is universally acknowledged to be a breach of the law. I believe that a subtle distinction is drawn, by way of salving the conscience, between the act of killing the fish and that of eating it when someone else has taken it, and although the class of fishermen is a considerable one, they are despised by their fellows as degraded beings who will have to be cleansed hereafter by severe punishment from the taint of their daily sin.

I am afraid that the gentle Burman also indulges in cockfights, and that the excitement of the sport is enhanced by heavy betting, though how he reconciles this entertainment with the dictates of his conscience I know not.

It is equally evident that under no circumstance can the slaying of a fellow-man be justified. Yet in our Burmese wars the untrained peasants fought hard against our invading armies, a proof that the innate love of a man's own country is a stimulus to action, so strong as even to overbear an abstract moral principle when, what we are wont to call, patriotism demands it.

It is, however, remarkable, if the statement to that effect be accurate, that when the whole country was rising against us during our invasion of Upper Burma, none of the religious teachers of the nation either fought against us, preached any crusade against the infidel, or incited the people to resistance by word or counsel, but that they remained in their monasteries, performing their usual routine of daily duties, reciting the precepts of the Law, gathering their pupils about them as usual, and conducting the elementary education of the young as regularly as if no stirring events were taking place around them.

After all, the professors of Buddhism are not the only ones whose practice is not always in accord with the binding precepts of their religion. The Christian is not generally averse to laying up treasure 'where moth and rust doth corrupt', nor does he commonly turn his left cheek to him who has smitten him on the right; wars are not unknown among nations who for 19 centuries have sung of 'on earth peace, good will toward men'. Let us not, therefore, judge too harshly the inconsistency of the Burman who eats fish or who fights for his country against the Western invader.

One word more, and an important one, as to the real faith of the Buddhist. It is sometimes said that he is an atheist. If an atheist be one who professes to believe that there is no great Spiritual Power at the back of the great laws of the Universe, and ruling it for good, the Buddhist is at the very antipodes from such a man. On the contrary he implicitly 'believes that the world is ruled over by everlasting, unchangeable laws of righteousness', that the great laws which govern his being are perfect, far beyond his comprehension, eternal, immutable, marvellous; that 'the world is governed with far greater wisdom than any of his—perfect wisdom that is too great, too wonderful, for his petty praise'. Of the conception of the Almighty as a being to be conciliated by sacrifice, or influenced by entreaty, he has no idea. He holds, therefore, by reason of this unquestioning faith, that his only duty in life is to act in harmony with the laws themselves, and that no prayer of man ever did alter, or ever will alter, in the faintest degree, the eternal sequences of good or ill involved in obedience to, or disobedience of, them. Hence, he neither praises the Almighty for his earthly gifts, nor ventures to pray to Him to alter the eternal course of things for his benefit. When you see the Burman telling his beads or laying his offering of flowers before the shrine, or hear him repeating his devotional exercises before the image of the Great Teacher, be sure that he is not performing an act of worship, as we hold worship to be, to the Almighty, still less to the Buddha, for he is no idolater. He is contemplating the hollowness of life and seeking, by meditation on the precepts of the Master, to cultivate that abnegation of self which alone can raise him one step higher in his progress towards the Great Peace. That is all. Everything is done in token of profound veneration of him, veneration which fills the heart of every one of his disciples. This sense that every man has his spiritual welfare in his own keeping, a sacred and inalienable trust, that he alone can mould his own soul into the image of

149

good or ill, has one very important consequence. He feels that there is neither necessity nor room for the intervention of any other mortal man between himself and the Author of the everlasting Law of Righteousness. Hence from end to end of the land there is no priestly caste, no man claiming to be a necessary intermediary between his fellow-men and their Creator.

Bear in mind, therefore, once for all, that the Buddhist brothers, the Pôngyis and Rahans, are in no sense priests. This is the last thing they are, or would themselves claim to be, since each man is keeper of his own conscience, and none other can help him, save by exhortation, instruction, or advice.

Sunny Days in Burma, privately printed at the Midland Counties Herald Press, Birmingham, 1905, pp. 58–66.

22
A Dane Becomes a Novice Monk

JØRGEN BISCH

In his youth, Jørgen Bisch had spent a lot of time studying psychology but had developed a liking for travel. Before visiting Burma he had been to places as far apart as Lake Titicaca, Uganda, and Singapore, and while in Africa had climbed the continent's highest mountain, Kilimanjaro. He had written articles, some of them published in the United States, which included accounts about how he had fought with an anaconda, had visited headhunters, and had climbed an erupting volcano. Bisch, a Dane, now wanted to go to Burma, his aim being to seek out the famous 'giraffe women' of Kayah State whose necks, encircled with metal coils, appeared grotesquely elongated.

He had read books about Buddhism but little did he know as he bought his Copenhagen–Rangoon air ticket how deeply involved with that religion he would become. He found the Padaung women and obtained the photographs he sought; but partly out of fascination and partly for the sake of giving authenticity to his writing, he entered a monastery in Loi

Kaw. His studies there persuaded him that Buddhist ideas offered an antidote for 'the cynical materialism of the western world'. In this extract he is still taking lessons from the hsaya-daw, *or abbot, but is about to become a novice in the monastery—a* ko-yin *(here, 'koo yien').*

DURING the final days the lessons became increasingly shorter. I suppose the abbot had realised that there was no point in repeating the same thing again and again, with only formal variations (as certain Christian priests do), when the interpreter's vocabulary was only sufficient to express the gist of the matter. Also the interpreter often had difficulty in keeping awake. Sometimes I had the feeling that he did not really understand anything of what he was translating.

We always sat on the floor during these conversations. My legs went to sleep and I tottered when I had to stand up, but as usual the lovely green cigars fully compensated for any temporary discomfort.

The day before my ordination the lessons were interrupted in a pleasant way. A charming old lady, from the town's aristocracy, came in to ask if I would object if she and two friends gave the feast for me. She had an intelligent face, friendly eyes and a beautiful smile—funnily enough she reminded me of a Douanier Rousseau portrait. She was called Daw Sao Mya and she arrived with two men, U Win Myint and U Kyaw Pe, and they all three wanted to thank me and support me in my wish to become a *koo yien*.

The three friends sat down on the ground, and the abbot continued his instruction quite unaffected by their presence.

'During the ceremony your hair and beard will be shaved off, and when they fall you can think that this symbolises the decay of the body. To-day you are proud of your hair and beard, but to-morrow they will be like a hair that you find in your food; you will loathe them. And when the body is dead it, too, is only dust. Now remember that you must never pray to Buddha for anything. When you kneel before Buddha you should think about his good deeds and his good example. Buddha does not save us, he has just left us his good example, and our conscience must decide whether we follow it and improve ourselves. And when you become a *koo yien*, you yourself must set a good example. So you must obey the

'Novices Returning to their Monastery with their Alms Bowls', from Noel F. Singer, *Burmah*, Kiscadale, Gartmore, 1993.

ten commandments I have already given you, and continue to do so until you take off your robe.'

My last lesson before becoming a *koo yien* was finished. I stood in my cell and gazed out over the countryside. There was a wonderful view from the monastery. To the west I could see the meandering River Pilu, with its bridges and swarms of human beings. To the north lay the little town, its inhabitants going about their daily tasks—I was already beginning to feel detached from the world—and to the east lay the lovely lake, encircled by a forest of blue water hyacinths. Behind the lake some enormous kapok trees grew on the slope, and behind them again a string of hills, which looked blue in the distance. From the steps of the monastery, I could see as many as fifteen pagodas, set on top of each peak in the area; highest of all was the Pagoda of the Split Rock, Taung Gwe, with its four stupas.

To the south there were big meadows, where herds of water buffalo were grazing. It is forbidden to kill them, and whether or not you are a Buddhist, this is common sense, because the country has had a shortage of draught beasts ever since the brutal Japanese invasion during the last war. Farther away to the south there were mountain chains—not steep and rugged, but low and friendly like the people of Burma.

What have you really let yourself in for? I asked myself. Can you do what you're going to do with a clear conscience? Well, I thought I could, because in my view the basic tenets of Buddhism are either identical with, or better than, those of Christianity. And from the human and ethical viewpoint it can only be good to try and forget for a time the turmoil of the outside world and have peace to think about life.

Darkness fell quickly, and the cicadas started to sing. Somebody was hammering away on a giant gong shaped like a half-moon, and each beat made such a deafening, penetrating sound that all the dogs howled as though they had been stung. From the other cells came the murmurs of the monks, as background music for the clatter of my typewriter.

I crept out into the big hall. A score of wax candles were burning in front of the big Buddha—it seemed an ample supply.

'Good Buddha, may I borrow one? *You* don't have to use a typewriter.'

Was it sacrilege to steal from Buddha? In any case he did not seem to be angry.

'Good Buddha, are you also in this game? And are you smiling in spite of it? Are you now quite sure that in me you have gained yet another adherent to your great following which makes up such a large part of the world's population?'

As I crept by with the candle it seemed as though the Buddha winked. But what he thought of me, Buddha alone knows.

To-day my scalp will be shaved as smooth as a billiard ball, and I will don the saffron robe. The abbot gave me one more short tutorial.

'To-day, when you become a *koo yien*, you are going to be regarded as a child, and so you will have a young girl to accompany you the whole time and help you to avoid transgressing the monastic rules. And you must not leave the monastery grounds.'

'Oh, won't I be able to go out to collect food?' I asked.

'Yes,' laughed the monk. 'That's an exception from the rule, but even then you won't be alone, for whilst you are still only a few days old there will always be someone to escort you and look after you. This is so that you quickly accustom yourself to all our rules, so that you don't offend the people outside. Do you think that from now on you can live on only one meal a day?'

'Sure,' I replied in American. It sounded a little blasphemous, and the abbot must surely have known the word, for he laughed again when the interpreter had translated it.

I was just about to tell him about an elephant hunt, where for three months we only fed in the evenings, because we could walk faster on empty stomachs. But then I remembered that the abbot abhorred killing, and also the elephant is a sacred animal.

'So now I can no longer go on safari?' I said.

'Yes, you can later on, if you really want to. But not while you are wearing the *tchingan*, not while you are clad in the saffron robes. But it is always wrong to kill, so it would be better if you didn't do it. It would also be a good thing if you never drank alcohol. But this is one of the most difficult things to get people to give up,' he said and laughed, as though this obstinacy in some way appealed to his sense of humour.

154

Now, at the eleventh hour I had to ask one more question before my ordination, a question I had long thought about.

'Holy abbot,' I said, 'I have great sympathy with Buddhism and to-day I can completely hold to the rules which apply to a *koo yien* but I cannot promise that in, say, six months or a year, I will still be thinking along the same lines. I am not familiar with what you call meditation, and my understanding of rebirth is not completely clear. Would it be wrong for me to become a *koo yien* on this basis?'

'No, my friend,' replied the abbot. 'You can certainly become a *koo yien*; it will be a gain both for you and for us, regardless of what your future may hold. But naturally we hope that you will return to live with us in the monastery on some future occasion. And we hope that when you write your books you will tell your people what it feels like to become a *koo yien*. We are all very grateful to you, because by your efforts you have set an example for others to follow.'

The town was in festive mood, with everyone smiling happily. Hundreds of the leading townspeople would be arriving here, led by the mayor, and there would also be many of the abbots from the neighbouring pagodas and monasteries. I was really rather embarrassed at all the fuss.

Once more I stood in my cell and watched as the brilliantly clad people climbed the hill. Men with pleasant, happy faces, chattering women, and children who looked like china dolls. The drums began to play in the big hall—in a few moments I would be ordained. And I intended to do the thing properly.

I washed my hair—it was easier to do this while it was still there. I was so tied to worldly vanity that rather than throw it away I wanted to keep it as a memento. I had just finished doing this when there was a knock on the door....

Bat Ears stuck his head in and said there was somebody waiting outside for me.

'Is it the police?' I asked. But when he opened the door wider I saw the Loi Kaw friends who were sponsoring my ordination. There was Daw Sao Mya, the old lady with the Rousseau face; she waited outside whilst U Win Myint and U Kyaw Pe came in with a green *loongyi*,* which they wished to present to me.

*A kind of sarong worn by both men and women.

'It is more practical than European clothes, when the time comes for your change into the saffron robe,' said U Kyaw.

'Well, yes, that I can well believe. But I should like to be allowed to pay for it.'

'You must get accustomed to forgetting that there is anything called money,' replied U Kyaw. 'And you also know that good deeds carry their own reward,' he added with a smile. 'So we are not losing anything.'

I stopped protesting and changed into the *loongyi*.

'Remember also to put away your wrist-watch and wedding ring whilst you are a *koo yien*,' said U Myint, when he saw me putting my European clothes and pocket-book into a chest.

'Can't I walk around with a watch?' I asked in astonishment. 'How will I know the time? Is there something vain about a watch? Surely it's a necessity.'

'Perhaps the watch itself is all right, but certainly not the gold strap. But it would be quite in order for you to take off the watch and tie it to the monk's belt which you'll wear under the saffron.'

A *koo yien* came to say that it was time for me to come. So with my friends alongside I walked slowly and solemnly through the big hall towards the Buddha.

The place was almost completely filled with spectators from Loi Kaw, and through the big door I could see that the courtyard was crowded with jeeps in which the more prominent visitors had arrived.

When they saw me the music rose to a loud crescendo—a kind of flourish, I thought, a little blasphemously. I glanced at the conductor of the orchestra and recognised him. His last engagement had been to play at the theatre show put on by the casino proprietor. On that occasion there was a piano and a trombone in the orchestra, but now he had to make do with drums, cymbals and other percussion instruments, which are considered correct for a solemn occasion such as this.

I had to turn my back on the orchestra and kneel before Buddha with everyone's eyes on the back of my neck.

Loi Kaw's saffron-clad monks sat side by side on a dais near to the Buddha. In front of them stood a row of large basins, which were filled with wax candles, matches, sardines in oil, condensed milk and other articles which had been presented to the monastery in honour of the occasion.

The eldest monk recited some verses in Pali which I had to repeat. Suddenly I became very nervous. I was sure that yesterday I knew all the verses inside out, but now I just could not recognise the words. I thought back to what my Minifon had said and by speaking sufficiently low and indistinctly I managed to get through it all without anyone complaining of mistakes.

Last of all came the most important clauses. These I knew well, so not only could I repeat them aloud, but also with conviction:

> *Buddham saranam gachami,*
> *Dhammam saranam gachami,*
> *Sangham saranam gachami.*

Which means:

> I base myself on Buddha
> I follow his teaching
> I support his monastic order.

The time was approaching when they must shave my head. The town's mayor sat down by my side and, through the interpreter, expressed the gratitude and sympathy of his fellow townsmen. As he took leave of me I almost felt like a prisoner about to be led to the scaffold. But it was still some time before my scalp would come under the knife, for suddenly all the monks and visitors left the monastery hall to partake of a feast in one of the adjacent buildings. Only a couple of my friends and I, the direct objects of the feast, were left behind to starve.

After half an hour they all returned, and the orchestra began to boom away again. I was taken into a side room, where the executioner stood ready with the guillotine—no, sorry, where the local barber was waiting with two pairs of scissors and three razors.

U Kyaw dropped his ring into the basin. This is an old custom, which is performed by the future *koo yien*'s father or foster-father—in my case U Kyaw was foster-father. The barber wetted my hair and then started cutting it, using scissors and razor alternately. I was surprised that he did not ask whether I would like the hair clippers on my neck.

The razor scratched against my scalp as the hair fell. It sounded like a nail against sandpaper, even though the orchestra was still thundering away in Buddha's hall.

I had hired the local street photographer and a wheel-wright from the town to operate my cameras. I had previously told them to fire away for all they were worth, in the hope that I might get at least one usable picture.

The street photographer managed fairly well—indeed he ought to have had some knowledge of the job—even though the pictures I had seen in his show-case in the street suggested that this was not very detailed. The wheelwright was not so good. What was the use of my having carefully explained the apparatus beforehand, if he held his thumb in front of the lens the whole time?

Whilst my hair was falling off I should have been thinking that this symbolised the frailty and decay of the body. Thinking too about how to live an exemplary life, so that all the inhabitants of Loi Kaw could respect me, as they had looked forward to doing, so that through my good example they themselves should come to lead a good and moral life. Instead of this I could not help thinking of that blockhead of a wheelwright and his wretched thumb.

In fact I did *try* to be serious, and I was really rather ashamed that I did not succeed. But in my own defence I must say that the good barber, his assistant and my two sponsors from Loi Kaw, were all being a little frivolous.

Suddenly it dawned on me that there was no need to be too pompous about it all, for ceremony itself is not of great significance for Buddhists. The ordination is only a festival, a kind of examination party, to celebrate the fact that I was now being promoted into a higher class.

In the same way—apart from the fire hazard—it was in no way offensive that Maung Maung Hong puffed away at a big cigar whilst holding the cloth into which my hair was falling.

Perhaps it was this simple happy atmosphere that was so attractive. True enough we had our Buddhist monastic Latin, the sacred Pali tongue, but to me it did not inspire the awe of Roman Catholic church Latin. Far more important than the ordination ceremony itself was whether in the coming days I should be able to keep the rules of the monastery.

The orchestra was playing a little less loudly, and soon afterwards a couple of men looked in.

'It's taking longer than usual,' they complained.

'It's the beard,' answered the barber as the last red tufts fell to the ground.

Tonsured and clean-shaven by the careful barber I was finally led into the hall, and with the orchestra playing forte fortissimo the saffron robe was draped around me; the worldly green *loongyi* fell to the floor behind me and I was led up to the dais.

I had become a *koo yien*.

People touched their foreheads to the ground in front of us. Now this really *was* a solemn occasion—that is, until the twenty-year-old *koo yien*, whom I called Yul Brynner, nudged me in the ribs, winked and whispered:

'O.K.!'

This was the only English he knew and perhaps it sounded more emotional in his ears than in mine.

Why Buddha Smiles, Collins, London, 1964, pp. 103–11.

23
Traditional Mon Beliefs About the Unseen

ROBERT HALLIDAY

Robert Halliday was a Scottish missionary who in the early 1900s was stationed for some years in Tenasserim, the narrow southern strip of Burma that for many centuries has been home to (among others) the Mon, a people historically related to the Khmer of Cambodia and long subject to oppression by their Burman neighbours. Many Mon had sought and found refuge in Siam. Like the Karen, another Burmese minority group, they are still to be found on both sides of the Burma–Thailand border. In some of the first passages quoted in this book we saw the glory and power of Pegú, the four-teenth century Mon capital; Halliday was clearly sympathetic to the aspirations of this once proud and powerful people, whom others had dubbed the 'Talaing', and set about studying their way of life. He was able to observe his chosen subjects on both sides of the border and was also given access to the National Library in Bangkok whose curator provided the services of his Mon assistant to complement the Burmese Mon who was already helping Halliday.

159

The resulting book is even today acknowledged to be a pioneering anthropological account of Mon culture. This passage is taken from a chapter headed 'The Belief in the Unseen'. Halliday uses the name Talaing, *although* Mon *is the name preferred by the people designated.*

THE spirit of most importance to the Talaing is probably the house spirit, *kalok sṅi*. It is, of course, a very difficult matter to get anything like satisfactory information about the belief in spirits and the practices connected therewith. When you mention the subject to them, some will say the practice is so and so, but it is all nonsense. Others will profess not to know anything about it. An intelligent Siamese Talaing explained to me that many did not wish to speak of these things to strangers lest questions were asked which they could not answer satisfactorily, and further lest, when they could not explain, one should say to them: 'Well, why do you believe in such things and why do you keep up the practices?' The only answer forthcoming to such questioning is usually: 'Our fathers did these things and we simply follow.' This friend said to me: 'I tell you what I know about these things, little as it is, because I see you are interested and want to know about them.' Speaking about the house spirit he confessed that he did not know much about the origin of the belief, but he said that he had heard it explained in the following manner.

In the time of a certain king, the kalok used to appear at regular intervals and demand the body of a subject on each occasion. This went on for some time and the king became anxious and began to reflect that if this continued his kingdom would soon be depleted of people. So it happened, as he gave voice to these reflections, a courtier heard him and thought of a way out of the difficulty. He therefore spoke up and advised that a great feast should be prepared and the kalok invited to the feast. He urged that in this way it might be possible to make him the people's friend instead of their enemy. The king saw the wisdom of the suggestion and preparations were set on foot for a great feast. All kinds of foods and drinks that the people could think of were brought together and the kalok was invited to feast with them on his next appearance. The plan worked well, the kalok was pleased and became their friend at once, but it was soon apparent to everyone that there would be the old danger of the kalok reappearing and demanding his victim unless the feasts were continued for each appearance. So it was decided that on each appearance of the kalok another great feast should be made. All things went well and the kalok was now the friend of the people, because he was treated as a welcome guest. This, however, was rather an exacting service to keep up, as the appearances seem to have been rather frequent. A compact was therefore made with the kalok, for he had become so friendly now that it was possible to get him to listen to reason, and the frequency of the feasts was reduced until it became recognised as an annual or even triennial occurrence. We must, I suppose, presume that the kalok at the same time made it plain to his friends that, whilst he agreed to the reduction in the number of feasts, he must be duly honoured on the occasions and in the practices set forth in the tradition.

This story has a certain resemblance to one related in the *Mahavamsa** to this effect. The yakkha [ogre] Rattakkhī made the people to have red eyes and then ate them. The king alarmed fasted and said he would not rise till the yakkha came. On the arrival of the latter, the king remonstrated and the yakkha wanted a district reserved for him to which he would confine operations. Then in the course of negotiations he agreed to the acceptance of one man as an offering and the king offered himself. This the yakkha refused to accept and it was finally agreed to make offerings at the entrance of every village. Thus the pestilence was stayed.

To guide us to an understanding of matters, we not only have the evidence that meets the eye in every Talaing village and the little bits of information which come out in friendly intercourse with the people, but we have in writing, scattered through various books for popular use, formulas for ceremonial and for diagnosis of sickness and fright in which the claims of the kalok are more or less exhibited. There is little reason to doubt that many of the observances in connection with house building and the form which different parts of the house are to take have something or other to do with the kalok.

---

*A Ceylonese chronicle compiled in the sixth century AD.

The *kalok sñi*, or house spirit, is quite an important personage in Talaing village life. The Talaings in Siam are just as assiduous in the observance of the traditions as their compatriots in Burma, if not even more so; and they always say that the tradition was brought over by their forefathers from their native land. Some even go the length of telling you to which district in Burma their house spirit belongs. It looks as if originally the kalok had marked a kind of tribal distinction, though nowadays it is more of a family affair. Here is a typical instance of the way in which it appears now and it may be seen in any village. You find a family in which there are three or four brothers, the various members of which have all married and are living in their own houses in different parts of the village. The eldest brother as being the nearest representative of the deceased father is recognised as the head of the family. In his house are kept the requisites for the kalok. These consist of articles of clothing and adornment and are kept in a basket hung on the *dayuṁ kharoṅ*, or spirit's post. This, in a house of the Talaing pattern, is the post at the south-east corner. All the brothers with their wives and children are said to be of one kalok, and when any need arises for using the kalok property or for examining as to the condition of the various articles members of the family must repair to the house of the head of the family. The kalok follows only the male line, and when the sisters marry each becomes attached to the kalok of her husband's family. The women are said to be *luṁ ta*. What this means exactly is not apparent, but after marriage the woman and her husband are required to perform the *luṁ tā* rite. They repair to the house of the head of the family bearing presents of food, and only enter the house after making the circle of it three times. They bring with them, or at least ought to bring with them, a fish (*ka kanon*, 'the banded snake-head') of the size of one's wrist. The fish is tied with a nose rope to represent a buffalo, and is led or at least pulled round the house in making the circuit three times. On each occasion on reaching the kalok post a stop is made and apparently a question asked. The words used have no meaning to any one now and may be quite different from the original formula. In Siam it is *di ma ni dok* and is understood to be the equivalent of asking whether the kalok is yet satisfied with what has been done. On the third round, it is understood that satisfaction has been given. The fish is then taken up into the house, and having been cut into seven pieces is cooked. The seven pieces of fish with seven portions or dishes of rice are set out in the centre of the floor as an offering. The feast is then proceeded with and portions are sometimes thrown down for the spirit. This is probably the rite referred to in the *Burma Census Report*, 1911, Part I, page 149, in section 132 headed 'Totemism'. As it is one of the things that may be put off until a more convenient season, it is quite likely to take place often at harvest time. It is only attended to once for each woman and it seems to be called for often when there is need felt for honouring the kalok. The women are not exactly cut off from the connection, as they are still bound to come when a kalok dance is arranged in the family.

Often it happens that in a Talaing village you find a man of other race married to a Talaing woman and using the Talaing language. The issue of this marriage is to all intents and purposes Talaing. Since, however, the kalok follows the male line only, such families have no *kalok sṅi*, or house spirit. The only connection they can have with the kalok is through their wives, but the men are not bound to observances and seem invariably to disclaim any connection with the kalok. I have met men in Talaing villages whose fathers had been Siamese, Talaing apparently in everything except in this deference to the kalok, and even speaking Siamese with a Talaing accent like other Talaings. One old man I met at Lophburi, not distinguishable from other Talaings in language and manner of life, told me that his grandfather was a Brahman, and that he had no connection with the kalok. This all proves that the kalok follows the male line, and that the woman is more or less cut off from her original connection and hence cannot transmit the connection to her issue.

When a man who has been the head of the family dies, the position descends to the next of kin in the male line, first to the sons in order of age, then to brothers, and even to nephews. Failing an heir in the male line, the kalok or family becomes extinct. I met with a case near Ayuthia where the natural head of the family, the eldest brother, refused to have anything to do with the cult of the kalok. In that case the next brother is the head of the family as far as the kalok is concerned, and the kalok property is kept at his house. The wife of the eldest brother recognises the kalok by giving money to help when any outlay is necessary. I had my information from the mother of this family of three sons and some daughters who of course do not count. This old woman told me that her father was of Burmese race from Ava and that he brought his own kalok with him to Siam. He had a cocoanut adorned with red and white cloth hung on the south-east corner post just where the Talaings hang the basket with the vestments and ornaments of the kalok, and that no one dare go near it. After his death the family removed the post bodily. I give this as pointing to a distinction between Burmese and Talaings.

When on account of distance or any other inconvenience in attending to the various functions it is thought desirable to hive off and start a new kalok or family circle, those who wish to make the new departure must come to the original shrine and get exact copies of all the vestments and ornaments. Everything necessary must be as before. The same colours and the same checks and patterns must be used. It is the same kalok and must be treated in exactly the same way.[*]

There are persons male and female who are supposed to know all about the kalok, the various things necessary for observances, and to be able to interpret the kalok's mind. They are called *doñ*, which we ought probably to translate 'medium'. They are the chief assistants at the kalok dance. I made the acquaintance of one, a very decent old woman at a Talaing village on the Meklawng, and got from her some interesting information with respect to the kalok. It is not always that you can get people to speak freely of such things and I was all the more indebted to her for the ready way in which she gave her information. She said she was called to Talaing villages far and wide, visits to some of which meant putting out to sea. She was intensely in earnest and quite believed in the efficacy of a due deference to the kalok. She had seen some marvellous recoveries from illness by just acting on the assumption that the kalok was angry. One youth with a chronic affliction, she was sure, would have been free

---

[*]Marriage is not permitted within the kalok. That is, a man must seek his wife from a family having another kalok. The Talaings are thus exogamists in principle. The probability is that they were originally regular exogamists, but as will be seen there is now a tendency to hive off and split up the clan.

from it long ago, if his people had but given the kalok his due. She had of course met with cases where the limit of life had been reached and nothing could avail. I wrote down to her dictation in Talaing some lists which I propose to use. There is no doubt somewhat of local colour about them, but in the main they agree with what one sees in Burma, and with the references to such matters in the writings. These, however, will be better given in describing the dance.

THE KALOK DANCE

The spirit dance, known to Burma people as the 'nat' dance, is frequently seen in Talaing villages. It is held in connection with sickness or calamity, and is generally with a view to the alleviation of sickness, though sometimes it is in consequence of a vow in case of recovery. In Siam this dance seems to be confined to the Talaings and their kinsfolk the Cambodians. The Siamese come frequently as onlookers. A booth is erected in front of the house, in Burma often right in the roadway. This booth or shed is called *sni kanā* or simply *kanā*, and the dance *leh kanā* or *leh kalok*. An orchestra is hired consisting usually of drum, clarion, bamboo clappers and cymbals. The men erect the booth and then very often in Burma, at least, leave things pretty much to the women. The men it has seemed to me have appeared rather shamefaced when found taking part in the ceremony.

The list of food-stuffs as given by the *don* is as follows:-

'100 red cakes mixed with jaggery;

100 white cakes unmixed with jaggery;

100 packets of cake mixed with jaggery and wrapped in plantain leaf;

100 pieces of jackseed pudding [the jack seeds are made of stiff batter];

100 portions of parched rice, a slab of stirred batter pudding.

Having danced from morning till midday take a fowl. When the sun is getting low in the west you must take a tortoise,

four strings of Abhik flowers,

nine trays of flowers (of any kind),

one tray of plantain-leaf packets,

one *galun* (a kind of eel).'

The food-stuffs are all eaten by the company. Before eating the fowl a portion must be offered to the kalok with these words: 'We have cooked a fowl and give of it to the *kalok sṅi* to eat.'

Similarly, in presenting a portion of the tortoise, they must say, 'We have gotten a tortoise and we give of it to the *kalok sṅi* to eat.'

To this feast all the houses pertaining to the kalok must come or must at least send representatives. The *doṅ* must be there dressed up in the vestments as representing the kalok and must lead off the dance. The women of the family then take part as they feel the kalok's influence. They seem actually for the time possessed. In replying to any question put to them whilst in this state of ecstasy, they are understood to be speaking for the kalok. Passing along the street in a large village in the Amherst district, we saw an old woman at one of these functions dancing in quite a frenzy, and not long after we saw her pass on the way home quite herself again, but carrying in her arms her present of cocoanut, plantains, etc. She was no doubt a medium. I heard an old midwife, who had been an eyewitness, relate an incident which took place in a Talaing village in Siam and which gives some idea of the way in which this possession by the kalok manifests itself. A young girl was taken ill of what seems to have been plague. When in a very low state and quite unconscious, another girl suddenly commenced dancing and was understood to be possessed by the kalok. On being questioned about the sick girl the answer was given that she would recover. Just then the sick girl showed signs of reviving and even asked about her father who had been absent in the fields and her brothers and sister, and whether an uncle who had been to the city had returned. She also took food given to her. Then the other girl had a second turn of dancing, but nothing could be got from her but dumb show. It was but a momentary revival with the sick girl and she died soon after. It was understood that the kalok had first expressed his intention to release the girl and then had become indifferent.

In Talaing villages in Siam the dance is often a great affair lasting the whole day, and strangers gather round to look on.

The list of vestments as given by the *doṅ* is as follows:-

'Put in the kalok basket:

Nine bamboo cups filled with *sat*[*] leaves.

A coverlet twelve cubits long.

A loin cloth four cubits long.

A scarf or shawl five cubits long.

A red cloth three cubits long.

A white cloth four cubits long, with a band of red sewn on it.

One ring with a red stone.

One bracelet.

These are the vestments of the *kalok sṅi*. If we Mons do not reverence the kalok there will be sickness and pain.'

When sickness comes in the family it must be seen to that everything is in good condition. If moth has eaten, rat bitten, or fire burned any of the clothing, or if a stone has dropped out of the ring or any little damage been done, renewals must be made at once.

It is on account of reverence due to the kalok that a pregnant woman is not allowed to lie down in another's house. She may walk up into the house and go about any of the outer parts and she may even sit down, but she must not lie on any part of it at all, not even on the open space at the top of the stair, and she must on no account enter the inner house. To allow her to go into the forbidden part, or to lie down anywhere, would be to bring down the wrath of the kalok. This brings about a state of things sometimes that causes one to think the people inhospitable and unkind when the motive is not understood. Here is a case which came under my notice in the Amherst district. A man died leaving his wife and children destitute and without a house to call their own. The widow was in the family way and wanted to stay over her confinement in the house of a family who had been very friendly, but they refused her though they allowed their daughter-in-law to come from a distance and be confined there about the same time. Evidently the kalok was the difficulty. The son's wife was of their kalok whilst the widow was of another kalok. According to the Lokasamutti[†] it is allowable to build a shed for a homeless pregnant woman

---

[*]Probably *Pandanus odoratissimus*.
[†]A book on the arrangements to be made concerning death.

by the house of a relative and let her be confined there. Should a pregnant woman inadvertently lie down in a house where it is not allowed, a dance must be arranged at the woman's expense.

It is much the same when an accident has taken place from home. If a person is brought to a house wounded and bleeding, no matter how bad he is, nor how much the people may pity his condition, he must first be laid down outside, the bleeding stopped and the wounds properly dressed before he can be taken in. I was witness of a case where a youth was badly gored by a bull. I helped to wash and dress his wound on the spot where the accident happened and saw him carried away by his friends, but when we were passing the house some little while after the wounded youth was lying on the ground. They had not been satisfied that he was quite fit to be taken in. This was in Burma and I have heard of cases of the same kind in Siam.

THE HARVEST OFFERING

When the first fruits of the harvest are brought home a feast is due to the kalok, but should it not be convenient to have it at the proper time, a cocoanut and a basket of rice must be brought and placed by the kalok post in the south-east corner as an earnest that the feast is to be duly given. The cocoanut and the rice can of course be used when the feast takes place. There are some peculiar customs observed by certain Talaings at harvest time which must have something to do with the deference to the kalok. In rural districts in Burma there is a good deal of borrowing and lending just before and in the early days of the harvest. Those who are fortunate in having early crops are sometimes asked to supply the pressing needs of those who are not so fortunate and whose last year's supply is finished. Some Talaings when approached for a loan of paddy will turn a deaf ear and appear to take no notice of the borrower. Later in the day, however, the borrower will find a basket set out on the path somewhere with the needful supply. Others again whose custom is known are not approached on the matter at all. The borrower simply takes a sickle and goes and cuts the grain to supply his needs. There is a similar custom with regard to the tortoise. When one has need of a tortoise and knows of a person who has some, he simply goes and takes one. If he went and spoke to the owner about the matter it would be useless. He might talk till he was tired, but he would simply have to go and take what he wanted in the end.

THE TORTOISE TRADITION

There is a special tradition regarding the tortoise as may be seen both from the above and from the reference to it in connection with the kalok dance. When a Talaing sees one and cannot get it for his own use or does not want it at the time he must say, 'It is rotten, it smells,' and pass on. Should, however, a tortoise by any chance be taken home, it must then be cooked; but, before any one has partaken of it, what is due to the house spirit must be offered first of all. To this end the head of the tortoise, together with what is called the head of the cooked rice (the top part of the rice in the pot), must be offered. Sometimes the feet and the tip of the tail are also offered, thus making a complete tortoise. This rule is general amongst Talaings who give heed to such things. When eggs of the tortoise are eaten, one must first be offered to the spirit. This tradition is referred to in Part I, *Burma Census Report*, 1911, at pages 148–9 under the head of 'Totemism', but 'turtle', which is misleading, is used instead of 'tortoise'. This seems an easy mistake for observers working through Burmese or Siamese. Talaing has a distinct name for the tortoise. Talaings make no trouble about the sea-turtle or its eggs.

A Talaing up the Menam above Bangkok told us that his brother once brought home a tortoise, and, having cooked it, ate it without taking any heed to the tradition. The same evening he was taken ill, and died soon after in great agony. Others vouched for the severity of the illness and its end. Our informant looked upon the matter as a mere superstition on his own part, but he seemed to think that those who accepted the tradition must obey the instruction to the letter. This tradition is general amongst Talaings.

As will be seen from the account of the kalok dance, fowls come in for similar treatment. A portion has to be offered to the kalok.

THE SNAKE TRADITION

There is a similar custom with regard to snakes but that does not seem to be general, only those subject to it having to give heed. Should a Talaing belonging to the tribe or class subject to the snake see a snake he must cry out, 'Our grandfather and grandmother', and pass on. He must not strike it or try to harm it in any way. A Talaing woman at Lophburi in Siam told us that she belonged to the snake class, and that it was not permissible for them to harm a snake in any way. The cobra most of all is not to be touched. She was the mother of one son then a monk. When he was born as she lay by her fire a snake came and coiled itself on her bosom. She simply did nothing. Suitable offerings were made and it went away. It then coiled itself round the baby and again went when offerings had been made. And at each special occasion of the child's life the snake again appeared. We can place what construction we like on the woman's story, but it is a statement of the belief of a certain class of Talaings.

The Talaings, Superintendent [of] Government Printing, Rangoon, 1917, pp. 94–107.

24
The Venerable White Elephant

FATHER VINCENTIUS SANGERMANO

Early accounts (see Passages 2 and 4 for example) tell of the great esteem in which the Mon and Burman peoples held the so-called 'white' elephant—one whose eyes are pale and whose skin is in parts lighter than usual. Not only was this creature, according to Hindu mythology, one of the symbols of universal kingship (chakravarti); *for Buddhists it was also the form adopted by the spirit that descended into Queen Maya's womb before she gave birth to the child who was to become the Gaudama Buddha. A further Buddhist belief was that Gaudama had been a white elephant in a previous existence. The creatures were consequently held worthy of veneration by the Burmese kings who strove to possess them and were even prepared to go to war in order to steal them from other monarchs.*

Father Vincentius Sangermano saw for himself the beliefs and behaviour of one Burman monarch with regard to the possession of a white elephant. Sangermano was an Italian Barnabite missionary who was sent out to Burma and arrived there in July 1783. He immediately went up the Irrawaddy to the capital city of Ava where he found that Bodaw-hpaya, having made himself king and carried out the usual massacre of possible pretenders to the throne, was about to evacuate the city and establish nearby a new capital which he would name Amarapura. Sangermano was later recalled to Rangoon, which was to be his base for the next twenty-three years. Here he became well-known to foreign visitors; the British in particular valued him as an informant on Burmese matters. Returning to Italy in 1808, he became president of his own Order in Arpinum, his home town, and prepared his writings for publication. In 1819, just as he was about to set sail for Burma again, he died.

His manuscript might have remained unpublished had not the Roman subcommittee of the Oriental Translation Fund argued that the treatise, though written by an Italian, was an 'oriental work'. It was first published in Italian, and the English translation preserved the Italianate spellings. Consequently Badon-saw-shin, *one name for Bodaw-hpaya, is here spelt* Badonsachen. *The king's ministers are referred to as* 'Mandarins'.

NOTHING was now wanting to the pride of the Burmese monarch but the possession of a white elephant; and in this he was gratified in the year 1805, by the taking of a female one in the forests of Pegù. This anxiety to be master of a white elephant arises from the idea of the Burmese, which attaches to these animals some supernatural excellence, which is communicated to their possessors. Hence do the kings or princes, who may have one, esteem themselves most happy, as thus they are made powerful and invincible; and the country where one may be found is thought rich and not liable to change. The Burmese kings have therefore been ever solicitous for the possession of one of these animals, and consider it as their chiefest honour to be called lords of the white elephant. To excite their subjects

'The Palace at Amarapoora, with the White Elephant', from Henry Yule, *Narrative of the Mission to the Court of Ava in 1855*, Smith, Elder, London, 1858.

to seek for them, they have also decreed to raise to the rank of Mandarin anybody who may have the good fortune to take one, besides exempting him from all taxes or other burthens. Not only white elephants, but also those of a red colour, spotted ones, and such as are perfectly black, are greatly prized, though not equally with the former; and hence have the Burmese kings assumed in their proclamations the title of lords of the red and spotted elephants, etc.

To convey an idea of the superstitious veneration with which the white elephant is regarded, I shall here give an account of the one taken whilst I resided in the country, and of the manner in which it was conducted to the imperial city. Immediately upon its being captured it was bound with cords covered with scarlet, and the most considerable of the Mandarins were deputed to attend it. A house, such as is occupied by the greatest ministers and generals, was built for its reception; and numerous servants were appointed to watch over its cleanliness, to carry to it every day the freshest herbs, which had first been washed with water, and to provide it with everything else that could contribute to its comfort. As the place where it was taken was infested by mosquitos, a beautiful net of silk was made to protect it from them; and to preserve it from all harm, Mandarins and guards watched by it both day and night. No sooner was the news spread abroad that a white elephant had been taken than immense multitudes of every age, sex, and condition flocked to behold it, not only from the neighbouring parts, but even from the most remote provinces. And not content thus to show their respect, they also knelt down before it, with their hands joined over their heads, and adored it as they would a god, and this not once or twice, but again and again. Then they offered to it rice, fruit, and flowers, together with butter, sugar, and even money, and esteemed themselves most happy in having seen this sacred animal.

At length the king gave orders for its transportation to Amarapura, and immediately two boats of teak-wood were fastened together, and upon them was erected a superb pavilion, with a roof similar to that which covers the royal palaces. It was made perfectly impervious to the sun or rain, and draperies of silk embroidered in gold adorned it on every side. This splendid pavilion was towed up the river by three large and beautifully gilded vessels full of rowers, and was surrounded by innumerable other boats, some filled with every kind of provision, others carrying Mandarins, bands of music, or troops of dancing girls, and the whole was guarded by a troop of 500 soldiers. The towns and villages along the river, where the train reposed, were obliged to furnish fresh herbs and fruits for the animal, besides all sorts of provisions for the whole company. At each pause too it was met by crowds from every quarter, who flocked to adore the animal and offer it their presents. The king and the royal family frequently sent messengers to bring tidings of its health, and make it rich presents in their name. Three days before its arrival, Badonsachen himself with all his court went out to meet it. The king was the first to pay it his respects, and to adore it, presenting at the same time a large vase of gold, and after him all the princes of the blood, and all the Mandarins paid their homage, and offered their gifts.

To honour its arrival in the city, a most splendid festival was ordered, which continued for three days, and was celebrated with music, dancing, and fireworks. A most magnificent house was assigned to the elephant for its residence, adorned after the manner of the royal palace; a guard of 100 soldiers was given to it, together with 400 or 500 servants, whose duty it was always to wait upon it, to bring its food, and to wash it every day with odoriferous sandal water. It was also distinguished with a most honourable title, such as is usually given to the princes of the royal family; and for its maintenance were assigned several cities and villages, which were obliged to furnish everything necessary for it. All the vessels and utensils employed in its service were of pure gold; and it had besides two large gilt umbrellas, such as the king and his sons are alone permitted to make use of. It was lulled to sleep by the sound of musical instruments and the songs of dancing girls. Whenever it went out it was accompanied by a long train of Mandarins, soldiers, and servants carrying gilt umbrellas, in the same manner as when attending the person of the king; and the streets through which it was to pass were all cleaned and sprinkled with water. The most costly presents continued daily to be brought to it by all the Mandarins of the kingdom, and one is said to have offered a vase of gold weighing 480 ounces. But it is well known that these presents, and the eagerness shown in bestowing them, were owing more to the avaricious policy of the king than to the veneration of his subjects towards the elephant, for all these golden utensils and ornaments found their way at last into the royal treasury.

The possession of a white elephant filled Badonsachen with the most immoderate joy. He seemed to think himself in some manner partaker of the divine nature through this animal, and could not imagine himself anything less than one of the great emperors of the Nat [spirits]. Besides that he now expected to conquer all his enemies, he confidently supposed that he would enjoy at least 120 years more of life. As a symbol of this number the members of the royal family were making ready 120 glass lamps and other things to the same number, which, according to the advice of the Brahmins, were to be presented to the great Pagoda, when the elephant disclaimed all pretensions to divinity by a sudden death, caused by the immense quantity of fruit and sweetmeats which it had eaten from the hands of its adorers. It is impossible to describe the consternation of Badonsachen at this disaster; for as the possession of a white elephant is esteemed a pledge of certain good fortune to a king, so is its death a most inauspicious omen. So that he, who but lately was elated by the most presumptuous pride, was now overcome by the most abject fear, expecting every moment to be dethroned by his enemies, and imagining that there remained to him but a few days of life.

At the death of the elephant, as at that of an emperor, it is publicly forbidden, under heavy penalties, to assert that he is dead; it must only be said that he is departed, or has disappeared. As the one of which we have spoken was a female, its funeral was conducted in a form practised on the demise of a principal queen. The body was accordingly placed upon a funeral pile of sassafras, sandal, and other aromatic woods, then covered over with similar materials, and the pyre was set on fire with the aid of four immense gilt bellows placed at its angles. After three days, the principal Mandarins came to gather the ashes and remnants of the bones, which they enshrined in a gilt and well-closed urn, and buried in the royal cemetery. Over the tomb was subsequently raised a superb mausoleum of a pyramidal shape, built of brick, but richly painted and gilt. Had the elephant been a male, it would have been interred with the ceremonial used for the sovercign.

The consternation of Badonsachen on the loss of his elephant was not of long duration, for, a few months later, some white elephants were discovered in the forests of Pegù. Instantly, the most urgent orders were issued to give them chase; and after several unsuccessful efforts one was at length captured. It was to arrive at Rangoon on the 1st of October 1806, the very day on which I sailed from that port for Europe; and it was generally supposed that, being a male, it would receive greater honours than its female predecessor.

A Description of the Burmese Empire, Compiled Chiefly from Burmese Documents, translated from the Italian and Latin by William Tandy, first published in Rome 1833; 3rd edn., with a preface and note by John Jardine, published by Archibald Constable, Westminister, 1893; reprinted as 5th edn. by Susil Gupta, London, 1966, pp. 76–80.

25
The Hill of the Snake

HASSOLDT DAVIS

It was just before the outbreak of the Second World War. Armand Denis and his wife Leila, resident in New York, were entering Burma on their way to China, India, and Nepal; as they proceeded, they would be making a documentary film. Armand had at various times been a scientist, an explorer, a soldier, and a monk, and his wife accompanied him on his travels. On this trip they were accompanied by Hassoldt Davis, the son of an American millionaire. Davis was a journalist and traveller who had spent more than a decade travelling through the South Pacific, North Africa, and elsewhere, noting the folklore and cultures of various peoples. In the coming war he would combine journalism with soldiering and would be decorated more than once for gallantry in the field. At this time, however, the party was driving north from Rangoon, having acquired an improbable companion on the way: a young native American chief named Thunderface who had drifted into Burma and had actually become the headman of a village. Also in their party was an Irish American mechanic called Jack.

A century earlier, a missionary named Hurston had made notes about a sacred snake hill, a bare black mountain near a village he called 'Kensi'. The ancient cult of naga[1] worship was not yet dead in Burma, and Armand Denis was intent on finding this 'Hill of the Sacred Snake'. Driving through the Shan States and following clues that led southwards towards Thailand, the party eventually had to leave their vehicles with a teak forester and borrow his working elephants and their mahouts. Finding a village at the foot of a dark pyramid-shaped mountain, the group heard strange music and spurred the elephants forward.

---

[1] A mythical, snake-like dragon believed to reside underground.

'Burmese Snake Charmers', from Noel F. Singer, *Burmah*, Kiscadale, Gartmore, 1993.

WE entered the village slowly, with the dignity befitting white men. The musicians didn't pause; they scarcely looked at us. Some had kidney-shaped violins, some had the usual narrow drums with clay daubed on the heads to raise the tone, and some were playing floppy flutes which seemed to be jointed in several places. The half-naked village men, their long hair twisted into topknots, had eyes only for the procession of musicians that was winding through the single muddy street, and the women, wearing embroidered red skirts similar to the Kengtung kilts, sat before their huts and moaned. Only a few of the younger men, who looked less entranced than their elders, reached for pellet bows and watched us suspiciously.

'Don't stop,' Armand advised us; 'follow the procession slowly.' But my mahout waited to point through the open door of the hut beside me.

'*Bhang!*' he said. The old man of the house had been smoking hemp, I judged from the accessories around him, and was now lolling on a filthy mat. At three more huts I saw the same thing, and when my mahout pointed at one after another of the spectators to the procession, saying '*bhang! bhang! bhang! bhang*'—like a boy cowboy shooting

Indians—I assumed that most of the village was drugged. He spoke for a moment to one of the older men, who fairly shouted his reply, a long complaint accompanied by gestures which unmistakably indicated the nature of it, then hurried on to reach Thunderface so that I might have it interpreted.

'Great fortune!' said Thunderface. 'Not one son has been born in this village for over a year, and they are going to try to get their sacred serpent to fix it up.'

'Great fortune indeed,' said Armand. 'Will they mind us watching?'

'We can try. They don't seem to have spirit enough even to be curious about white men, which most of them have never seen. This race,' said Thunderface pontifically, 'is decayed.'

When we caught up with twelve musicians we noticed that a woman was now leading them, a woman who might well have been a creature of the infamous Dr Fu Manchu. She was dressed in the purest white from throat to ankles. The *longgyi* skirt was wound tight around her waist and the long-sleeved blouse fitted like a dazzling skin, a strange contrast to the sombre nudity of her companions. Her face was farded white with some heavy paste, and her agate eyes were those of a snake.

'Hsa-pu,' said my mahout—her name, I supposed.

Riding beside her, and staring fascinated at her, I had forgotten the sacred hill ahead, and it was not until she left her musicians and started off alone that I looked up. It was Hurston's hill and no mistake. Before us was the serpentine stairway, a foot wide, winding into the clouds, and slowly along it climbed the weird Hsa-pu, followed by a fattish youth who bore a roll of mats and a tray with offerings of coconut and fruit and rice.

We knelt our elephants and got down. Hsa-pu was far ahead by now and we followed hurriedly in single file. Each step of the stair was shaped like a scale of the Naga, crudely cut of flagstone, and where the rain had settled upon it and thin moss grown it was slimy as a serpent's skin. I turned to look at the musicians who still were playing, and the half-drugged villagers with their pellet bows held indecisively, but they made no move to stop us. We climbed for half a mile, slippery step by step, until we reached the lowering mists.

The stairs levelled here and seemed to go directly into the solid earth. We had expected to find some sort of temple at the top, but the grassy court where we stood, watching Hsa-pu, led to a low precipice which was honeycombed with small caves. Thunderface was at my side and the mahout beside him, explaining as best he could this extraordinary ritual.

There was just light enough to see, far in the depths of the largest cave, a low cot woven of vines, and flower garlands suspended from pegs above it. Hsa-pu went in slowly, followed by her servant, and in a moment he came backing out, looking neither to right nor left but abjectly laying the mats straight before him. The mahout was whispering. Hsa-pu had gone to propitiate her god, Hsa-pu whose ancestors for centuries had exclusively had the knowledge of the snake and the secret of placating him. And Hsa-pu it must be of this generation to discuss with the god all matters of fertility, whether of crops or beasts or women. This year no sons had been born to Kensi, and so Hsa-pu had come to exert her powers.

We could dimly see her raise the tray of offerings to the height of her eyes, scoop a fistful of rice, blow upon it and flick it in all directions, to appease the other gods, I assumed. Then she put the tray upon the cot and knelt beside it.

It was nearly dark by now; the sun beyond the mist was sinking and the orange light that reached the cave was whitened suddenly with a flare of lightning. We could hear the music far below, muffled by mist, and from the cave came strange noises, alternately sibilant and explosive, that sent a shiver up my spine. Hsa-pu was squatting, backing towards us, talking to the snake that lived within, drawing him out along the mats.

We too backed off and stood breathless before the creature we saw.

This was the King Cobra, or Hamadryad, at least fourteen feet in length, as large, I believe, as they ever grow. His hooded head arched four feet above the ground, on a level with Hsa-pu's breast as he wove after her.

'My God!' said Armand, who cherishes snakes. 'Do you suppose it has its fangs?'

The mahout was whispering hoarsely to Thunderface who passed on the message to me. These snakes, he said ('serpents,' he corrected himself), were caught in the jungle and brought once a year to the sacred mountain, where Hsa-pu made a pact with them, promising to return them within twelve months to their homes. She would be bitten, she knew, if she broke faith. The snakes were then content to remain within the cave, where she fed them with frogs once every five days and besought their boon when the need arose. The fangs and the venom were untampered with—you can't pull the teeth of your god—and since the King Cobra, because of his enormous secretions, carries over a hundred times the lethal dose of venom, we realized that we were witnessing perhaps the most dangerous religious ritual in the world.

Now the woman and the snake were upon the mat before the cave, Hsa-pu squatting, approaching and backing with quick smooth movements of her heels, drawing the attention of the god with her left hand and striking it lightly with her right, as a boxer might do. Now she rose to a crouch and curved one arm over it, farther and farther back until the snake rose erect as far as it could reach and she could gently bring down her hand upon its head, forcing it flat upon the ground. She would humble it thus, remind it of her power, before she wheedled it for the village sons.

The snake, the god, sprang back hissing when she released it. Squatting again less than three feet away she tempted it with her knees, swinging them together from side to side, opening and closing them, until the snake lunged and she could catch it beneath the throat with the side of her open hand. Lightning forked across the dusk like a snake tongue threatening us.

Hsa-pu backed round in a circle now, always squatting, and the huge snake pursued her. With forefinger pressed to thumb of her left hand she seemed to draw it towards her, as if by a thread, while with her right hand she made curious lithe gestures similar to those used in the Tibetan worship. Her face was set hard as a mask. Sweat beaded her forehead and ran down in grey lines across her powdered cheeks.

Roy was beside me. 'This is incredible!' Leila started to speak, then suddenly pointed to the cliff. From the holes beside the cave of the god three common cobras were slowly emerging.

'Jack, look!' Jack looked, and reached for a boulder, but the mahout stopped him. A fourth cobra, six feet long, had raised its head within striking distance of his thigh. The mahout nodded reassuringly.

The music from below grew gradually faster and Hsa-pu's movements quickened with it. Rain was falling now, and the great snake glistened as he tried to get close enough to his tormentor to strike. She bent forward, protruded one knee, and when the snake flung towards her, hurtling half its body from the ground, she received its fangs in the taut skirt which her knees had spread. A stain grew slowly there.

I could hear Armand muttering, and from the corner of my eye, I saw his finger point. 'There's another.' Another cobra, a small one, was within five feet of us. This was getting a bit thick, I thought; we were interested in strange cultures, but—but I was as fascinated as the snakes by this amazing woman. I scarcely felt the rain that was flailing against us now.

Hsa-pu lowered her head almost to the ground and looked sidewise at her god; and he rose and remained motionless above her, hood expanded and jaws wide to strike again, while she talked to him gently. She laid her hand upon her abdomen and then upon the earth, and along the muddy print where the snake had fallen when he struck at her, she drew her two hands caressingly then cupped her breasts with them.

The rain was blinding. We shielded our eyes and leaned forward, trying to watch the other snakes and the god at once. The lightning was continual now, and the sound of thunder drowned out all the music with the exception of the whining flute. I realized with a sudden chill in the marrow of me that neither Hsa-pu nor the snake had moved in a very long while, but had remained watching each other's eyes, she crouched and he overlooking her like a god.

Then with almost imperceptible motion her head was rising. Her head was curving across the green, lightning-lighted sky till it was level with her god's, and slowly it came forward. There were but two feet between them now. Now there was but one.

Hsa-pu, her hands behind her, leaned slowly down and pressed her mouth against the poisonous mouth of her great god, and the trembling that ran through her whole body seemed communicated to his before he swung his head to one side and moved off into the cave.

Hsa-pu remained kneeling, her forehead in her hands. My breath came slishing out and I was aware suddenly that the storm had swung with all its fury upon us, lashing leaves in my face and pressing me towards the stair which led to supper and sanity, and a long hot drink.

We spent seventeen days at Kensi, waiting for the weather to clear sufficiently for us to film Hsa-pu and her amazing ritual. She was perfectly willing. Although the great duty of her life was towards her own village and the Naga, the serpent god, she had several times travelled to the west and south of Burma, 'charming' common cobras at the five-day markets and drawing the snakes from the estates of white men, an inexplicable feat performed by no one else in Burma though it is quite matter-of-course in India proper.

Surely, she felt, it could do no harm to implore the god's favours once again in behalf of the sonless village women, particularly when for her pains she would receive some very natty apparel which Leila had outworn. But what really clinched it, I think, was Jack's offer of a gift to the god.

Jack was the only one of us who could be called a hunter. He had shot bear and moose in Maine, and here it was his heart's desire to try his skill with tiger or binturong, the bear cat, or the great rhinoceros which is now found only in this wild corner of Burma near the Siamese border. And more exciting even than these was the report of a creature, the Kung-lu (the Mouth-man), which has terrified the people for centuries. The Kung-lu, according to Thunderface, was a monster that resembled a gorilla, a miniature King Kong, about twenty feet tall. It lived on the highest mountains, where its trail of broken trees was often seen and descended into the villages only when it wanted meat, human meat. Elephants roamed hereabout, we learned, and we were told also that no one in Kensi had been eaten by the Kung-lu for more years than the eldest could remember.

Despite this anti-climax the story was interesting because it was common all along the borders of Chinese Yunnan, French Indo-China, and Siam. Another curious thing about it was that the Mouth-man never ate fat people, as one would expect, but the very thinnest of them; what he liked was bones.

Jack disdainfully went over our small arsenal of revolvers, deploring the lack of any proper gun, and chose Armand's Colt .45 as the best available weapon for Mouth-men, tiger, or rhinoceros. All night he kept vigil in a thick clump of brush outside the village, until about three a.m., when the rest of us were shaken in our cots by the sound of a shot. Jack crept back to the tents with a giant frog in his hand.

'There's your Mouth-man,' said he. 'Thought he might make a nice gift for the lady's god.'

Hsa-pu was so pleased with this gallant gesture that we could no longer doubt her promise to let us film the Naga rite if the weather cleared. If it cleared. The period we spent at Kensi waiting is the sort that is usually skipped in the tales of explorers, and rarely envisaged by those who think of exploration as high adventure. We sat and soaked, bored to tears. Gloomily we slopped through the village to try to learn something of the half-drugged people whom Thunderface had aptly called 'decayed'. There wasn't much to learn. They were a branch of the Muhso tribe, it seemed, which made a wretched living smuggling opium and *bhang* across the borders of the three frontiers near Kensi. They were not always so languid with drugs as on our first day, apparently because that was a ceremonial occasion, but they were never sprightly. If we wanted chickens, for instance, we had to give them twenty-four hours' notice so that they could debate the matter and, finally, irresolutely capture them. If we wanted a jungle fowl the hunters would first deliberate, eventually shoot the bird with their pellet bows, then excise the bones from it and return them to the place of the kill, for otherwise the nats [spirits] would prevent all future hunting. Eventually we ate.

Our most careful questioning, relayed through Thunderface and Gongue's mahout, failed to elicit any satisfactory answer as to the origin of the Naga cult in Kensi. Whether it had come from India across Burma or via the ancient Khmer kingdoms of Cambodia and Siam was a dilemma equally tenable by either horn. There were of course no written records, and with the exception of the winding, snake-like staircase there was no sculpture which could give us a clue. The staircase resembled somewhat the Naga causeways of Angkor Thom. It also resembled any practical, carefully built path up any mountainside.

Of more immediate interest to us was the problem of why a village of seventy people should have had no sons born in it for over a year.

It was a curse, we were told by one old woman, a curse of the *nats* because one of their favourite trees had been carelessly burned. She was certain, however, that the Naga could remove this curse. The infant mortality of Kensi seemed in general to be very high. Back and forth across the stream at the edge of Kensi there ran many fine threads whose significance baffled me for some time. It was finally explained that children were buried on the farther shore and these threads had been stretched from tree to tree across the stream so that the small ghosts could hold to them when coming to visit their parents.

The rain at last abated sufficiently for us to film Hsa-pu's strange ritual. We worked feverishly, Roy and Armand with the two big moving picture cameras and the sound recorder, I with the Leicas and Ikontas.

We were a considerably shaken expedition after making the close-ups of that fourteen-foot King Cobra's venomous head. We made tests in the evening, as we did for every scene, developing about eight inches of the exposed film in a Leica tank. It was good, said Roy; focus, exposure, composition. The piece of film we developed showed Hsa-pu's head and the snake's almost filling the frame with that deific kiss.

We were jubilant. This was rare material, and we took it as an augury of better things along the Burma–Yunnan Highway which we should now follow into China.

Thunderface left us in Kensi, for he had his own village to attend to, said he, and the quicksands to guard. We watched him regretfully, as he turned from us, that lost redskin, high aboard an elephant in the Burma jungles.

Nepal, Land of Mystery, Robert Hale, London, 1942; Readers Union edn., 1943, pp. 77–86.

26
Word-play and Word Magic

GERRY ABBOTT

In 1988 the whole of Burma was in a ferment, an unrest caused firstly by the failures of General Ne Win (popularly known as 'Number One') and his oppressive military government, then by the killing of some students, and finally by a demonetization that wiped out many people's savings. Since

Ne Win's takeover in 1962, there had been no appreciable progress; in fact the country seemed to be going backwards.

But the Burmese people had shown a remarkable resilience in which their sense of humour played no small part, and the author was privileged to see it in action. A London-born man in his fifties, he had spent his life teaching English, and training teachers of English, in various countries—including Thailand, Jordan, Uganda, Yemen, and Malaysia—and now he was working at the University of Mandalay. Here, he shows how the traditional love of word-play also finds expression in a form of magic known as yaddayá, *belief in which is still strong in Burma.*

IN circumstances that are embarrassing, frustrating or bewildering most Southeast Asians release tension not by snarling or shouting but by laughing. In some cultures this is just a fairly humourless reflex, but the Burmese have a well-developed sense of the ridiculous and derive a great deal of real pleasure from seeing the funny side of even quite shocking things.... The government's handling of everything was so inept, everything was so topsy-turvy, that political criticism was being more and more openly expressed.

The only truly national exponent of political humour that I knew of was a brave stand-up comedian who called himself Zā-Ganā ('Pliers') because he was—or had been—a student of Dentistry. His humour was simple and allusive but, in such an oppressed society, deliciously daring; his stories, passed on by word of mouth, were rays of sanity in the gathering gloom. There was one typical little tale that used an image ubiquitous in Burma—the clapped-out vehicle—to represent the misguided State apparatus. His forbidden topics sent frissons of nervous delight running through a population riddled with fear—even a joke as simple as this one, freely rendered into idiomatic English:

There's this ancient patched-up jalopy, full of people, you see, and it's chugging down a busy one-way street in Rangoon. And it's going the wrong way. [Giggles] And it's going backwards. [More giggles of anticipation] So a traffic policeman sees this and stops the car and tells the driver to drive properly.

'Can't be done,' says the driver. 'This old contraption only seems to go backwards.' [Knowing grins as people cotton on to the imagery]

'Nonsense,' says the cop. 'Use your gears. Try number one.'
[Gasps]

'Number one's no bloody good.' [Guffaws] 'Been no good for years.' [Hoots]

'Well, what about number two then?' says the policeman.

'Number two's useless as well. It's no good. We're stuck in reverse.'

And so on. No doubt there was more innuendo, but the references to Ne Win and to San Yu, the President, were daring enough. I wondered if Zā-Ganā joked about Number Three, Sein Lwin, in the same way. I wouldn't give much for his chances of survival if he did. Sein Lwin had not only been in charge of putting down the student unrest a few weeks earlier; he had, in Ne Win's first months of power, been involved in quelling the student riots of 1962. His nickname was 'The Butcher'.

The once-affluent country, still potentially rich, was now classified as being of 'Least Developed Status' and was plumbing such depths that people found themselves laughing at just about everything. The students knew that university education was of pitifully low quality. The BA (English) had been dubbed the ABC (English), and the BSc (Maths) had become 123 (Maths). Whatever their main subject they all had to study English, and they joked that there was a gold medal for any student who failed that exam. The older generation had long been amused by what Ne Win called 'The Central Organs of Power'—the various State bodies through which he exerted his own power—and now, because he had just taken yet another wife, a woman only in her twenties, the ladies in the staffroom were laughing heartily at the current description of Number One: the leader of the least developed country with the most developed organ.

Just as in English the words 'road', 'rode' and 'rowed' sound exactly alike though they are spelled differently, so in Burmese (but far more so) many a syllable heard on its own is ambiguous. For instance, the flame-of-the-forest tree (*Butea frondosa*) is *sein-pan*; but each spoken syllable in isolation could mean 'immerse in water' and 'penis'. The scope for puns and word play is therefore enormous. One of the more respectable jokes of the day played upon the phrase for boiled sweetcorn, or maize; *pyaungbu-pyouq*. Separately, *pyaung* means 'alter' and *pyouq* can also mean 'dismiss'; *ma ... bu*, like the French *ne ... pas*, makes verbs negative. So one topical catch-phrase was:

pyaungbu pyouq	*ma-pyaung-bu*	*ma-pyouq-bu*
The boiled corn-cob	won't change,	won't be ousted

Then, during July, what the Party manifesto had called 'social antagonisms' erupted, civil disturbances all of which appeared to involve acts of racial enmity towards Muslims and which followed such a set pattern that I assumed the troubles were being deliberately fomented by the government's *agents provocateurs* in order to divert public resentment and discontent into a conventional channel. At this time, the troubles were mainly in Taunggyi and Pye (Prome). There were none in Mandalay. Much later, some rumours confirmed my hunch; according to these stories, the government had instigated these riots as a form of *yaddayā*, to ward off major catastrophes. The logic (if that is the right word) behind *yaddayā* is similar to that of some superstitions that I had come across elsewhere: for example, that if you have a minor accident in your new car, you will henceforth be protected from a major one. Months later, back in England, I noticed a form of *yaddaya* pictured in the *Guardian* (London): some self-styled witches had, on a hilltop in Kent, burned a model train in an attempt to prevent Channel tunnel trains being routed through their unspoiled environment.

That form of witchcraft attempts to influence a reality by operating upon an image of that reality—in this case by burning a model train, in another by sticking pins in a doll, and so on; but another kind of image of a reality is its name. The *yuddayā* that Number One was said to be operating at this time almost invariably rested on a linguistic base: on a pun of some sort, in fact. There had been riots not only in Taunggyi and Pye but also in Myedeh; and it was said that the disturbances had been designed to prevent the disasters represented by these phrases:

taung-gyi hpyo	('destroy big mountain')
pye-gyi pyet	('devastate the country')
mye-deh hlan	('overturn the earth')

As with all folklore, it is difficult to tell whether this was indeed what was done, or whether it was simply what people ascribed to Ne Win and his like; but it was believed by many quite well-educated people familiar with their leader's ways.

During September 1987, Number One had started on a series of trips to sacred and venerable places, including Pagān and Sagaing, for the purpose of *yaddayā-kyi*—which I can only express in English as 'the warding-off of evil'. What might a European leader do to ward off further troubles when his (or her) country was in a mess because all government measures had patently failed? Well, in some countries perhaps special prayer meetings might be held in the hope that the community might obtain supranatural assistance. But *yaddayā* is different from this, in that it is not a communal act, or one which a person carries out on behalf of a community. Ne Win was not trying to help his country; Number One was looking after Number One. Considering the plight the country was in, I found this apparent self-centredness offensive; but my colleagues knew that a Buddhist is responsible for his own salvation (to borrow a Christian term) and they appeared to hold no grudges against Number One on this account.

Later, just before leaving Burma, I swapped a few tales with the Ambassador and learned of three more *yaddayā* incidents. The first two were rumours that had reached his ears; the third he could vouch for.

The first was that Ne Win, having been warned of an assassination attempt, had stood in front of a large mirror and had shot at his reflection, 'killing' his own image. The second story was that he had sent for human blood, which had been brought from a hospital, and had trampled it into the ground. The purpose of the first was clearly to protect himself from the assassin's bullet; the second was also presumably to prevent his own blood being shed. The third did not concern Ne Win. There had been several ferryboat disasters during my two-year stay in Burma and, several months earlier, the Inland Waterways office had been warned that there was going to be another disaster on an identified route. The official in charge had promptly ordered the construction of a model ferry, and this craft had been ceremonially scuttled in that very river in order to avert the predicted disaster. Not long afterwards a ferry did indeed sink on that route, and many lives were lost. You might think that such an event would be enough to destroy one's faith in the efficacy of *yaddayā*. Not so. It wasn't a demonstration of supernatural fallibility or caprice; simply a case of human error. Some time later, a high-ranking Inland Waterways official was dining with the British Ambassador and the conversation turned to the topic of the ferryboat disaster.

'Unfortunately,' the official explained sadly during the meal, 'unfortunately, we made a model of the wrong ferry.'

When we had learnt that Ne Win, now aged seventy-five, had taken a new young wife—a sixth, I believe—after performing *yaddayā*, no official announcement was made; but the rumours were confident. He had been advised by an astrologer to marry, and the choice had been the daughter of a well-to-do Arakanese official, a good-looking woman in her twenties. The Burmese word for 'Arakanese' is pronounced *ya-khine*, and these two syllables sound similar to two verbs meaning (roughly) 'get' and 'cling to'. It was said that Ne Win had been influenced by this word-magic even in his choice of consort.

Back to Mandalay, Impact Books, Bromley, 1990, pp. 147–51.

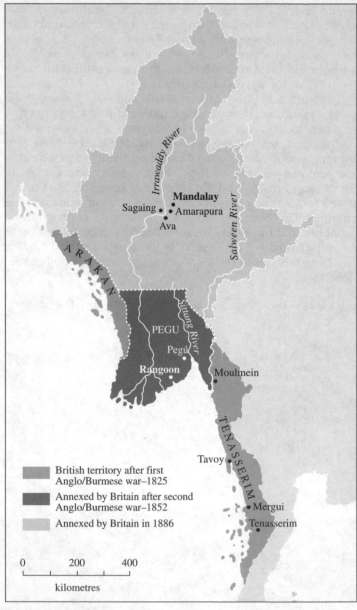

British territory after first
Anglo/Burmese war–1825

Annexed by Britain after second
Anglo/Burmese war–1852

Annexed by Britain in 1886

Burmese Territory Annexed by Britain.

The Anglo-Burmese Wars

27
The First War: The Death of Maha Bandula

MAJOR JOHN JAMES SNODGRASS

*In 1600 the British government had chartered the East India
Company to trade in the East Indies but, on being ousted by
the Dutch, the Company had developed commerce with India.
In the process it had become rich and powerful, benefiting ter-
ritorially from disputes among local groups, and was soon a
formidable political power. In gaining complete control of
Bengal in 1757, the Company had brought itself into contact
with Burma. In 1811 there began a series of border incidents
in which rebellious Arakanese bands were crossing the Naaf
River and using Bengal as a base for mounting incursions
into Burma. These incidents caused tension between the
Company and Burma, a tension which the powerful king,
Bodaw-hpaya, did not lessen when he annexed Manipur and
marched into Assam. He died in 1819 leaving unfinished the
massive Mingun Pagoda with its giant guardian* chinthe[1] *(see
Passage 13). His successor, Ba-gyi-daw, sent his charismatic
general, Maha Bandula, to Arakan with orders to take Bengal
and bring back the British Governor-General in chains.
Bandula and his men duly crossed the Naaf and struck the
first blow, whereupon the East India Company declared war
early in March 1824.*

*While some British troops attacked Assam, the main force
was sent south by steamship to the delta so as to capture the
Burmese ports and strike north up Burma's lifeline, the*

[1]Mythical, lion-like creature.

Irrawaddy. When the main forces under General Sir Archibald Campbell landed in Rangoon with naval support, they found that Ba-gyi-daw had evacuated the town and that consequently there were no local provisions and services to rely on. The monsoon was at its height too, and Campbell's troops were soon decimated by malaria, cholera, and dysentery. Nevertheless, superior firepower soon drove the Burmese out of their timber stockades in spite of their 'invulnerables'— warriors supposedly protected from the bullet by magical means. Meanwhile, Bandula and his men on the northern front were ordered south by Ba-gyi-daw and, despite arriving in a state of exhaustion, fought bravely. When his war-weary band was obliged to retreat, Bandula decided to dig in at Danubyu by the Irrawaddy, vowing to beat the British or die in the attempt.

Accompanying General Campbell as his military secretary for most of the war was Major John James Snodgrass from whose journal is drawn the following extract, in which we learn how Maha Bandula kept his word. (The war went on after Bandula's death: while the Burmese Court prevaricated over the terms offered by Campbell the British continued to advance upriver and were only about 72 kilometres from the capital, Amarapura, when the Burmese surrendered and came to terms at Yandabo on 24 February 1826.)

THE stockade of Donoobew extended for nearly a mile along a sloping bank of the Irrawaddy—its breadth varying according to the nature of the ground, from five to eight hundred yards. The stockading was composed of solid teak beams, from fifteen to seventeen feet high, driven firmly into the earth, and placed as closely as possible to each other; behind this wooden wall the old brick ramparts of the place rose to a considerable height, strengthening the front defences by means of cross beams, and affording a firm and elevated footing to the defendants. Upwards of a hundred and fifty guns and swivels were mounted on the works, and the garrison was protected from the shells of the besiegers, by numerous well-contrived traverses and excavations.

Bandoola's force at this time did not probably exceed fifteen thousand men, but it was chiefly composed of the veterans who had accompanied him from Arracan, and, generally speaking, men of more tact and military knowledge than the raw levies, which had been raised upon the spur of the occasion. A ditch of considerable magnitude and depth surrounded the defences, the passage of which was rendered still more difficult by spikes, nails, holes, and other contrivances. Beyond the ditch several rows of strong railing were next interposed; and in front of all, an abatis, thirty yards broad, and otherwise of a most formidable description, extended round the place, except on the river face, where the deep and rapid Irrawaddy presented a sufficient barrier—its breadth at this season not exceeding seven hundred yards; and not a boat could pass without being exposed to a heavy fire from the stockade.

Before the right face, or that lowest down the river, two strong outworks were constructed, the first of which had been taken by the marine column, the second having proved too strong to be carried by so small a force. A heavy and extensive jungle intervened between the right and rear faces, covering about a third of the latter, beyond which, however, a fine open plain extended to the river; upon this plain, at long-shot distance from the fort, the division was encamped, and preparations immediately commenced for breaking ground and proceeding systematically against the place.

The camp being pitched, the enemy at once desisted from further annoyance, and the heavy fire which he had kept up all the morning entirely ceased; but there was a something in the calm, in the sudden disappearance of the defendants from their ramparts, the occasional patroling of small parties of horse, and the long-continued observation of our line by a party of chiefs, from an elevated watch-tower, that foreboded a very early interruption to the present stillness of the scene. Even the careless soldiers seemed to regard the momentary repose as seamen do a treacherous lull between the violent gusts of the increasing storm; and each sentinel, when the night had closed, stood prepared upon his post for the sudden appearance of an enemy—listening anxiously for some sound which might indicate where the conflict would begin: nor were they long kept in suspense or doubt. The clock had struck ten, and the moon was fast approaching to the verge of the horizon, when sharp musketry, and the loud war-cry of the enemy, roused the sleeping camp. The wearied soldiers, starting from a profound repose, mechanically seized their muskets, which every man had carefully placed by his side, and were quickly drawn up in readiness to receive the noisy visitors, who had so unkindly robbed them of their rest.

The line was scarcely formed when the enemy's intention became apparent: his columns were distinctly heard moving in an oblique direction towards our right, for the purpose of turning it; at the same time keeping up a distant fire upon the left and centre, to encourage a belief that these were the selected points. On reaching and out-flanking our extreme right, apparently at no great distance, the two regiments on the right of the line rapidly changed front to the right, and kneeling, to insure a better aim, kept up a rapid running fire, which instantly checked the advancing columns; and although they repeated their attempt more than once, every succeeding effort became more feeble, until they at last returned in hopeless silence to their irritated and disappointed commander, who did not fail to give the usual Burmhan reward for failure, to such as had been most conspicuously unsuccessful on the occasion.

The night was very dark, and enabled the enemy to carry off their killed and wounded, which could not be few. On our side, only two or three men were killed, and twenty wounded.

MARCH 26th. No communication having yet been opened with the marine column, a party of one hundred European infantry and a few cavalry were sent early this morning to march round the enemy's works, keeping at a respectful distance, in order to reach the fleet at its station below Donoobew. The road lay partly through a thick jungle, but, with the aid of three elephants, a passage was forced, and the party reached the fleet without firing a shot. After requesting the naval commander to move up, and form a junction, the party endeavoured to return, but found the jungle so strongly occupied by the enemy, that it would have cost many lives to force a passage through them; and as there was no particular object to be gained, they were prudently ordered back, to come up with Brigadier-general Cotton on the following day.

A little above Donoobew, the river forms an island, the channel on either side being about four hundred yards broad. In the farther channel lay the enemy's war-boats, fifteen in number, from which they occasionally turned their prows round the corner of the island, and fired into our camp. A party of seventy men, with a few rockets, were, in consequence, crossed over to the island: the boats at first drew up, and appeared inclined to maintain their station, but the unpleasant hissing of a shower of rockets quite disconcerted them; and if they did not shew much gallantry on the occasion, they at least gave us a tolerable specimen of their chief merit—that of flying with incredible speed.

An old pagoda, about three hundred yards from the enemy's defences, being chosen as the most eligible point for breaking ground, it was accordingly occupied by His Majesty's forty-seventh regiment early in the night. The working parties immediately commenced operations, and at day-light a considerable extent of trench was completed. The ground about the pagoda was found mined and loaded, but owing to the inexperience of the miners, it did no harm; indeed, if it had gone off, it would have done no more than scorch the standers by.

27th. At nine o'clock this morning, the flotilla was seen in full sail up the river; and they were no sooner observed than the garrison sortied in considerable force, infantry and cavalry, with seventeen war elephants, fully caparisoned, and carrying a proportion of armed men. This attack was, as usual, directed upon our right; and while the flotilla came up in full sail, under all the fire of the fort, the cavalry, covered by the horse artillery, was ordered to charge the advancing monsters: the scene was novel and interesting; and although neither the elephants nor their riders can ever be very formidable in modern warfare, they stood the charge with a steadiness and courage these animals can be rarely brought to show. Their riders were mostly shot, and no sooner did the elephants feel themselves unrestrained by the hand of their drivers, than they walked back to the fort with the greatest composure. The flotilla having passed the fort, with trifling loss, anchored on our left. During the heavy cannonade that took place between the boats and the stockade, the Bandoola, who was superintending the practice of his artillery, gave his garrison a specimen of the discipline he meant to enforce in this last struggle, to retrieve his lost character and reputation. A Burmese officer being killed while pointing a gun, by a shot from the flotilla, his comrades, instantly abandoning the dangerous post, could not be brought back to their duty by any remonstrances of their chiefs; when Bandoola, stepping down to the spot, instantly severed the heads of two of the delinquents from their bodies, and ordered them to be stuck up upon the spot '*pour encourager les autres*'.

28*th*. The working parties continued making approaches towards the place; and the steam-vessel and some light boats, pushing up the river after the enemy's war-boats, succeeded in capturing nine of them (four gilt): their crews, when likely to be run down by the steam-boat, jumping into the river, where they are quite in their element, effected their escape.

29*th, 30th, and* 31*st*. Continued constructing batteries, and landing heavy ordnance; the enemy on their part remaining very quiet, and busily employed in strengthening their works. On the evening of the 31st, a Burmese came out of the fort with a piece of dirty canvass, containing the following laconic epistle from the Bandoola:—'In war we find each other's force; the two countries are at war for nothing, and we know not each others minds!!!' The bearer, on being interrogated as to the meaning of such obscure and bravadoing language, as well as to the insulting manner in which the message was delivered, said he was merely a common soldier, and knew nothing of the matter, but believed his chief wished to make peace: on being threatened, however, with punishment as a spy, he at last confessed there had been a grand consultation held in the Bandoola's house; and it was thought in the garrison, that his intention was to sally upon us at the head of his whole force, the first favourable opportunity, and to conquer or perish in the attempt.

APRIL 1*st*. The mortar batteries and rockets began the work of destruction this morning, and continued firing, at intervals, during the day and succeeding night, the enemy remaining under the protection of their works, and making little return to our fire.

2*nd*. At day-light the breaching batteries opened, and almost immediately afterwards two Lascars,* who had been prisoners in the fort, came running out, and informed us, that Bandoola had been killed the day before by a rocket; and that no entreaty of the other chiefs could prevail upon the garrison to remain, the whole having fled or dispersed, during the preceding night. The British line was, in consequence, immediately under arms, and the place taken possession of. Sufficient proof remained in the interior, of the hurry

---

*Bengal native seamen or soldiers.

and confusion of the flight; not a gun was removed, and even the large depôt of grain which had been formed, remained uninjured—the dread of detection having prevented the enemy from putting the torch to what they well knew would be a most valuable acquisition to the British army. In the fort we found a number of wounded men, who all concurred in saying their general had been killed; and one poor fellow, with both his feet shot off, related the story so circumstantially, as to leave no doubt whatever of the fact: it was as follows:— 'I belonged to the household of Menghi Maha Bandoolah, and my business was to beat the great drums that are hanging in the viranda of the Wongee's house. Yesterday morning, between the hours of nine and ten, while the chief's dinner was preparing, he went out to take his usual morning walk round the works, and arrived at his observatory (that tower with a red ball upon it), where, as there was no firing, he sat down upon a couch that was kept there for his use. While he was giving orders to some of his chiefs, the English began throwing bombs, and one of them falling close to the Wongee, burst, and killed him on the spot: his body was immediately carried away and burned to ashes; his death was soon known to every body in the stockade, and the soldiers refused to stay and fight under any other commander. The chiefs lost all influence and command over their men, every individual thinking only of providing for his own personal safety.' But, even in a desultory and disorderly flight of this nature, the characteristic cunning and caution of the nation was conspicuous, effecting their retreat with such silence and circumspection, as would have been a lesson to the best-disciplined army in Europe.

The character of Maha Bandoola seems to have been a strange mixture of cruelty and generosity, talent with want of judgment, and a strong regard to personal safety, combined with great courage and resolution, which never failed him till death. The acts of barbarous cruelty he committed are too numerous to be related: stern and inflexible in all his decrees, he appears to have experienced a savage pleasure in witnessing the execution of his bloody mandates; even his own hand was ever ready to punish with death the slightest mark of want of zeal in those he had intrusted with commands, or the defence of any post. Still his immediate adherents are said to have been sincerely attached to him; uncontrolled license to plunder and extort from all who were unfortunate enough to meet Bandoola's men, may no doubt have reconciled them to their situation, and confirmed them much in their attachment to their leader. The management of a Burmese army, for so long a period contending against every disadvantage to which a general can be subjected, evinced no small degree of talent, while the position and defences at Donoobew, as a field-work, would have done credit to the most scientific engineer; but it is difficult to account for his motives, or give credit to his judgment, in giving up the narrow rivers of Panlang and Lain, where a most effectual opposition could have been given, to fight his battle on the banks of the broad Irrawaddy, where the ground was favourable to the regular movement of disciplined troops. During the days of his prosperity, Bandoola seldom exposed his person: in the battles of Rangoon and Kokeen, he was never under fire; but he did not hesitate, when circumstances required it, to allow himself to be hemmed in at Donoobew, where he boldly declared he would conquer or die, and till he actually fell, set his men the first example of the courage he required in all.

Narrative of the Burmese War, etc., John Murray, London, 1827, pp. 165–77.

28
The Second War:
The Storming of Shwe Dagon

WILLIAM F. B. LAURIE

By the terms of the treaty concluding the First Anglo-Burmese War, the Burmese were required to cede 'in perpetuity' the two coastal strips of Arakan and Tenasserim and to have a British representative (or 'Resident') at the Court. Here, the Burmese monarch continued to rule over his greatly diminished kingdom. First Ba-gyi-daw and then his successor, Tharrawaddy, became subject to fits of insanity; also, the East India Company withdrew its Residency in 1840. With little contact there was no further cause for Anglo-Burmese friction until 1851 when the Burmese arrested and summarily convicted

two British sea captains of offences that included murder.
Protesting their innocence, the two were fined heavily and
they turned to the Company for reimbursement. The Company
decided that they should receive a sum of £920 and that the
Burmese Court, now presided over by King Pagán, should pay
it. A British representative, Commodore George Lambert, was
sent from Calcutta to Rangoon to sort things out. But instead
of following his carefully sequenced orders, he took precipitate
action by withdrawing Britons residing in Rangoon, seizing
some of the king's ships as indemnity, and declaring that the
Burmese ports were now under blockade. Initially annoyed at
Lambert's rashness, the Governor-General of India neverthe-
less backed him. The terms of the ultimatum sent to King
Pagán were so harsh as to constitute a declaration of war in
that, if he were to meet them, he would in effect yield up his
country's sovereignty. On 6 April 1852, Admiral Charles
Austen (Jane Austen's brother) assembled his fleet of
steamships to bombard the shores of the Rangoon River, and
Lieutenant-General Henry Godwin's troops went into action.

The author of the following passage was a lieutenant in the
Madras Artillery who, having already published a book called
Orissa and the Temple of Jagannath *(now long forgotten),*
had some literary aspirations. As can be seen in this extract
from his narrative of the war, he tended to glorify the British
officers and men and to despise their Burmese counterparts.
He quotes the account of someone he calls 'an intelligent
Armenian' but does not indicate who this might have been,
and in his final remarks there is a very modern sounding
reference to the arms trade of his day.

TUESDAY, the 13th of April, was a busy day in camp. In
addition to the Artillery already up, four eight-inch iron
howitzers were required by the General for the grand
advance on the great Pagoda. This was fixed for the morrow,
when, many believed, from what had already been experienced, the enemy would make a desperate resistance. The
whole of this day was employed in disembarking and taking
into camp these noble pieces of ordnance. The Naval Brigade
rendered us the most hearty assistance in this arduous task.

At one spot on the field might be seen a knot of artillery-
men, under some zealous officer, cutting and fixing fusees;
at another, the Infantry cleaning and examining their trusty

percussion muskets and bayonets, the best Infantry WEAPON after all; at another, a cluster of talkers, very eloquent some of them, discussing the operations of the previous day; the sun, apparently, being quite disregarded in the zeal of a wordy contest. In the shade—and a good deal was afforded by the surrounding jungles—the thermometer stood considerably above one hundred degrees.

The King of Ava, no doubt, all this time, believed that, through the re-agency of such troops as those composing 'Shway-Pee [Pyee] Hman-Geen,' or the Mirror of the Golden Country—a body of Royal Guards—and other bodies equally well gilt, the English would soon be driven into the river; and that then the Tenasserim Provinces would be taken from us, and even Calcutta might become submissive to the Golden Feet! 'On the night of the 13th,' writes an intelligent Armenian, one of the oppressed, 'orders came to send us up to the great Pagoda. We were accordingly conveyed thither in files of ten men, three Armenians and seven Mussulmen. Rockets and shells [from the ships] poured down on every side. Our escape must solely be ascribed to the mercy of Providence. To have escaped from the shells, some of which burst near us—from the Governor's hand, and the hands of the Burmese soldiery, that had already commenced pillaging the new town—must be set down as a miracle. However, two files of our comrades had scarcely gone, when the guard placed over us thought it prudent to save themselves from the impending danger by flight; yet their chief stood with his drawn sword. We shekoed,* prayed, and conjured him to save his life and ours. In my long experience of the Burmese generally, I have never found them wantonly cruel in nature. It is the system of the insane Government of Ava that produces monsters. So the man released us, and, with good grace, after seeing us depart, departed himself also. We at first returned to our abodes, but found them uninhabitable. A portion of the houses in the new town were in a blaze from the rockets. We then thought of our safety: some tried to escape to the river-side—they fell among the Burmese soldiery, were maltreated, stripped even of their upper garments, and obliged to return, and hide themselves under a Kioun [monastery]; others took shelter under the foot of the

*Made salutation.

great Pagoda, and a few disguised got safely out of the town through the kind assistance of their Burmah friends. This night was a night of flight.'

We have been informed that, shortly before the fleet arrived, the Governor called a sort of Cabinet Council together, to deliberate over the probability of beating back the English. An old and respected inhabitant of Rangoon, who remembered the last war, and many years before it, was called on to give his opinion. The old man was afraid to speak out what he thought would be the result; but being pressed to do so, *as there was no fear he would suffer for telling the truth*, he declared that the British, on account of their superior skill and discipline, would certainly be victorious. 'With them,' said he, 'one mind guides all; with the Burmese, each guides himself in the fight; what if we have fifty to one, the Europeans will conquer!' The fine old fellow was immediately ordered to be branded, and otherwise tortured, for his candour.

An idea of the strength of new Rangoon may be gathered from the fact that the new town, already mentioned, upwards of a mile from the river, was described as 'nearly a square, with a bund, or mud wall, about sixteen feet high and eight broad; a ditch runs along each side of the square, and on the north side, where the Pagoda stands, it has been cleverly worked into the defences, to which it forms a sort of citadel.'

Wednesday morning beheld the force moving on. The troops were certainly in the finest temper for dealing with the enemy. The halt of yesterday had refreshed them considerably, notwithstanding the intense heat; and recollection of the 12th prompted them to double exertion, if such were possible, to-day. [The author was with the D Company, 3rd Battalion of Artillery, in reserve.]

H. M.'s 80th Regiment, with four guns of Major Montgomery's battery, formed the advance, covered by skirmishers. About seven o'clock, the sound of musketry fell upon the ear. It seemed to those composing the reserved force in rear to proceed from the dark jungles, through which our march lay. The troops in our front had come into action; and the enemy were being driven before the fire of the European and Native Infantry. But this was not effected without some loss, as several *doolies* [stretchers], with their wounded, which passed by us, clearly testified.

The sound of artillery, from a Madras battery, likewise told that the guns were in position.

Major Montgomery, having brought one nine-pounder, and a 24-pounder howitzer into a favourable position, had opened fire at a distance of about 700 yards from the stockade. Passing on through the jungly way, we at length came within range of the enemy's jingals,* which appeared to fire at us from beside a small pagoda. A succession of well-directed shots were now launched against the reserved force, in rear of which the heavy eight-inch howitzers were being nobly brought along by the gallant Naval Brigade. Our guns inclined to the right, and halted to make way for the coming young giants of ordnance—all the while, the fire proceeding from the enemy near the small pagoda by no means abating.

Again we marched on, and came upon a large body of our troops, the Europeans, with fixed bayonets, as if ready for an attack as soon as a breach could be made. The 40th Bengal Native Infantry were likewise in this position, a petty *midan* [open space], sheltered by a small hill covered with jungle. Shot from the Burmese guns, as well as jingals, fell fast and thick upon the plain. The troops wisely remained under cover of the hill, passing an occasional remark on the correct range the enemy had attained, as shot after shot bounded along only a few yards before us; and then would come a jingal, with its strange whistling sound, over your head, making a man thankful he was not quite so tall as men are represented in ancient writ. In spite of all philosophy, such music must sound very strange to all ears, for the first time! At length, the greater portion of the Infantry moved on.

The D Company's 3rd Battalion Battery, under Captain Cooke, was ordered to remain in the old position till required. Certainly, it is galling to be under fire, without any order to advance; and such was our case for about four hours. It was amusing enough to observe the cattle attached to the guns, while the shot continued to fly about. Strange to say, not one bullock of the reserve battery was struck, nor did they seem to be at all affected by the firing of the determined enemy!

The Burmese soon got the range more exact than ever. Probably guessing that some of the troops were under cover

*A heavy musket several feet long, mounted on a swivel.

of the small hill, they gave less elevation, when their shot fell very near us, and the jingals continued to whistle with fearful rapidity. An intelligent Bengal officer, who had been engaged in several of the great Punjaub battles, declared to us that he had not, on those occasions, 'bobbed' his head as much as he had done to-day. At length, the range of one of the enemy's guns entirely differed from the previous practice; which led us to believe that the devoted warrior, who had shown so much skill, was no more.

Major Montgomery's battery had, no doubt, done considerable execution. It may have laid the aforesaid warrior low. The gallant Major himself came past us while the jingals were flying, his Lascar* orderly following him. A spent ball struck the unfortunate orderly in the forehead, when he immediately fell, but not dead, as at first supposed.

About this time, our Assistant-Surgeon, Dr Smith, was slightly wounded. A tar of the Naval Brigade we also saw struck while giving assistance in bringing along a heavy gun; and several others, European and native, were wounded near the spot we occupied. The 9th M. N. I. had gallantly driven back a body of Burmese skirmishers in our rear.

At about 10 A.M., the heavy howitzer battery, under Major Back, manned by the Bengal Artillery, was, after great labour, brought into position. We were delighted to hear the howitzers sounding forth in the advance, as they opened fire against the great stockade. This continued about one hour and a half, under a very galling and well-directed fire from the enemy's guns and wall-pieces, from which our troops suffered considerably. The artillery operations of the Wednesday were under the direction of Major Turton, of the Bengal Army, whose accustomed zeal was fully displayed throughout. Colonel Foord had not recovered from the *coup de soleil* in time to proceed with the force; nothing could have disappointed him more.

It may be mentioned that, just before the heavy guns were dragged into position, Major Turton told Lieutenant Ashe, of the Bengal Artillery, to take his gun, a 24-pounder howitzer, to the left of the heavy battery, to dislodge some Burmese skirmishers from the bushes in front. This was the only Bengal light field-gun engaged that day; and it was highly

*Here, an Indian artillery-man of low rank.

necessary, as those determined skirmishers were fast closing in on the crowded mass of our troops, who with great difficulty kept down their fire.

At about half-past eleven, Captain Latter, the Interpreter, proposed to the General an attack on the eastern entrance of the great Pagoda; for ten of our troops now being killed or disabled, we would lose but one with a storming-party; which would naturally draw off the enemy's attention, and excite their surprise. This sensible advice was by no means disregarded.

Eventually, Captain Latter asked General Godwin's permission to lead the storming-party. The gallant General replied, 'With the greatest pleasure, my dear friend!' This reply was quite characteristic of our brave and courteous Commander....

From the elevated position—on which were our heavy guns—to the Pagoda is a sort of valley to be crossed before reaching the eastern entrance; the distance might be about eight hundred yards. The hill on which the great temple stands is divided into three terraces, each defended by a brick and mud rampart. There are four flights of steps up the centre of each terrace, three of which are covered over; the east, south, and west. On went our gallant troops, crossing over to the Pagoda in the most steady manner, under a heavy and galling fire from the enemy on the walls. At length, they reached the desired gate, which was immediately pushed open. Captain Latter had beheld Lieutenant and Adjutant Doran, of H. M.'s 18th Royal Irish, rather in advance of his proper position: on being spoken to, we believe he said that his regiment was in rear. Now, a grand rush was made up the long flight of steps they had discovered. The storming-party, however, suffered from the shower of balls and bullets which immediately came down upon them with dreadful effect; but nothing could ever check the determined rush of British Infantry! Near the foot of the steps fell Lieutenant Doran, mortally wounded; and by his side fell also two men of his regiment. The young hero lay pierced by four balls. Colonel Coote was also wounded. But our troops nobly gained the upper terrace. A deafening cheer rent the air! The Burmese defenders fled in all directions before the British bayonet. The Shoé Dagoon, or say, 'Dagon the Great', had fallen for the second time into our hands! The blow had been struck; the first grand act of the drama was over!

'On the 14th,' writes the Armenian, 'there were but a few thousand Shwaydown and Padown men, say about five thousand in all, that kept to their post on the Pagoda, under the immediate command of the Governor. They held out until noon, when the Governor, in despair, gave orders to retreat, himself setting the example of flight. His men, distinguished by their gilt hats, remained to the last. They stood the first onset of the British, and then fled to the west'; that is, towards Kemmendine. 'Had there been a brigade of cavalry, or a division of troops, at the north-west, the Governor could not have escaped. He had, a few days previously, despatched his plunder to his country Shwaydown, in charge of one of his trusty relatives. Thus dispersed the grand army of Rangoon, computed at about 20,000 strong at the beginning, some of whom did not even exchange a shot with the English, and many were driven away by the rockets and shells.'

The reserved force moved on. A loud cheer from the advance made us long to get near the heavy guns. There was enough in that hearty cheer to tell that Rangoon was entirely in the British possession. Having proceeded a short distance, the battery halted in rather dense jungle. There, among other sights, we beheld three of the 40th B. N. I. lying dead on a bank—all three, including a bullock, having been struck down with a shot from one of the enemy's eighteen-pounders. Ascending a little, we found the four eight-inch guns in position; and a good view of the piece of country at the base of the Shoé Dagoon was presented, to all appearance, jungly and confined. We were now informed that the General and his Staff had entered the Pagoda.

After our Europeans had refreshed themselves with a little tea—and nothing is more refreshing on the field—the Artillery were ordered to proceed in a southerly direction, and take up quarters where they best could till the morrow. These were on the cold ground, as on the two previous nights. To get thither, we had a short march through the jungle, and while passing along, we frequently came across a Burmese soldier who lay dead, with a look of determination, and a smile of apparent contempt on his countenance. Curious enough, many of them had adopted a sort of red jacket as a portion of their costume; this had been frequently a source of confusion to our troops, who could with difficulty distinguish them from our own skirmishers. The *Burmese* muskets were old flint ones from England, 'condemned', the excuse for their being sold to our enemies, and with the dah or dhar—a sharp, square-pointed sword with a long wooden handle; and with other weapons, such as a British bayonet stuck on the handle of a spear, the Burmese Infantry equipments were found to be tolerably complete.

Towards the south side of the pagoda we passed a *Pongee* [priest] house in ruins. Gaudamas of huge size gazed upon the stranger with beneficent countenance, as if they were giving him a hearty welcome to the new land. A huge tree, lying across the road, was speedily cut asunder, to make way for

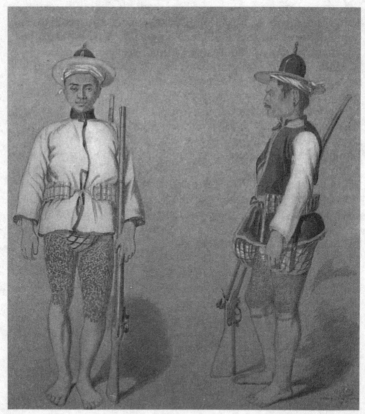

'Burmese Soldiers', from Henry Yule, *Narrative of the Mission to the Court of Ava in 1855*, Smith, Elder, London, 1858.

the light field-guns; after a short period a portion of the heavy battery arrived. When the guns were all in position, preparations were made for the night's bivouac. Beside our halting-place we found a fine tank and well. Many had never before enjoyed a bathe or a wash so much as they did upon this occasion. After a comfortable night's rest in the open air, in the morning we moved into a Pongee-house for breakfast.

Some necessary stores for hot weather campaigning had found their way to us through the faithful followers, who, since the capture of the Great Pagoda, had been streaming forth to the camp, some of them, during the early part of the day, having nearly fainted from fear, while performing their philanthropic duties, as the enemy's bullets flew about rather too near to be agreeable. Where we now were stood various ruins of the new town. The remainder of the force passed the night in the covered entrances and immediate vicinity of the pagoda. By the route we had come, it was expected there would be no very great difficulty in placing our guns on the ramparts for the defence of Guadama's Temple.

The Second Burmese War: A Narrative of the Operations at Rangoon in 1852, Smith, Elder, London, 1853, pp. 83–95.

29
The Third War: The Taking of Mandalay

COLONEL E. B. SLADEN

In settling with the British after the Second Anglo-Burmese War, the monarch (by that time, King Mindon) had been obliged to cede Lower Burma. King of a landlocked realm, the reasonable and pious Mindon had established Mandalay as his capital and tried unsuccessfully to regain the lost territory by peaceful means. But he was now dead, and his young successor Thibaw was allowing the kingdom to subside into a near-anarchic state. This fact, taken by itself, was none of Britain's business; but France was at the same time gaining influence at the Court in Mandalay. This threatened to spoil Britain's plans for an overland route to China, along which she could channel her exports to a vast market. But once

207

*again it was a squabble over money that provided the British
Government with the opportunity to issue an ultimatum; and
once again the terms imposed were so truculent that they
amounted to a declaration of war. The year was 1885 and the
dispute was between the Burmese Court and the Bombay
Burmah Trading Company.*

*Even before the 10 November deadline for acceptance of the
terms, British troops were disembarking in Lower Burma. A
few days after it, a flotilla, 8 kilometres long, was chugging
up the Irrawaddy—the famous 'Road to Mandalay'—under
the command of General Sir Harry Prendergast. His chief
political officer was Colonel E. B. Sladen who in Mindon's day
had been the British Resident in Mandalay and who therefore
knew very well both the town and the walled city within it (see
Passage 15). Of course, the British gunboats won the day.
Mandalay was taken on 28 November 1885 and on the following day Thibaw with his Queen Su-hpaya-lat were
deported to India. On I January 1886 Upper Burma was
annexed, making the whole country part of the British
Empire. Meanwhile, in Ratnagiri the royal couple continued
to live in exile until the death of Thibaw in 1916, whereupon
Su-hpaya-lat was permitted to return to Burma and live out
her last years in quiet retirement.*

*The following passage is extracted from one of Sladen's
official reports (dated 16 December 1885), in which he lays
out in numbered paragraphs his version of the last few days of
the kingdom of Burma. We join his narrative when the flotilla
is about 16 kilometres south of Mandalay, but the most
intriguing episode must be the events of the night of
28/29 November, when the townswomen of Mandalay (and
possibly others) were allowed to enter the gates, and the palace
buildings were looted.*

6. An hour or two of daylight still remained, and the fleet
made progress up the river the same evening in the
direction of Ava. A King's steamer came in sight,
moored to the bank. This was taken possession of, and was
found to be heavily armed and to have troops on board, all of
whom (57) were taken prisoners.

At first it was alleged that the steamer was covered by the
flag of truce, but this proved to be false, as all evidences
tended to show that she had not come with the Envoys from

the capital, but had been engaged for some days conveying troops and materials of war between the Ava forts and the military defences at Myingyan.

The fleet anchored that night (26th November) 7 miles below Ava opposite Kyaukta-lôn. The sites of Ava and Sagain were both visible in the distance. There was some delay in making the start the next morning owing to fog, but all was in readiness for an attack on the forts in our front, and gunboats and steamers were under weigh, when at 10 A.M. the Burmese Envoys of the previous evening were again seen coming down stream in their golden war-boat, flying a flag of truce.

7. The delay in their movements was soon explained. It was intelligible enough to any one who realised the intensity of the position, and the difficulties in the way of getting Burmese Ministers in such a predicament, to give an immediate reply to so complete and peremptory a demand as that put forward, *viz.* the surrender of King Thibaw and his country.

8. The telegram from Mandalay, in reply to our demand, was as follows:–

'When the English ships arrive you are on no account to fire on them. Let all our troops keep quiet. Publish this abroad everywhere. The King concedes unconditionally all the demands made by the Commander of the English forces as contained in his letter (of yesterday's date). You are to let the English Commander know this as quickly as possible.'

General Prendergast's reply was that we could not pass up to Mandalay and leave strongly armed forts in our rear. Forts and arms must be surrendered at once.

The Envoys professed their inability to act in this matter on their own behalf, and again they left for the shore and sought communication by wire with the capital.

They agreed, however, to point out a channel through the sunken obstacles opposite Fort Sagain, and went with the General Officer Commanding and Colonel Sladen on board the *Palow* to do so.

When the channel had been discovered and buoyed by the naval survey party, delivery of the arms was again demanded. The vessels containing or towing flats or barges armed with artillery, took station for attack, and the transports prepared to land troops half a mile below the Ava redoubt.

It was 2 o'clock P.M. before any reply was received from Mandalay, and by that time the whole fleet was abreast the

Fort of Ava on the left bank, and Sagain on the right with [the forts of] Shwe Kyetyet and Thabyadan ahead, all gay and bristling with arms, soldiery, and golden umbrellas. The slightest contretemps would have produced immediate battle.

9. The interval was one of intense interest. The wire reply, which arrived at 2 P.M., was to the following effect:– 'You are to surrender all arms as required by the English Commander-in-Chief.'

Steamers were ordered to moor alongside the shore, and I was deputed by General Prendergast to land and facilitate the surrender of arms at the Ava forts.

The Burmese Envoys accompanied me, and at first a mere handful of officers and men entered the principal fort. The Burmese troops were ordered to withdraw. They did so. Twenty-eight guns in position in the fort and in batteries facing the river were secured and parked outside.

Small arms were brought in by the soldiery and heaped in stocks on the river's bank. The Burmese troops seemed in no way disconcerted, and many groups of them, with whom I conversed, readily understood that they were acting for their country's good.

10. Similar operations were being conducted on the opposite side of the river at the fort and redoubts of Sagain by Brigadier-General White and the Hampshire Regiment, who were as successful ere nightfall in carrying out the disarmament on the left bank as we had been on the right. The fort of Shwe Kyetyet and Thabyadan were details which could be left till the morrow, but their eventual surrender was already secured, and a few river obstructions having been peacefully removed during the day in full view of the Burmese troops on either bank of the river, there was nothing to prevent an immediate advance on the royal capital.

11. On the morning of the 27th the fleet was only (12) twelve miles distant from Mandalay, and weighed anchor at 6.20 A.M. At 9 o'clock A.M. it was abreast the steamer ghâts of Mandalay, at which, instead of an hostile demonstration, thousands of persons, of apparently all nationalities, had assembled to greet the army which was to dethrone Thibaw.

In consultation with General Prendergast, I wrote a letter to the Chief Minister, informing him of our arrival, and saying that in terms of the telegraphic Despatch of the previous day we expected him on board with King Thibaw by midday, otherwise the troops would land.

The Minister's reply did not arrive till after the hour fixed for landing the troops. He said he would be on board at 3 P.M.

12. The disembarkation of troops was not delayed. The military arrangements were complete, and the preparations were proportioned to all contingencies.

With the General's consent, I attached myself to the brigade which would advance on the southern city attack.

Knowing the road, I rode ahead with guides in the hope of meeting the Chief Minister, who, I felt sure, would take the same line of route from an opposite direction in making his way to the shipping as I was proceeding by in order to reach the city.

I heard on my way that he had been seen on the central route, and sent a mounted scout to tell him to come to me as quickly as possible to the southern city gate.

All along the suburbs the population had turned out and lined the roads, as if intent on some ceremonial festival.

I crossed the moat at the central southern gate exactly at 3 P.M. and entered the city without interference or obstruction of any sort.

Inside the city the same placid curiosity was observable, large crowds in quiet amazement wondering what was going on.

13. It was evident that the Government had collapsed. The questions which suggested themselves were–

(1) What were we to expect at the palace?

(2) Would it be defended or deserted?

(3) Was Thibaw still there? Would a stand be made at the last?

All that could be learned during the morning from the European and Native residents was that Thibaw was in his palace up to 9 A.M. of that day, but that he was prepared for flight, and that (50) fifty elephants with trusty friends were in waiting for him at Shemaga, 12 miles up the river, to convey him to the old dynastic stronghold of Shwebo.

14. I proceeded as hastily as I could through the city and arrived at the east gate of the palace enclosure with only my guides, my head assistant, Mr Nicholas, and Captain Morgan, of the Irrawaddy Flotilla Company's Steamer *Shensawboo*.

The gate was open and I might have entered. The idea struck me that we were too late, but the palace guards were on duty, and no actual evidences of discomfiture or desertion were apparent.

Only a few minutes intervened before the Minister's elephant was seen in the distance coming in full haste.

After greeting, his first words were—'On no account let the troops enter the palace. Will you come in with me alone?'

I agreed on his representing to me that he did not know what might occur (alluding significantly to Thibaw's flight) if troops entered abruptly.

I left a note at the gate to be delivered to General Prendergast on his arrival, begging that troops might not enter the palace till he heard again from me.

14. After this there was no delay. I entered the Hlut-Daw and sat down for a few minutes until King Thibaw had been communicated with. It was an immense relief to find in a few minutes he was still there, and willing to see me.

He received me as if at an ordinary public audience. The Queen and Queen's mother were present. The usual palace guards were also in attendance.

The King spoke nervously at first, and asked whether I remembered him; then he went at once *inmedias res*, and in a very formal and impressive manner he said, 'I surrender myself and my country to you. All I ask is, don't let me be taken away suddenly. Let me have a day or two to prepare. I will leave the palace and go into a summer-house in the palace enclosure.'

Subsequently he gave me to understand that he was anxious on the Queen's account to remain until her confinement, an event which was expected in three or four months.

It would be in vain to describe my own feelings during this interesting and trying interview.

My reply to the request for grace was to the effect that the General-in-Command of the troops was supreme, and would act in accordance with the orders he had received from the Government of India.

I would not myself, I said, press for harsh measures, though my own belief was, that, all interests considered, the best course for the King was to prepare for an immediate departure from his capital and country.

15. My interview was continued to an extent which I knew would be trying to the troops outside; but it was well to know also that the slight delay which occurred allowed sufficient time for the several brigades, which were

Note by General Prendergast.

All the gates of the town and place were of course secured by the troops as they marched on. Colonel Sladen being with the advanced guard could not see this.

advancing on the city in different columns, to arrive and secure all the palace gates and outside enclosures.

I informed the King that the only respite it was in my power to grant was that he would not be interfered with in his palace that night, that the immediate palace precincts would not be entered by troops; but that I would come in the morning with General Prendergast, and that he would then, as now, consider himself our prisoner.

To this he assented, and when I hinted at the possibilities of attempted flight, he said seriously, 'Where can I go to? I have no wish to go anywhere. I wish to remain now that you are here. I know you will see that I am not ill-treated. I will go anywhere with you. Will you come with me when I am taken away?'

I took assurance from the Ministers in attendance, and left Thibaw's presence perfectly satisfied that he was in safe keeping for the night, and would not attempt to make good his escape.

I may add that the assurances granted by the Ministers amounted in effect to a strong guarantee that they would deliver the King to me the next morning, or pay the penalty with their lives.

16. On my return from Thibaw, I met General Prendergast at the eastern gate of the palace, and communicated the news of the King's surrender.

The troops were ordered to enter and immediately occupy the outer enclosure, as far as the Hlut-Daw, or main entrance to the inner palace.

Note by General Prendergast on my draft.

The custody of the King was entrusted to Brigadier-General White and his Brigade, who took the requisite military precautions.

I slept, or rather passed the night in the Hlut-Daw, and was roused at dawn on the following morning by a message from the Teindah Mingyi, who had slept that night with a strong guard inside the palace, in charge to Thibaw.

'The Burmah Expedition: Deposition of King Theebaw—General Prendergast Gives Him Ten Minutes' Grace', *Illustrated London News*, 30 January 1886.

The Mingyi was waiting outside my room. He had come to tell me, he said, that Thibaw was in very troubled state of mind, and had worked himself into a sort of panic by fancying every moment that soldiers were about to break into the palace and put an end to his life. The Mingyi begged I would at once accompany him inside.

I did so and found Thibaw in his private apartments in evident alarm. The Queen and Queen-mother were with him. They were almost unattended. The guards of the previous evening had most of them withdrawn, only 17 female attendants remained with the Queen out of (300) three hundred who had been faithful up to the previous evening.

Note by General Prendergast on my draft Copy.

By request of Colonel Sladen and the Ministers, women were allowed to go in and out of the west gate of the palace, which they said led only to the Queen's rooms.

I remarked that 'women are very clever, how shall we be sure that some one who should not go out will not pass as a woman?' One of the Ministers proposed that the sentry should examine them all—a delicate task for a private soldier.

Further Note by Colonel Sladen.

My request was that 'Palace' women should be allowed exit and entrance through the western gate leading into the Queen's apartments. I admit I was wrong.

Their place seemed to have been taken by a number of common women of the town, who, by some means or other, had gained admittance through the western gate of the palace, and had already commenced to seize and carry off everything they could lay their hands on in the royal apartments. The King argued in his own mind that if people of this class could enter the palace at will, men and troops might soon follow, and his life was not safe. The Queen and Queen-mother called me away to their own portions of the palace, in order that I might see for myself what was going on there.

It was evident that without further assistance we were powerless to keep back the women, who were streaming in through all parts of the western palace.

I rejoined the King and told him that for his own safety and the protection of his property it was necessary that he should leave the palace, and that I should go and bring in a European guard, then in attendance at the palace gate. I found that during my absence he had collected at the entrance of one of the rooms a large quantity of gold jewelled vessels, which are used by the Sovereign on all State occasions.

I felt sure that these would soon be looted unless placed under a guard, and without further ado, I left the King and soon returned with an officer and 25 men of the Hampshire Regiment.

Sentries were dropped as we passed through the several State apartments of the palace; and on reaching the place where I had left the King, I found that Thibaw and the Queens had taken my advice and retired to the summer-palace.

I followed him. Sentries were placed round the little building he occupied, and he was my prisoner.

The same afternoon I handed him over to General Prendergast, and as soon as the necessary preparations could be made, the dethroned King walked out of his palace with the Queen (Soopia Lat), the Queen-Dowager (Maidawpyah), and a few female attendants. They passed between double files of European troops, who lined both sides of the road from the steps of the palace to the eastern gate-way. Here native carriages were in attendance to convey the whole party to the steamer, which was reached only at nightfall.

A crowd had collected at the landing-place, and darkness may have added somewhat to the responsibilities of the situation. Here and there were heard wailings of women, and the crowd, in their anxiety to see what was taking place, showed slight signs of impatience; but the demonstration, if it may be called one, was feeble, and the embarkation took place without further hitch or incident.

'Report to H. M. Durand, Esq., C.S.I., Secretary to the Government of India, Foreign Department, dated Mandalay, 16th December 1885', in *The Third Burmese War: Diary of Events*, India Office Records: L/MIL/17/19/32/1.

A Few of Burma's Minority Groups

30
The Sad 'Sea Gypsies'

LEOPOLD AINSWORTH

With dozens of minority groups living within her borders Burma is a multicultural country. Though the Burmans have been historically in the ascendancy, other large groups such as the Shan, Karen, Chin, Kachin, and Arakanese have played important roles and continue to do so. Since limitations of space prevent us from looking at all these, three groups are selected here. These groups are among the smaller, less well-known, more disadvantaged groups.

The Selon (or Selung or Mawken) have been called 'sea gypsies' because they live on boats for much of the time, rarely staying at one place for more than a week at a time. They are said to be the only Burmese group that is not of the Indo-Chinese family, being Malayo-Polynesian, and it is possible that they are remnants of the earliest inhabitants of Burma. At the beginning of the twentieth century they were thought to be dying out—perhaps because of the alcohol and opium that traders sold to them or paid them off with—but a number survive to this day, moving around some of the beautiful, seldom visited islands of the Mergui Archipelago.

One evening in the late 1920s, an Englishman called Leopold Ainsworth was sitting in a Penang hotel reflecting on the twelve happy years he had spent working as a surveyor in Malaya. He was on his way to Casuarina Island in the Mergui Archipelago to do further survey work with Airt, his Malay assistant. While he was staying in the hotel a British timber merchant sought him out and persuaded him to supply him with timber from the island. Ainsworth and Airt took a steamer to a town near Victoria Point, the southernmost tip of Burma, and hired a sampan to the island. We join them on Casuarina Island as they set about making a dug-out canoe in order to be able to reach the mainland.

IT was essential to complete the boat and get across to Victoria Point or Renong and endeavour to pick up some woodcutters and Chinese sawyers, or, if these were unobtainable, to send a message through the coasting steamer to my agent in Penang, who would send me out a number of Chinese labourers.

We were destined, however, not to have to complete this boat ourselves; for on the morning of about the tenth day we awoke to find three queer-looking craft in the bay, about fifty yards out from the shore. They were probably the Sea Gipsies or Salones, as I had heard them called by Airt, and they had obviously run into the bay to get fresh supplies of firewood and water for their families. We both shouted to them in Malay, in the hope that they would understand us and come ashore, for it can be readily imagined that we were most anxious to persuade them to land. Subsequent events proved that we were very fortunate to strike these three boat-loads, who were less afraid than most of these sea people, and did not immediately turn their boats seaward and take to flight when they saw signs of any strangers, particularly a white man.

After much consultation among themselves, two of the men dived into the water and swam ashore, and to our delight we found that they understood our Malay, which they spoke themselves with a very broken accent, mixed with a number of Siamese and other words which we could not recognise at all. We talked for over an hour, eventually persuading them to work for us, felling trees and floating them round to our head-quarters, where we intended to store them, in readiness for sawing up when we secured the necessary labour.

We found that these Sea Gipsies had very little knowledge of money or measurements, and when arranging remuneration for transport work or for felling trees, I found it necessary to cut pieces of rattan of various lengths which they could use as a guide for the length and circumferences required. I gave them a number of these, explaining what each length of rattan was worth to them when they brought in the corresponding sized logs. It was agreed that I should give them rice, tobacco, opium and cloths in exchange for the logs which they brought in, and they insisted that we should settle up each night for the day's work. They seemed to have no interest in coinage, and their one desire was to secure a supply of food and opium.

The men were short, I should say on an average, about 5 feet 3 inches in height, whilst the women appeared to be even shorter. They were brown-skinned and varied in colour, some being much lighter than others. Their hair was straight and usually black, though one or two amongst them had curly or frizzy hair, which was quite auburn in colour and had the appearance of having been bleached by the sun. Both men and women were well built, with particularly good chest and shoulder development like the Malays. They had no hair to speak of on their faces, though I noticed one elderly man amongst them who had grown an apology for a beard—about half a dozen hairs, I should say, and about 12 inches long. I was rather struck by their faces, for most of them had better features than the average Malay. They had high foreheads, quite strong chins, and red lips, not too thick. Some of them had noses that were flat, whilst others were Grecian in shape. One and all had wonderful eyes, dark brown or black, well set apart, and an intelligent look on their faces. They resembled Airt and all Malays in respect of their eyes and facial expression. The younger men and women had nice, small, even, white teeth, but the elder members seemed to have lost them, or the few that remained were badly discoloured a red brown by the chewing of betel nut, which, with opium eating, appeared to be customary among them.

One or two had a kind of skin complaint which gave them the appearance of a fish, quite scaly. I imagined this must be due to the amount of salt which they absorbed from the atmosphere, their food, and continual immersion in salt water. They were scantily clad in old bits of rag which they used as loin cloths only. They were dirty and unkempt in appearance, and the hair of both men and women looked positively matted and tangled for want of attention. They appeared serious-minded, even to the young children, and did not laugh or make jokes with one another or pass critical and humorous remarks as a boatload of Malays would have done, and later they gave me a very sound reason for this air of sadness.

So much for their appearance. Now as to their boats. They were first and foremost dug-out canoes of a type I should say about 25 feet in length and quite 4 feet 6 inches wide amidships. But, to make them more seaworthy and to prevent them from being swamped through lack of free-board, they had added a bamboo strake from bow to stern and built up the sides a foot or more with pieces of palm stem bound tightly together with rattan. Part of the boat was decked in with split bamboos tied together in such a way as to make a rough deck, upon which six or seven Salones were sitting in each boat. The after part of the boat contained a crude awning made of leaves, under which they slept and kept their pots and pans. This awning could be rolled up when required and kept at the side of the boat. The canoes were propelled by very roughly fashioned oars in the same way as the Venetian gondola. Men, women and children could all handle these oars, and they stood up to row, generally one in the bow and one in the stern, and balanced themselves in a most dangerous fashion on the extreme edge of the boat. The rowlock consisted of a tough branch of a tree which had a natural fork in which to rest the shaft of the oar, which, instead of having a leather block to keep it in place, was made fast by a piece of green rattan, which was still pliable with sap and could be tied after a fashion. Incidentally I found later that these pieces of rattan were a confounded nuisance and most inefficient; they always seemed to break at the most critical moment, just when one was negotiating a difficult part of a channel with a swift current and all hands were needed.

In addition to oars, each boat had a single mast which could be put up and be rigged with a square sail made of palm leaves plaited together. Like the roof, this sail was kept rolled up at the side of the boat when not required, and was run up to the masthead quite easily by a piece of rattan or thin line, looking more like an old mat hung out to dry than a sail. The mainsheet to this sail was also of rattan or a piece of fishing line.

The boats, one and all, seemed to have their full share of bilge-water in the bottom, and the smell that came up from below was terrific, the reason being that all garbage, fish entrails, pot washings, etc., were poured into the bottom of the boat and only baled out periodically when they happened to be in a sheltered, shallow bay near land. The reason for this unhygienic state of affairs was that if they threw garbage overboard at any time, sharks would get into the habit of following their boats, and as they spent a great deal of time diving for pearl oysters, sea snails and slugs this would never do. These boats were called *kabangs* by the Sea Gipsies, and were floating homes in which these sea-people lived the whole year round, except on rare occasions in the very bad south-west monsoon weather, when they would run into some sheltered bay on one of the large distant islands, build a most primitive shelter on the beach, and live there until the bad weather was over.

During these first few days with the Sea Gipsies, Airt and I were most interested in their boats, and asked them many questions regarding the way they were made, and it was during one of these conversations that one of the men gave me this account of a construction of the freeboard of one of these boats. This extra piece of freeboard is particularly interesting, as the Sea Gipsies have derived their own name from it. The freeboard is marked by a bamboo rib, called by the people the *Maw* or Drowning, as without it the boats used to be swamped and the occupants drowned. *Oken* is their word for salt water, so these two words seem to have been joined together, and the one word *Mawken*, which is the name they call themselves, would appear to mean Seadrowned.

They, therefore, consider themselves to be the Seadrowned people of the Mergui Archipelago, which is a stretch of the Indian Ocean containing several hundreds of beautiful islands running parallel to the southern coast of Burma and stretching from Mergui in the north to a few miles south of Renong in the south, a distance of well over two hundred miles. I asked them where they came from and who they were, and they appeared from their own accounts to be the Sea Gipsies of these islands, and their *kabangs* had perpetuated their history. Airt was very curious to know why the Mawkens, as I shall now call them, had taken to living in boats. 'They must be mad,' he said to me. 'Fancy leaving a nice house on shore to live in that smelly boat.' I told him he had better ask them why they had done so. At first they were very reluctant to say anything, but in the course of a few days, during which time Airt and I spent the whole of our time with them collecting logs and floating them round to our base in the bay, we gradually extracted what appeared to be the most interesting part of their history. Briefly, this was what they told us, and it seems to be a reasonable and, in fact, the only account of their origin that exists, for they have no literature, neither have they any script to their language, so there is no record handed down in any written form.

'Generations ago,' they told us, 'our fore-fathers lived on the mainland of Burma and the northern shores of the Malay Peninsula. They had settled homes there. Then came the fierce Burmese hill tribes from the north and the piratical Malays from the south, both of whom were wild and lawless. They drove us Mawkens out of our settlements, robbing and killing whenever they came. We were not fighting people, so we left our inland settlements and moved towards the sea coasts, eventually crossing the shallow waters to the various islands in the Mergui Archipelago, making one or two settlements on the larger islands, such as St Matthew's and St Luke's. But again we were persecuted by Malay pirates, who robbed, killed and enslaved some of our people during the north-east monsoon weather, when these Malays could sail about and commit acts of piracy on the seas and around these islands. Our people could not bear these attacks any longer and decided to build boats large enough to take their families, and in which they could escape hurriedly during the fine weather season when they were open to attack from the Malay pirates. Finally, our people found residence on the islands impossible, so they took to living in their boats entirely, as we do now. We had come to take shelter in this bay and to find some food for ourselves as our supplies were exhausted, and owing to the south-west monsoon we have been unable to secure any sea slugs, or snails, or birds' nests to barter with the Burmese and Chinese traders.'

'What did you expect to find to eat here?' Airt asked.

One old man, Bhatoo by name, replied: 'We can usually get a good number of limpets and crabs from the beach and rocks, when we have driven off the monkeys, and then we send our mongrel dogs on shore to help us hunt while we spear wild pig and deer. There are plenty of them on this island. Now that we have found you and the white man here, we may be fortunate enough to obtain enough rice and opium to keep us going through the bad-weather season and until we can go diving for pearl oysters again.'

'Will your people fell trees for us regularly?' demanded Airt.

'Yes,' replied Bhatoo, 'so long as you feed us every day.'

Their great need during these bad-weather days was food and opium, and it seemed, therefore, that we were lucky in coming to the islands at this time of the year, as there would be a chance of securing a certain amount of labour. Had we arrived in the north-east monsoon, when the fine weather prevailed, it is doubtful whether we should have seen these people at the island, as they would all have been out with the pearl-fishing schooners.

* * *

The *Dharacotta* made the journey to Victoria Point once a fortnight, and was due to arrive in two day's time. On the morning that the steamer arrived at Victoria Point, Airt and I were taken across by the Mawken, and I shall always remember that first trip, even though it was a short one. I sat with three women on the bamboo floor. All of them without clothes to the waist. Two men navigated the boat, one using the oar to steer and propel whilst the other looked after his primitive sail, first hauling it up to the masthead and then sitting aft with the main-sheet wound round his big toe. We were almost running before the wind, which, incidentally, is practically the only occasion on which the sail can be used, as the Mawken boat has neither keel nor leeboards. There were two small children, a girl and a boy. The boy, aged about seven, remained permanently in the bottom of the boat acting as a sort of human bilge pump, baling out the water, which seemed to trickle in slowly the whole time through the almost transparent freeboard. The little girl sat under the roof, and stared at me most of the time, occasionally making some remark to the women in the Mawken language which I could not understand. At other times, she would dreamily pick her head and examine her find, just like monkeys at the Zoo; when that bored her she would take up the sharp knife used by the menfolk for cleaning fish and shave off some of the hard skin from the soles of her feet. The principles of hygiene obviously conveyed very little to these simple folk. The smell in the boat was appalling, even though we were in the open air, and made me almost sick.

A Merchant Venturer Among the Sea Gipsies, Nisbet, London, 1930, pp. 15–25.

31
The 'Flowery' Lisu

BEATRIX METFORD

In the mountainous north of Burma live the Lisu. Although most of this ethnic group live across the border in Yunnan, scattered communities are found not only in the Kachin mountains but also southwards through Shan State territory. Traditionally, they lived only on mountain ridges, practising taungya *(slash-and-burn cultivation) and keeping to themselves. Even as late as the 1930s, when the next passage was written, very few people outside the region knew anything about their language and culture.*

Beatrix Metford, as the wife of a British official serving in Burma, was able to accompany him on tour and travel widely in the Kachin Hills and Shan States. She was even able to observe the 'frontier meetings' by means of which British and Chinese magistrates jointly administered justice in cases involving both countries. The couple lived first in Sinlumkaba, two days' march from Bhamó, and later in Bhamó itself.

Given the Lisu's geographical distribution, it is only to be expected that Chinese influence on the group would be strong. The Chinese distinguish between 'White' and 'Black' Lisu. They also call certain communities 'Flowery' Lisu because of the pretty dresses of the womenfolk, and their regard for the group as a whole is much higher than for the Kachin. Intermarriage between Chinese and Lisu is common, as the author says; but such marriages have almost always been of Chinese men to Lisu women.

NEXT to the Kachins the largest and most important of the frontier tribes is the Lisu. Both of these tribes belong to the Mongolian race of mankind and have spread south from an aboriginal Tibetan home, but the Lisus are tall and spare and have frequently straight or even aquiline noses, while the Kachins retain the short, stocky figure and broad, flattened nose of the Mongolian. Probably the tall, war-like Aryan tribesmen of north-western India, who for centuries made repeated raids across the Himalayas into Tibet, mingled their blood with the Mongolian ancestors of the Lisus.

The main habitat of the Lisus is the valley of the upper Salween River in north-west Yunnan, a country of precipitous mountains and deep ravines covered with dense jungle. Save on the mountain tops, the climate is very oppressive, and poisonous plants and insects abound. Of roads there are none, and the so-called paths are but ledges in the cliff-sides, so narrow as to be almost impassable to the European, though the Lisu, even with a heavy bundle on his back and his cross-bow in his hand, walks along them and up and down the steep hills as easily as if he were striding along a wide level road.

Only about half a dozen Europeans have penetrated this upper Salween valley and seen the 'black' Lisus, as the Chinese call these wild, uncivilized tribesmen, and of this handful of travellers two, Dr Brunhuber and Herr Schmitz, were murdered there by the natives in 1909. But from their secluded home the Lisus have wandered far and wide over the mountainous districts of Yunnan and of the Burma border land. By contact with their Chinese and Shan neighbours, they have become 'tamed' or civilized, and their customs and ever their dress have altered. It is these civilized Lisus whom I have met and of whom this chapter mainly treats.

The costume of the black Lisu woman is, according to travellers' accounts, crude in the extreme. Just a short coat of coarse hempen cloth, with a skirt of the same material reaching only to the knees. Shoes and stockings are unknown, but they wear gaiters of the same grey homespun as the dress to protect the legs from thorns and from snake bites.

These gaiters are common to all the frontier tribes, and I once queried their usefulness, seeing that the feet are bare. 'On bare feet there's nothing to be feared from snakes,' I was told. 'Snakes always strike high; about calf high.'

Round the hair the Lisu women wear a bandeau of red cloth about an inch wide and studded with silver or bone buttons or with cowrie shells. They love jewellery and wear as many bracelets, necklets, and armlets as they can get hold of. As red is the favourite colour and coral the favourite stone of the Kachins, so the blue turquoise is the preferred colour and jewel of the Lisus. Dozens of strings of this stone, which is found in large quantities in Tibet, adorn the neck of a black Lisu belle, who also loves silver ornaments if she can get them. The poorer women and girls have to content themselves with cowrie shells, bone buttons, or dried seeds.

The dress of the civilized Lisu women is very striking and full of colour; the Chinese call them 'flowery' Lisus on account of their varicoloured garments. Over short loose knickers of dark blue cotton, they wear a long coat of the same material, which reaches just below the knees but with the front half cut away from the waist downwards, something like a man's dress coat. Over the shoulders, and reaching to the waist back and front, are broad bands of cloth of three different colours, varying slightly according to locality, such as brown, white, and green, or red, white, and blue. The coat tail is ornamented with many small patches of the same three colours, and with rows of white seeds or cowrie shells. The gap in front caused by the cutaway is covered by an apron similarly ornamented with coloured patches and white seeds. A coloured woven belt and a triangular 'tail' with tassel complete the costume, which is so neatly put on as to give the illusion of a skirt. Tubular gaiters of blue cotton, also ornamented with coloured patches, are worn to protect the legs. The hair is roughly bobbed or even cut short and then completely covered by a huge turban of dark blue cotton, with the ends ornamented with coloured patches and a fringe of reddish yarn. Over the turban is frequently worn a bandeau of red cloth edged with blue, on which are sewn a row of large white bone buttons. Silver earrings and necklaces, torques and bracelets are worn, together with as many as a dozen blue glass necklaces; even though they are unable to obtain the turquoise beads worn by their grandmothers, they still retain a predilection for blue ornaments, and I have never seen a Lisu woman wearing red jewellery, like her Kachin neighbours.

The dress of the Lisu men consists of short loose knickers such as the women wear, a long coat reaching to the knees, and gaiters, while the pigtail they usually affect is concealed by a large turban. Among the black Lisu all these garments are of whitish hempen homespun without trimming of any kind. The flowery Lisu, however, wear broad bands over the shoulders as the women do, but of plain dark blue; while between the shoulder blades on the back of the coat is a small square of blue and black patches. The gaiters are edged with blue, while turban and belt of dark blue cloth complete a very striking costume.

It is a pity that most of the flowery Lisu men are now forsaking this stately long coat for the short, but no doubt more convenient, coat of the Chinese. In a few years' time one more tribal costume will be a thing of the past.

Like the Kachins, all Lisu men carry a long sword in a wooden sheath, but their characteristic weapon is the crossbow, with which they are exceedingly skilful. The usual bow is about three feet broad, and is made of wild mulberry wood, which is exceptionally tough. I bought one of them and tested it by pulling the string back to the trigger with a spring balance, and the dial showed 160 lb! I could never string a bow myself, and found that not many European men could do it. The Lisus pressed the butt against their stomach, bent forward grasping the bowstring, and then threw the body backwards so as to bring its whole weight in play. Even they doubled up their coat into a pad for the butt to rest against, and my friends found at least a sofa cushion necessary to avoid bruises!

The arrow is made of bamboo, and is only about a foot long and the thickness of a wooden knitting needle. It is feathered with a little piece of bamboo sheath. The arrow can be bent or broken by the fingers almost as easily as a match, and yet it is shot from the bow with such force that at twenty paces it will go right through an inch plank.

These plain arrows are used for practice and for shooting at birds; even when marching along with a heavy load on his back the Lisu always has his bow in his hand, ready for a practice shot at any bird he sees. They are marvellous marksmen, and some can hit quite small birds at fifty yards. I amused myself one day in a Lisu village by sticking up some silver dollars as targets, and the men hit them once in three times at twenty yards. They thoroughly enjoyed the sport, but I found it too expensive to continue!

For big game hunting and for war the arrows are more carefully pointed—sometimes an iron barb is fixed on with twine—and behind the point the shaft is carefully pared thin and then filled up again with poison paste made of wild aconite and resin. A wound, even the slightest scratch, from a poisoned arrow is said to be fatal within half an hour. When Lisu hunters have hit a deer or such large animal they and their dogs follow in its tracks until it drops, and a wounded animal always runs in a circle, they say, so the chase is not too long. A huge piece of the flesh round the poisoned wound is cut out and thrown away, and the rest of the carcase is said to be quite free from poison and good to eat. If a Lisu is himself hit by a poisoned arrow he at once draws his sword and cuts out a big piece of flesh; it is the only way he can save his life.

The black Lisu men are said to have special weapons for war: five-foot wide bows, five-foot long swords, and five-foot high shields of ox-hide. They also wear caps of deerskin adorned with the horns as a protection against head hits, and hang strings of cowrie shells round their necks and blacken their faces to terrify the enemy. A black Lisu raiding party must offer an awesome spectacle.

Like all hillmen, the Lisus are very lazy; although keen hunters and untiring climbers, they much prefer spending their time squatting round the hearth or in the sunshine puffing away at a pipe. Their wants are few. A little plot of jungle is cleared in the spring, and amid the charred tree stumps enough Indian corn is grown for the year. Tobacco and opium poppy are also usually cultivated, and all their other needs—firewood, wild honey, meat, hemp to weave into clothes—are supplied by the jungle. Even when some Lisu family leaves the Salween valley and gradually becomes civilized, it is several years or even generations before they relinquish their nomadic jungle existence and settle down in permanent villages with tilled fields. Forest officers hate them for the damage they do to the forest by clearing each year a fresh patch for cultivation, and so destroying all trees.

The Lisu house is made of rough poles with walls of plaited split bamboo. The floor is raised three or four feet from the ground, and in front there is a small veranda. In the middle of the house—it is only about fifteen feet long and half that distance wide—is the hearth, where logs are continually burning and filling the room with smoke and fumes. Logs of wood or roughly made low stools serve as seats, while the floor serves as bed. I shall never forget the first Lisu house I entered. It was some minutes before my eyes got accustomed to the smoky gloom. Indeed, I stumbled over what looked just a bundle of blankets, but it let out a grunt. It was the granny of the family taking an afternoon nap.

My hosts begged me to 'eat wine' with them, and I reluctantly agreed. A large earthenware pot was produced from a corner of the room, along with two or three Chinese rice bowls and some roughly cut chopsticks. My host dipped from the jar a bowlful of fermented rice and handed it to me with a pair of chopsticks. I had expected a small cup of spirit! It did not taste so unpleasant as I expected; it was just rice malt.

The more civilized of the flowery Lisu usually build their houses on the ground, with a floor of hard beaten earth as in Chinese houses. The house is larger and is frequently divided into two rooms, but it is just as draughty and roughly built as that of their wild relatives. The Lisu can never throw off his hatred of restraint; he wants to be able to move to new hunting grounds the moment the spirit moves him, so what is the use of building an elaborate house?

The Lisus are animists, worshipping—or rather propitiating—the spirits of nature, but in addition they also pay reverence to the spirit of their ancestors. This latter worship they have probably adopted from their Chinese neighbours, who rate the Lisu far higher than any other frontier tribe. Intermarriages of Lisu and Chinese are by no means uncommon, and are not deemed by the Chinese such mésalliances as are marriages with 'wild men', as they style the Kachins. The principal spirits worshipped by the Lisus are Misi the god of the jungle, Mina the god of the earth, Muhu the god of lightning, Mihi the god of the winds, and Makara the Lord of Heaven. The spirit of the ancestors is called Hini. Like most Oriental peoples, they celebrate the new year at the new moon which occurs about the beginning of February. These celebrations include, besides the usual feasting and drinking, dances in which, to the music of reed pipes, men and women shuffle round and round a big circle in the centre of the village. In the dim light of the stars and the glow of the fires this dance is most impressive.

Marriage customs are very simple. The man courts the maid openly, and when she accepts his wooing she gives him as a token a bag she has woven and ornamented with a diamond pattern in white seeds. He then gets some elders to act as middlemen and arrange with the girl's parents for the wedding. All preparations having been made, the bride is escorted to her groom's house, where a large feast takes place. At nightfall the bride goes into the jungle with her parents, and the bridegroom has to hunt for her. When he has found her, her parents return to the house, leaving the young couple to spend the night alone on the hillside. This is done on three successive nights, while the feasting, dancing, and carousal continue all the time.

When the birth of a child is imminent, the father offers sacrifices to the god Hini, and invokes his assistance for a safe delivery. Directly the babe is born it is washed, and the priest then announces its safe arrival on earth to Hini and thanks him for his help. On the third day the child is given a spirit name, which is not used again until death. On the tenth, twentieth, and thirtieth days after birth, both the child and its mother are again bathed, but are forbidden to leave the house until the full month has elapsed. During this month the mother does no housework for fear that her uncleanness should infect others; her relatives and friends do all the work for her. Certain highly seasoned foods, such as chillies and bamboo shoots, sugar and spirits, are forbidden her. When the month has elapsed, the bed and bedding she used for the confinement are burnt, and the period of uncleanness is at an end.

When death is seen to be near, nine grains of rice and nine tiny pieces of silver are, whenever circumstances allow, given to the dying man to swallow. If it is a woman who is about to die, then the mystic number of grains is seven. Directly life is extinct two men seize the dead body by the arms and, calling out the deceased's spirit name, beseech him to return direct to his ancestors whence he came. The body is then washed and placed in the coffin along with some offerings, and other offerings are thrown into the nearest stream so that they may float away to the spirit kingdom. Funerals, like weddings, are

great occasions for feasting, so both are usually postponed
until after harvest, when provisions are in plenty. On the road
to the spirit world there are nine hills that the soul must
climb, nine streams it must cross, nine paths it must follow,
and the priest warns it against losing its way and following
animal tracks instead of the right paths. He also calls on Hini
to keep a good look-out for his child who is just starting on
his journey back, and to guide him whenever possible. The
coffin is then covered with earth, and the deceased's bow
and quiver, sword and bag are hung on a tree above the
grave. A bamboo or earthenware pot is also buried in the
coffin with its neck above the ground, so that the offerings
which are made regularly for the next three years can reach
the deceased.

Where China Meets Burma, Blackie, London, 1935, pp. 135–43.

32
The Proud Mon

AUSTIN COATES

For centuries the Mon and the Burmans were engaged in fre-
quent and bloody conflicts. We have seen in earlier extracts
that the Mon, influenced long before by the cultures of India
and Ceylon, were prosperous and powerful in the sixteenth
and seventeenth centuries; but the kingdom was conquered by
Alaung-hpaya in the mid-eighteenth century and thereafter
its culture faded. The two peoples were culturally quite dis-
tinct, Burmese being a Sino-Tibetan language while the
Mon–Khmer group forms a large part of the Austro-Asiatic
family. But though there are today more than five million
Khmer speakers there are perhaps no more than half a million
speakers of Mon, most of them clustered on either side of the
Thai–Burmese border. Nevertheless, this proud group has con-
tinued to see itself as distinct, as Austin Coates discovered for
himself.

*   Austin, son of the distinguished English composer Eric*
Coates, took delight in staying with Asian families, living (to
use his own words) 'as a son of the house' and conforming to

their way of life; consequently he had a wide circle of friends in India and the East. He consciously tried to 'shorten the mental distance between the continents', to find a way out of that sense of isolation that the European feels when trans-planted to an Eastern culture. 'Each traveller must find that gate for himself', he says in the Introduction to his book, 'because for each one it is different.'

Arriving from India as a tourist in the late 1940s, Coates came at a time when Burma was not only still feeling the after-effects of a world war but also suffering from internal strife. He was fortunate enough to be invited to stay in a rural Mon household in a riverside village on the Salween. Having hired a canoe in Moulmein to take him upriver he found the house of U Mya, who welcomed him and took him round the village.

THE most interesting people we called on that evening were U Mya's two younger sisters, who were school-teachers. One was a widow, the other a spinster, and both were again typical of Burma's forthright womanhood, courageous, practical and cheerful.

The village's education problems were peculiar. It was in one of those rare areas where Mon and not Burmese was the predominant language. The monastery schools therefore spoke and taught Mon; they were in fact the citadels of con-tinuing Mon identity. The Government schools, however, upon which some of the boys and all the girls depended for elementary education—until some of them were old enough to take further education with the Italian sisters in Moulmein—taught only Burmese and English, the attitude of the Burmese Government towards Mon being that it would be simpler for everyone if it died out entirely.

U Mya's sisters had therefore answered a prime local need by founding a Mon school which would take girls and any boys whose parents preferred lay to monastic education. They began with their own money, and some of the better-off villagers helped them. But in the long run the school, edu-cating for the most part poor children who could not afford to pay fees high enough to cover the school's expenses, needed a Government subsidy and therefore Government approval of its existence.

The sisters worked at a frightening rate. Having no text-books for Mon lessons, they had to plan out their lessons in every subject and help the other teachers do the same. They had to translate histories, essays and geographies from Burmese and English into Mon, and in addition there were the physical training, dancing and sports classes to be attended to. It is a peculiarity of India and Burma that there are virtually no nursery rhymes or folk-songs apart from those that have survived among aboriginal tribes, but the sisters had decided that community singing was an essential part of modern education in that it trained people to do things together in dependence upon one another. They therefore translated many European folk-songs into Mon. I remember one day coming to the school to find all the children singing '*Au clair de la lune*' in Mon, and they knew many other songs.

The sisters were themselves highly educated, speaking perfect English without trace of foreign accent, and good French. The elder one was a little stout, like her brother, with a deep musical voice and that pleasant combination of motherliness and intellectuality, sympathizing one moment and the next putting her finger on the weak spot in an argument, which every social reform movement knows if it has attracted women into its ranks. The younger sister was thin and quiet, a restful person with a gift for dealing with very young children. They were popular with everyone in the village, though of the elder one some were a little nervous.

In the days that followed I took every opportunity of meeting them, and I gradually realized they were the centre of a movement to revive Mon learning and culture. The movement was of course non-political, the only threatening political aspect of it being concerned with whether the Government would consent to finance Mon schools. Negotiations on this were just starting in Rangoon.

I had to admit to myself that in spite of the unquestionable Mon influence on Burmese art and monastic learning I could not see why, if by the process of history the Mon language had nearly died, there was any advantage to be gained in rescuing it at the eleventh hour.

During my stay various young people interested in the movement came to the village. Most of them travelled by boat, but one from thirty miles or so further north had come

'Portraits of Two Talain [Mon] Young Ladies', from Henry Yule, *Narrative of the Mission to the Court of Ava in 1855*, Smith, Elder, London, 1858.

down by road to Martaban at the opposite side of the mouth of the Salween to Moulmein, and from there had come like myself up-river by boat. He was a particularly interesting young man, of good education and interested in the promotion of Mon studies; he too had plans for a Mon school in his home town where Mon was the principal language spoken although the Government schools taught only Burmese.

It was interesting to see the village children playing. They would be amusing themselves in a simple and surprisingly grown-up way compared with English children, until suddenly a newcomer would come along and join the game. Before long this youngster would be shouting at the others and bossing them about till everybody did what he wanted.

Several times, passing a scene like this, I remember one of the sisters smilingly pointing out to me the tough little child.

'You see that one? He's a Burmese. The others are Mons.'

So it started as early in life as that, this mediaeval rivalry.

I found Burma on the whole culturally colonial or suburban in the sense that for the greater part of their mental stimuli her people looked abroad. They had few writers, the aim of the few being to write in or be translated into English and published in London or Calcutta. There had been a handful of talented artists—the best of them, Ba Nyun, coming from a Mon village not far from the one I was staying in. There was no film industry, no modern theatre; there was not that air, in other words, of being in surroundings where people thought originally and perpetuated their thoughts which there is in Paris or Berlin or Calcutta. Without this chemically unanalysable air life can never grow to its full graciousness, never lift itself up entirely from the level of being a mere round of toiling, eating and sleeping.

In the Mon villages, and with the hospitable family in whose houses and company I spent the best part of my days, I found for the first time in Burma a hint of that rare atmosphere.

'And how do you think we could have preserved that spirit without our language?' U Mya's elder sister asked one evening when I was dining in their house.

It was true, of course. The old gentle spirit of the Indian emigrants could only have survived through the language, a more melodic language than Burmese, which trained its children to think along certain tracks inevitably different from those in other languages where other grammatical technicalities, other modes of expression, drive the mind along differing courses.

The candles flickered on the luxurious table, teak and silver, the age-old produce of Burma, the two sisters in their glowing silk loungyis, our visitor from Pa-an with his keen eyes and intelligent enthusiasm for the Mon tradition. The younger sister served most of the dishes; as in India, servants were not permitted to hand food or drink to a guest. But once the dishes were on the table we helped ourselves Chinese-style, taking now this, now that, from the central bowls and mingling it with the rice on our plates—India and China combined, Chinese variety of dishes, but the Indian custom of taking rice as the neutral base with which to mix them; Indian highly flavoured preparations, but a moment later noodles served almost exactly in the Chinese manner. Another Chinese subtlety was that beside each person's plate was a small bowl of soup to be taken at any time during the meal when one felt thirsty. A Chinese spoon, made of porcelain, was provided to drink it with. These Burmese soups were generally clear and made of vegetables and fish; there were particularly tasty ones flavoured with the small green limes which are the East's substitute for lemons. Looking back now after having been to China I realize these soups were cooked in a Chinese way, but their taste was something specially Burmese, superior to most Chinese soups.

The elder sister presided at the evening's entertainment; with her greater intellectuality she was looked upon as the fountain-head of much to do with the movement, and, typical of Burma and the special position women occupy in that land, the young man listened to all she said and took his lead from her without any suggestion of resenting a woman's authority.

After dinner we sat cross-legged in the low teak chairs, made ourselves comfortable with cushions and talked far into the cool night. Whenever the slight wind dropped we fanned ourselves gently.

Monasteries, bandits, music and food

As in most Burmese villages there were areas where the air was heavy with the smell of rotting fish and the ground covered with hundreds of small fish laid out on mats to dry in the sun. This was the national dish being prepared.

The national dish—also a feature of Siamese cookery—is ngapí (Siamese, kapi), the juice of rotten fish, or else paste made therefrom, taken with rice, Burmese dwarf celery with its delicious peppery flavour, and a sprinkling of lime juice.

I found at first that no hostess would let me eat it. It is a peasant dish or one for informal occasions, and the general fear seemed to be that once I tasted it all my illusions about Burma would be shattered. Quite a dispute finally took place between one married couple on the question of whether or not I was to be allowed to taste ngapí. My hostess was determined to let me try and my host equally determined not to lose a friend over a plate of food. In the end of course the determination of the hostess and the guest's curiosity prevailed, and the fatal ngapí was brought for me to sample. It is of course delicious, something like *patum peperium*,[*] and

[*]A spicy paste.

every visitor to Burma should insist upon trying it if invited to a Burmese home.

There were many fine monasteries in the region, but the one at U Mya's village was the finest of them all. It consisted of several single-storey buildings set in a large walled and paved compound well planted with trees. Small bells suspended from the canopies of the higher pagodas swayed in the fresh wind giving a constant silvery music, another sound distinctive of monasteries in Burma. The pagodas were whitewashed, and it was only in the main Buddha shrine that the well-beloved Burmese gold dominated the colour scheme. Here the great statue of the Buddha was of gold and the surrounding walls were decorated with golden pillars separating the flat surfaces of the walls, which were mosaics of many-coloured glass. The candles burning before the statue and the odour of incense mingling with fresh flowers seemed to quicken the senses and produced on them the impression of great brightness and spiritual clarity.

I could not help comparing this spotless shrine with the refuse-strewn temples of India—and indeed with the Shwédagon Pagoda, after visiting which it was advisable not only to wash one's feet but put disinfectant into the water as well. The Burmese have inherited from India, possibly in the message of the Buddha himself, the traditions of country as opposed to city civilization, and it is only in the country that they are seen at their best.

It was interesting to observe how conscious these Mon priests were of the great contribution their people had once made to Burmese culture. U Mya's sister was an admirable interpreter, and with her help I was able to converse with the abbots of several monasteries.

Exquisite Burmese writings were shown me, written on dried palm-leaves lacquered all over in red or black and with the sacred Pali texts of Buddhism written on them in gold. These were kept in huge lacquered wood boxes with heavy locks, and some of them were several hundreds of years old; but it was pointless to ask to see anything other than the sacred texts—there was nothing else. All the writings were repetitions; there were no new commentaries, new thoughts.

It is curious to see how when a people is scattered in two countries, as the Mons have been scattered in Burma and Siam, unexpected links are formed in which national frontiers play no part. The Mons of Burma in their far-away villages looked towards the Dauna range of hills separating Burma from Siam as if no cartographer had ever depicted the two sides of them in different colours. Girls of the district married men of Chiengmai in Northern Siam, and sometimes a villager would bring back a wife born in Siam, often a very pale girl looking more Chinese than the village beauties.

The only alternative to boat travel was walking and this was rendered pleasant by the excellent brick pathways maintained to link one village with another, each village being responsible for the upkeep of the paths for half the distance to whichever other village the path led. Streams were crossed not by bridges but by curiously shaped trunks of trees laid across from bank to bank. Using the trunk's gnarled protuberances on which to balance or secure a good foothold, one hoped for the best and moved forward. In all this part of the country it was an advantage to walk barefoot.

Like so much of Asia the area was subject to banditry. The general areas used by bandits as their centres of operations were known; in fact the bandits themselves were known from the occasions, such as at Thadingyut, the autumn light festival, when they came into town like any normal citizens to take part in the celebrations. But it was difficult to catch them, and when they were in town the honour of the village was at stake not to molest them, for the bandit chief would go straight to the headman's house and crave hospitality, which by the traditions of his country the headman was bound to give. The bandit in this way slept the night in the village in perfect safety.

When they were out on a skirmish it was a different matter. In all the villages anyone possessing firearms had to surrender them at night for use by the village patrol, which consisted of eight or ten men, depending on the size of the village, every able-bodied man having to take his turn as a watchman under the headman's instructions. The bandits sometimes interfered with the elections of village headmen, intimidating the villagers to raise votes for their own nominee. Life had its raw side, as everywhere else.

In the houses where people of the older generation predominated it was customary for food to be served in the old Burmese manner, the guests sitting cross-legged round a table raising the meal about nine inches from the ground.

Most of the houses followed the same custom as U Mya's house in that when there were no guests everybody ate in the old style, though if there were guests the men took food from a table of ordinary European height for which chairs were required. In general the women did not take food from such tables, and U Mya's sisters were considered somewhat *avant-garde* in dining habitually sitting on chairs; it struck the others as being a masculine trait in them.

When guests came men and women dined at the same time but in different rooms, the men at a high table in the dining-room, the women at a low one in the room beyond. The guest of honour was placed at the head of the table. One of the amusing sidelights on such occasions was the ribaldry being shouted from one room to the other. The ladies of course ate in the kitchen section of the house, although as I have explained it was less like a kitchen than such a room would have been in a western house; it was a room in which all household affairs were looked after, accounts kept and stocks counted—a comfortable cool room.

There were pianos in some of the houses—the sisters of course had a piano, an old German upright with candlesticks, very necessary in the country. I took a look through their music. '*Les Millions d' Arlequin*' was the one on top of the pile, and beneath it pieces by Boccherini, Kreisler, Godard, and songs such as Schubert's '*Ave Maria*' and Mendelssohn's '*On Wings of Song*'. It was the first time I had found European music in an Asiatic home—in India interest in Indian music has resisted the encroachment of western music more than in the Far East, where music is less developed and thus more susceptible to outside influence. With a curious nostalgia I remember playing some pieces by Brahms in a part of the world where they had perhaps never been heard before.

In that village I met some of the most beautiful-looking people I have ever seen, particularly the old ladies with their soft expressions, the lines of their faces having an upward slant caused by the constant drawing back of the hair to tie it in the old-fashioned coil. Their perfect manners and surprising interest in everything to do with the outside world, their straightforward approach and frank conversation, all reminded me of the characterful old ladies Rembrandt painted and the Manchu women whose independence and forthright behaviour so delighted the first Dutch Embassy to

Peking. With all of them there was a son or a grandson to act as interpreter, and some of my best memories are of those low houses overlooking the river where we sat on mats laid over the teak floor, ate betel nuts from huge carved silver boxes, watched the boats pass and talked of different things. Calling on people is difficult in Burma if one has many people to see in one day because of the social law that every stranger crossing the threshold must be offered food and drink. It is impolite to refuse, and after a few calls I usually found myself incapable of further movement. As in India, alcoholic drinks were not usually offered although they would sometimes be taken before a meal.

I remember a young friend taking me to see his grand-mother, a silver-haired old lady wearing a magnificent grey silk loungyi. As she saw us arrive her eyes sparkled. She gave an instruction to her servant.

We sat on the floor beside her and chatted comfortably; I imagined the usual drinks, tea, coconut water or buffalo milk would be arriving in due course. This old lady had other plans, however, and when the servant returned it was with a fine vintage Burgundy.

'Those Japanese!' she scowled. 'I wasn't going to let them get my wines. I buried the whole lot under the house and didn't dig them up till they'd gone. They came to me and asked what I had, but I told them "I'm a poor old woman with nothing to interest you gentlemen".'

Acting and reliving the scene, she looked at me again at this point and we all burst out laughing.

'You like wine?' she asked, extending a full glass to me, and as with renewed merriment we drank she murmured again softly between two sips 'Those Japanese!'

Visiting other riverine villages

When going further afield than we could conveniently walk we went by boat. This with U Mya was quite a proceeding. There was no question of him embarking while the stern was unattached to the jetty or there was the least chance of him-self or his guest having to make any exertion in order to get aboard. Things had to be done properly, and no amount of orders were given before the two boatmen had everything ready, Koomba had packed the lunch in the right place so that we all had plenty of foot-room, and all things were attended to that needed attention; finally, like emperor and visiting monarch, we embarked, respectful people on the shore made suitable inclinations of the head, Koomba grinned from ear to ear, and we were borne slowly away into the stream.

On arrival at the village where we had decided to lunch someone's house would be commandeered and all the table things set out. I remember we were even going to bring our own water until I managed to restrain U Mya on this point. One or two pieces of cutlery also had to be commandeered and a leasehold obtained of part of the kitchen for Koomba to warm the food in. After this we sat down to eat and were served by Koomba just as if we had been at home, while the members of the commandeered household who happened to be there watched us and chatted generally.

Then, while we walked round the village and smoked Burmese cheroots, the washing-up was done, and everything was shipshape by the time we re-embarked. I never quite managed to work out what the reactions of the commandeered household must have been to all this, but presumably they would have done the same to us had they been visiting our village. And it is superfluous for me to say that U Mya had a way with him.

One afternoon I remember walking unexpected into his room to find him lying on his bed with a man standing on him and, balancing by keeping his hands on the ceiling, walking slowly up and down his body, giving him an ancient form of massage. I naturally showed no sign of amazement, said what I wanted to say, and went away. But in my mind I wondered whether the man was a professional masseur come up from Moulmein on the morning tide or whether he was a villager; I recalled having seen him in the kitchen earlier that morning. Later on, without appearing too inquisitive, I asked U Mya where the man came from and was told he lived at a village some miles down the river on the opposite bank.

After a day or so the facts fell out. The man was the owner of two coconut islands U Mya was interested in renting, but the price asked was too high. Accordingly my host had asked the man to come and see him, had entertained him and kept him hanging about all day with his 'Let's make a move' technique while at odd moments the price was mentioned, made the fellow give him a massage—after all, he had to wait several hours for the ebb—and sent him home in the evening with the price satisfactory and the deal clinched.

U Mya understood life.

Returning in the late afternoon was a pleasant experience, when we could relax in the boat after hours of walking in the hot sun and the boatman could paddle faster in the cooler atmosphere. Kingfishers of several varieties—'Very good eating,' remarked U Mya as I spotted the first one—flew along the bank and kept pace with our boat, and as we entered the main river and headed for home thousands of swallows flew across the Salween from the midstream islands and beyond, home to their nests among the roofs of the village. The farmers and their buffaloes were coming home across the river too, though with less noise than in the morning; as we passed along, a fleet of grey nostrils, eyes and horns swam steadily towards us. The bells were tinkling on the pagodas, children were calling their returning parents, the brightly clad cheerful people were making fast their boats and carrying home their bundles, and the sun was setting red across the river. We only had time to take our things from the boat and walk through the trees to the gate of U Mya's garden before looking back to find the sun departed, the river becoming dark and the air suddenly grown chill.

Five years later

When I returned to Burma five years later it was to find those villages no longer existed.

The demand for Government recognition of Mon schools grew from a small point on the horizon to an issue that came foremost in the minds of the people of that district. When the attitude of the Burmese Government, after the departure of the British, was seen towards the Karen's demand for a separate State within the Union of Burma the Mons began to realize for the first time what they were up against, and rightly or wrongly they interpreted what they saw as the intention of the Government to eradicate Mon language and culture. The Mons and the Karens came to an understanding to work together for their related aims of a separate state and education in their own language.

Their first demonstration was the peaceful occupation of Moulmein, which they took over from its Burmese administrators. The Government was alarmed and a Commission was set up to examine the claims made for a Karen State.

The Commission worked slowly, and again rightly or wrongly the people judged that the Government was deliberately letting things slide in the hope of resuming the administration. Finally, after many months, the Karen leader who was a member of the Commission walked out, the popular inference from this being that he considered the Commission was achieving nothing.

It was a moment of despair throughout the Karen–Mon region. For some time at the back of their minds, I suppose, had lurked the idea of armed insurrection if this was the only alternative to suppression by the Burmese. The moment seemed to have come.

There was hardly the need for an interchange of views between the Karen and Mon leaders. The Karens took to the field with arms, and U Mya's sisters called upon their people to support the Karens. The Mons rose in revolt.

A bitter struggle followed, the Government forcing the insurgents to retreat into wilder parts of the country, and finally Burmese troops were ordered to destroy the villages of the ringleaders.

The villages I have described were burned from end to end.

Many connected with the movement have not been heard of again; some are believed to be in prison, but whether they are to be released or even tried is not known. The young Mon who dined with me at the sisters' house that evening is one of those of whom there is no record.

When I last heard of them the sisters and many of their friends were in hiding in Siam and the little-known regions of the Burma–Siam frontier. Of the Mon movement little more was heard, although the insurrection and its ruthless suppression had observably increased the community consciousness of the Mons, whose language is now further from dying of neglect than when I first heard it spoken.

With personal friends on both sides, in the Government of Burma and among the former insurgents, it is difficult for me to judge these events, and at the time of my second visit to

Burma people were still too dazed by them to be able to discuss and sum them up. But I recall from that second visit the words of a Mon lady, one of my dearest friends, when she said in a troubled voice, as if seeking to convince herself:

'I'm sure what they did was right, Austin. That sweetness, that softness in our people and our language—we cannot let that die from the heart of Burma.'

Invitation to an Eastern Feast, Hutchinson, London, 1953, pp. 176–93.

The Independent Women of Burma

33
Obliging but Jealous Wives

ALEXANDER HAMILTON

Alexander Hamilton was born in Scotland in 1666 or there-abouts. There are no records of his early life, and in his book he tells us very little about himself. But we can assume that his family was poor because he does say that he had 'a rambling mind and a fortune too narrow to travel like a gentleman' and that he was very young when he began to work at sea, a student at 'Neptune's school'. He also tells us that he had earlier been on voyages around Europe and the north African coast, and to Jamaica. The first certain dates we have are of his voyage on board the Shrewsbury, *which left the Thames at the end of April 1688 and arrived in Bombay the following November. The young student at 'Neptune's school' very soon turned into a resourceful merchant sea captain, hiring ships and engaging in trade in eastern waters*

At the height of the war between France and England, he was heading for Burma with a cargo of Indian rice for sale in the city of Pegú when French vessels attacked, commandeering his cargo and scuttling his ship. Undaunted, Hamilton persuaded his captors to sell him a Dutch vessel that they had acquired; he then sailed on, reaching Syriam (the main port of Pegú) in February 1710. Among the details he gives of Pegúan culture the following remarks about Burmese women are particularly interesting, but it should perhaps be pointed out that for a long time now the Burmese woman's longyi, *a sort of full-length sarong, has been modest by any standard.*

THE Women are much whiter than the Men, and have generally pretty plump Faces, but of small Stature, yet very well shap'd, their Hands and Feet small, and their Arms and Legs well proportioned. Their Headdress is their own black Hair tied up behind, and when they go abroad, they wear a *Shaul* folded up, or a Piece of white Cotton Cloth lying loose on the Top of their Heads. Their bodily Garb is a Frock of Cotton Cloth or Silk, made meet for their Bodies, and the Arms of their Frock stretcht close on the Arm, the lower Part of the Frock reaching Half-thigh down. Under the Frock they have a Scarf or *Lungee* doubled fourfold, made fast about their Middle, which reaches almost to the Ancle, so contrived, that at every Step they make, as they walk, it opens before, and shews the right Leg and Part of the Thigh.

This Fashion of Petticoats, they say, is very ancient, and was first contrived by a certain Queen of that Country, who was grieved to see the Men so much addicted to Sodomy, that they neglected the pretty Ladies. She thought that by the Sight of a pretty Leg and plump Thigh, the Men might be allured from that abominable Custom, and place their Affections on proper Objects, and according to the ingenious Queen's Conjecture, that Dress of the *Lungee* had its desired End, and now the Name of Sodomy is hardly known in that Country.

The Women are very courteous and kind to Strangers, and are very fond of marrying with Europeans, and most Part of the Strangers who trade thither, marry a Wife for the Term they stay. The Ceremony is (after the Parties are agreed), for the Bride's Parents or nearest Friends or Relations, to make a Feast, and invite her Friends and the Bridegroom's, and at the End of the Feast, the Parent or Bride-man, asketh them both before the Company, if they are content to cohabit together as Man and Wife, and both declaring their Consent, they are declared by the Parent or Friend to be lawfully married, and if the Bridegroom has an House, he carries her thither, but if not, they have a Bed provided in the House where they are married, and are left to their own Discretion how to pass away the Night.

They prove obedient and obliging Wives, and take the Management of Affairs within Doors wholly in their own Hands. She goes to Market for Food, and acts the Cook in dressing his Victuals, takes Care of his Clothes, in washing and mending them; if their Husbands have any Goods to sell, they set up a Shop and sell them by Retail, to a much better Account than they could be sold for by Wholesale, and some of them carry a Cargo of Goods to the inland Towns, and barter for Goods proper for the foreign Markets that their Husbands are bound to, and generally bring fair Accounts of their Negotiations. If she proves false to her Husband's Bed, and on fair Proof convicted, her Husband may carry her to the *Rounday*, and have her Hair cut, and sold for a Slave, and he may have the Money; but if the Husband goes astray, she'll be apt to give him a gentle Dose, to send him into the other World a Sacrifice to her Resentment.

If she proves prolifick, the Children cannot be carried out of the Kingdom without the King's Permission, but that may be purchased for 40 or 50 L. Sterl. and if an irreconcilable Quarrel happen where there are Children, the Father is obliged to take Care of the Boys, and the Mother of the Girls. If a Husband is content to continue the Marriage, whilst he goes to foreign Countries about his Affairs, he must leave some Fund to pay her about six Shillings eight Pence per Month, otherwise at the Year's End she may marry again, but if that Sum is paid her on his Account, she is obliged to stay the Term of three Years, and she is never the worse, but rather the better lookt on, that she has been married to several European Husbands.

A New Account of the East Indies, John Mosman, Edinburgh, 1727; reprinted by The Argonaut Press, London, Vol. II, 1930, pp. 27–8.

34
Free and Happy Lives

ALICE HART

Unlike many British women of today, Alice Hart chose to be known by her husband's name. When in 1897 her book Picturesque Burma Past and Present *was published, her name appeared as 'Mrs Ernest Hart'. She was the wife of a distinguished surgeon, medical journalist, and reformer, and had herself been engaged in medical work and published a book called* Diet in Sickness and in Health. *But she was known neither as a writer nor as a traveller. When she accompanied her husband on a tour through Burma in the spring of 1895, she tells us she had no intention of writing a book about the country. The couple were travelling 'solely in the pursuit of health and enjoyment'. She did record some impressions which were published as articles in British journals, but it was only when she realized the extent of public ignorance about Burma that she 'undertook the task of writing a book on the subject'.*

A few years after the annexation of Upper Burma in 1886, British and American tourists (known at the time as 'globe-trotters') were arriving there by steamer, by train and even by bicycle. Unlike the typical British traveller of her day, Mrs Hart observed people at their everyday tasks and listened sympathetically to what they said. Many of those in Upper Burma, for instance, deeply regretted that they had lost their king and court, and the loss saddened her too. She concluded her book with the hope that Burma would 'give the world the example of a people who know how to be happy without caring incessantly to toil, and to be joyous without desiring insatiably to possess'. In this extract we can see that, as a lady of the Victorian era, Alice was particularly impressed by the happiness of her Burman counterparts, who enjoyed far greater social freedoms than she herself possessed.

WOMEN in Burma are probably freer and happier than they are anywhere else in the world. Though Burma is bordered on one side by China, where women are held in contempt, and on the other by India, where they are kept in the strictest seclusion, Burmese women have achieved for themselves and have been permitted by their men to attain, a freedom of life and action that has no parallel among Oriental peoples. The secret lies, perhaps, in the fact that the Burmese woman is active and industrious while the Burmese man is indolent and often a recluse. Becoming, therefore, both by taste and by habit the money-earner, the bargainer and the financier of the household, she has asserted and obtained for herself the right to hold what she wins and the respect due to one who can and does direct and control. Things are strangely reversed in Burma, for here we see man as the religious soul of the nation and woman its brain.

Burmese women are born traders, and it is more often the wife than the husband who drives the bargain with the English buyer for the paddy harvest, or, at any rate, she is present on the occasion and helps her easy-going husband to stand firm. So highly is trading esteemed, that a daughter of well-to-do parents, and even a young married woman, will set up a booth in the bazaar, and, dressed in a bright silk tamein [skirt] and white jacket, with a flower jauntily stuck into her coiled black tresses, she will start every morning with a tray of sweetmeats, fruit, or toys on her head, and, with a gaiety and grace born of the sunshine and the bounteousness of the land, will push a brisk trade all through the short and sunny day. The earnings thus made are the woman's own, and cannot be touched by her husband.

English officials told me that contracts for army forage and for timber were often made with women-traders, and that they well understood the art of 'holding up the market'.

The education of women was in times gone by *nil*, and all that is thought necessary to teach them at present is to read and write. To be pretty, to be religious, to be amiable and gay-hearted, and to have a good business instinct, are all that is demanded of a woman in Burma; presently, when she comes to learn the advantages which education confers in dealing with the ubiquitous foreigner, she will doubtless demand it as her right. At present she fulfils all expectations. To charm is her openly avowed aim, and few things human are more charming than a group of Burmese women going up to the pagoda to worship at a festival. With her rainbow-tinted silk tamein fastened tightly round her slender figure, her spotlessly clean short jacket modestly covering the bosom, and with her abundant black tresses smoothly coiled on the top of her head, in the braids of which nestles a bouquet of sweet-smelling flowers, the Burmese young woman knows full well she is an object to be admired.

Perfectly well pleased with herself and contented with her world as it is, she gaily laughs and chats with her companions while puffing from time to time at an immense green cheroot. Amiable she is, as a matter of course, for are not the laws of Manu and Burma very particular in their denunciation of all who speak harshly and who use abusive words? Besides, what is there to vex her soul? She has not the thousand and one cares which harass the poor European housewife. Her home, built of bamboo and plaited mats, costs but a few rupees to erect, and can easily be restored if burnt down in a fire or shaken down in an earthquake. Her household goods can be numbered on her five fingers, and could be carried on her back. Her boys are taught free at the monastery, and till her girls are old enough to have their ears bored, clothing for them is an item of the smallest expenditure, for little children are generally seen wearing nothing but a 'necklace and a smile'. Her stall at the bazaar will give her earnings enough to buy the brightest silk tamein to wear at the next pagoda festival or boat race, and perhaps the money to win 'merit' by purchasing packets of gold leaf to plaster on the stately statue of the holy Gautauma at the next full moon. Her husband treats her well; if not, if he neglects her, fails to provide for her, is unkind or abusive, she has but to go before the nearest magistrate and state her case, and he will grant a divorce, and she can depart with all her possessions and earnings. She has every reason to be happy, and to laugh gaily from pure light-heartedness as she carries her tray of goods to the bazaar, or her offering of fruit and flowers and gold-leaf to the pagoda.

Marriage in Burma is an affair of the heart. More often than not a Burmese girl chooses her own husband, but she is frequently aided in the selection by her parents, or by a go-between called an *oung bwé*. There are plenty of opportunities given for the meeting of young people of both sexes at the pagoda festivals, at the pwés or public plays, and at friends' houses on the occasions of marriages and funerals. Courting takes place in the evening, and a suitor for a girl's hand visits her at her father's house generally after eight o'clock. He does not come alone, but with his friends and supporters. The girl receives her lover alone or accompanied by a friend, and dressed in her best. The parents retire to another room, but, though not present at the interview, a bamboo house does not admit of secrecy, and the mother probably sees and hears all that goes on. Presents are exchanged, but not kisses and caresses, as these would be thought highly improper. When the young people have made up their minds to marry, the parents' consent is asked, and is almost invariably given, even though the intended husband may be very young, and not yet in a position to support a wife. But the happy-go-lucky Burman has great sympathy with love's young dream, and arrangements are made to take the young couple into the house of the parents, either of the bride or the bridegroom, for the first few years, till the husband can afford to start a separate establishment. The marriage ceremony is not religious, the celibate Buddhist monks taking no part in such mundane affairs; but a great feast is given by the bride's parents, and the public pledging of troth is virtually the marriage ceremony. It is said that these marriages of boy and girl in the heyday of life and love are generally happy; warm family affection is one of the national traits of character, and kindness to one another is a religion and a habit.

The following funeral dirge, written by a Rangoon man on the death of his wife, breathes the spirit of the purest devotion, as we Westerns understand it. The translation is by the Burmese scholar, Shway Yoe:–

Gone, gone art thou, sweet wife, gone far away,
    Fair still and charmful, stretched on thy cold bier,
As erst thou wert upon that joyous day
    When first I wed thee, gladsome brought thee here,
And joyed to think that thou wert mine. Ah, me!
    The butterfly's silk wings are shred no more,
Ne'er more to rest upon thy head, Mah Mee—
    Sweet name for wife affectionate! Deplore
Her death, ye Nats that forests rule and streams,
    The hills and vales, the greater ye who guard
The sacred law, the holy shrines, the beams
    Of silent moon, and sunlight baking hard
The hot scorched earth, nor scorched more and seared
    Than is the parchment of my tortured heart.

Ay, thou wert mine when last I trod the earth,
    Ere yet, all sinful, I was born a man;
And yet again, in yet another birth,
    I'll claim thee, when maybe a happier Kan,
A Fairer sum of merit, hardly won,
    Will lead us on, linked-armed to linkéd death,
That, so progressing, joyful may we run
    Through all life's changes, and with single breath,
Through heavens and Zahn and Rupa we may bound
    To Neh'ban, blissful home of rest.

    Bow me low, grant me the holy calm.

Marriage in Burma is easily contracted. A girl cannot marry before she is twenty without the consent of her parents or guardians. Should she not, however, obtain this consent, the marriage is considered valid after three elopements. Marriage is viewed by the Burmans in the light of a partnership in which the wife has equal rights with the husband; theoretically the husband is lord of his wife, and has the control of the household, the children, and the family property, but this power cannot be exercised arbitrarily without consultation with the wife, and as she is often the bread-winner, her wishes are naturally deferred to.

The equality of women in marriage is particularly shown in the disposition of property. Property is divided into personal and joint. There has been no need in Burma for a Married Woman's Property Act, for all property belonging to a woman before marriage remains hers absolutely when she becomes a wife. The joint property consists of bequests by the parents or husband at the time of marriage for joint purposes, all profits arising since marriage from the employment or investment of the separate property of either husband or wife, and all property acquired by their mutual skill and industry. The husband cannot sell or alienate the joint property of himself and his wife without her consent or against her will, except when he manages the business or acts as her agent; also during the continuance of marriage neither the husband nor wife has the right to the exclusive possession of the joint property. The fact, that in Burma all the male population pass through the phongyee kioungs or monasteries, and must for a certain time don the yellow robe and become monks, and also that an immense number of men remain monks and lead celibate lives, has led to women taking a very active part in business, and hence has arisen the idea of an equal partnership in marriage. If, however, the wife is not engaged in business, it is acknowledged that she fulfils her part in the partnership by bearing the children and attending to the domestic comfort, and she still retains her control over the joint property.

Divorce is obtained with facility. Buddhist law recognises the fallibility of man, and the fact that in marriage, as in everything else, he may act in error, and should therefore have the opportunity given of retrieving his mistake. To obtain divorce in Burma, it is simply necessary for the parties to agree together that their marriage or partnership should be dissolved. The marriage is thereupon annulled; each takes their separate property; they divide the joint property equally, the husband takes the male children and the wife the female. There is no scandal, and no opprobrium is incurred. Should only one party insist on separation, and there is no fault on the other side, the party who does not wish to separate retains the joint property. Marriage cannot, however, be put an end to simply at the caprice of one of the parties. Polygamy is allowed by the Buddhist law, though the practice is regarded with disfavour by the Burmese people. The taking of a lesser wife is not of itself considered a sufficient cause of divorce by the first wife. Desertion is a valid reason; if a husband leaves his wife for three years and does not maintain her, or a wife her husband for one year because she has no affection for him, then 'they shall not claim each other as husband and wife; let them have the right to separate and marry again'.

Exceptions are made in the case where the husband absents himself to trade, to fight, or to study, in which cases the wife has to wait eight, seven, or six years respectively before she can marry again. If a married man enters a monastery, the marriage is dissolved. Constant ill-treatment on the part of a husband is sufficient cause for divorce, but not petty quarrels. A husband may put away his wife or take another if she has no children or has only female children; if she has leprosy or disease, if her conduct is bad, and if she has no love for her husband. If a husband is a drunkard, gambler, or better, or is immoral, and has three times in the presence of good men made a written engagement to reform and yet continues these evil practices, his wife may put him away. If the divorce is due to the fault of one party, he or she is not entitled to any share in the joint property. The partition of the property is the actual test of divorce, for according to the Dhamma, 'If a husband and wife have separated and no division of property has taken place, neither shall be free to live with another man or woman. But if the property has been divided they may do so. Thus Manu has decided.' In every case the husband takes the male children and the woman the female.

Marriages so easily made and so easily broken must inevitably lead to a certain looseness as regards the marriage tie; but there are several points of view in the Buddhist law which may be commended to Western peoples, namely, the equal status of women in marriage, the equal control and

253

partition of the joint property, the division of the children of the marriage among the parents, and also the possibility of obtaining divorce without public scandal. As a matter of fact, marriages are happy in Burma, as a rule, and, whatever may be said to the contrary, illegitimate children are rare, except as the Eurasian offspring of Christian fathers, whose example is bitterly deplored by those who desire to see the Burmans take a higher standard.

Babies are well taken care of, and many are the pretty lullabies composed to lull them to sleep—a few verses from one of which, translated by Shway Yoe, I am tempted to give:–

> Sweet, my babe, your father's coming,
> Rest and hear the songs I'm humming;
> He will come and gently tend you,
> Rock your cot and safe defend you....

Mrs Ernest Hart, *Picturesque Burma, Past and Present*, J. M. Dent, London, 1897, pp. 135–42.

35
The Fascinating Burmese Woman

SIR FREDERICK TREVES

The young Frederick Treves (1853–1923) studied medicine at London Hospital where he became not only a full surgeon but also famous nationally as 'demonstrator' of anatomy. He was appointed as surgeon to Queen Victoria, and then to the two kings who succeeded her. He achieved an international reputation when he performed a successful appendectomy upon King Edward VII. He was also well-known for his treatment of the unfortunate 'Elephant Man', about whom a film was made some years ago. First knighted and then made a baronet, he followed up his earlier writings (mainly surgery textbooks and articles) with travel books and reminiscences.

In 1903, Sir Frederick set out by steamer on a tour that included stays in India, Ceylon, and Burma besides further ports of call on the way to California. In Burma his impressions tended to be extreme: on the one hand he found the

*architecture of the king's palace in Mandalay 'puerile' and
'pitiable', and on the other he could hardly find enough words
of praise for 'the fascinating Burmese woman'.*

IT is to be regretted that the traveller's first acquaintance
with the fascinating Burmese woman will probably be
made in Rangoon, as she is looking at French hats in a
European shop, or as she is waiting for a train at a distasteful
railway station.

The first glimpse of her should be on an old road, in a
Burmese town—such a town as has remained unsullied by
the West—where she would be found among surroundings
which have known no change for centuries, and which are,
above all, her own. The Burmese woman belongs to Burmah
of the old world, over which the wind of change has not yet
blown.

I can recall one such vision of the lady of the land in the
country as it was. There was inland a grey, still road, shaded
by trees and hushed by many palms, which made of the way
a sleepy aisle. Small pools and splashes of sunshine lay in the
road as if it had rained gold. Among the columns of the
palms, low houses with walls of mat and roofs of velvet were
dozing in the shadows. An inquisitive creeper had climbed to
a verandah, and had tumbled over the slender handrail into
the passage. Around each house was a yellow palisade of
bamboo lattice-work, and against such a fence two naked
children were leaning. The road itself was deserted. At one
end of it a far-off pagoda of gilt shone in a jagged gap of blue
sky.

From out of the cloister of the wood a girl came, who
halted for a moment in the road, hesitating which way she
should turn. She stood erect, like a queen. Her eyes were
dark and expressive, and there was a smiling mouth with
white teeth. Glossy black hair, with a red rose in it, made the
covering of her head. A simple jacket of white linen hung
from her shapely shoulders, and from her waist to her naked
feet was a skirt of glistening pink silk that sketched in simplest lines her perfect form. Two plain gold bangles on her
wrist complete the account of her—a delicate, cool little
figure, with a splash of sunshine at her feet, and the vision of
the pagoda at the road's end. Such is the lady of the land.

That her face is Mongolian in type is evident enough. She may hardly be pretty if judged by a European standard, but by no standard can it be declared that she is other than most fascinating. Her eyes, at least, are absolutely beautiful. Her expression is alert, vivacious, cheerful, so that she looks the embodiment of good temper. She is as neat as a nun, and as quaint as a Puritan maiden, but there is too much coquettishness about her to allow of these comparisons being made complete. She is a brilliant little personage, graceful in her slightest movement, infinitely feminine, full to her lips with the sparkle of life, yet dignified and even stately. She walks with a swing of her arms and a roll of her shoulders which mark her as one who thinks well of herself, and intends that all others should hold to the same belief.

She has excuse for some dignity of bearing, for it is the Burmese woman, and not the Burmese man, who is at the head of affairs. What business is to be done she does. She is ever astir in the market, buying and selling, since it is the woman who sits at the receipt of custom. Her husband or her brother may carry bales of silk for her, may unpack her cases of silver, may bring vegetables in from the country to her stall, but it is she who guides the enterprise and who manages the trading. She does it because she does it well, and because 'he' is so indolent and uncertain.

She sits on a low, yellow mat in her stall, and holds up to you a piece of silk. Her hands are pretty, and there are many gold bangles on her wrists. A sleek head and smiling eyes are visible above the rim of the silk. She holds it up as a child would hold up its last new toy for admiration. You ask the price of this trifle of amber and rose, and she shyly suggests a quite fantastic sum, as if she were playing at 'keeping shop'.

You propose to give her half the amount she has ventured upon. This amuses her beyond words. She is filled with laughter, for the jest is evidently much to her liking. Smiling, moreover, becomes her, as her teeth are exquisite. There is more movement of shapely fingers and of supple wrists; the silk is dropped, and another piece is held up with mute questioning. You renew the offer of half the price named for the piece first shown. She again becomes radiant with laughter, and hides her mouth behind the edge of the outstretched stuff. With infinite shyness she suggests a less extreme mutilation of her original price. She half whispers the sum, as if it were a possible answer to some absurd conundrum. You finally take the silk for exactly one half of the sum originally discussed. She is perfectly delighted, and appears to regard the long bargaining as the best of fun.

It is all excellent fooling, this playing at 'keeping shop' by a picturesque woman instead of by a child, but the woman—like the child—is never a loser at the simple game.

The ever-courteous little silk mercer is, without doubt, an alert woman of business, and yet matter-of-fact people who know her say she is careless, pleasure-loving, and hopelessly improvident. It would seem, then, that she is still a child, even when she is not playing at 'keeping shop'.

The blue-stocking lecturer on woman's rights should have one of these light-hearted, stockingless little people on the platform with her as an example. Harsh critics are apt to describe such a lecturer as sour of aspect, and also as lean, spectacled, and moustached. If there be any truth in this, the contrast between the advocate of women's rights and the possessor of them might be vivid. The association of the two may, however, arouse the suggestion that violent and per-spiring speech, a creaking voice, and a bony and mittened fist are less strong aids to argument than an amiable capacity and a readiness to undertake loyally whatever the particular hand may find to do.

There is in the world one matter of taste upon which unan-imity of opinion can never be obtained, and that is on the subject of woman's dress. It may as well, therefore, be stated—without the least hope of carrying conviction—that the dress of the Burmese woman is as nearly perfect as any female costume can be.

Its chief claim to perfection is that it is exquisitely, divinely simple. This will not appeal to the Western lady, who may hold that strict simplicity is only becoming to the workhouse inmate. The dress of the Burmese woman consists of a white linen jacket of the plainest possible type, without collars, ties, or cuffs, and a skirt of unstudied silk wrapped closely round the body down to the feet. This robe is marred by neither flounce nor frill, and, so far as the uninitiated can tell, it has escaped even the touch of needle or thread. Sandals to the feet and gold bangles to the wrist complete the costume.

Whatever may be the artistic value of this attire, it can at least claim to be perfect from the standpoint of health.

The Burmese woman 'does' her hair also with equal simplicity, in a neat coil severely fastened by the turning of the same upon itself. It displays the outline of her head with perfection, and no hair arrangement of the ancient Greeks could be more 'classical'. A fresh flower, or, possibly, a comb is the sole ornament. There is no attempt to contort the human hair into puffs or rolls, or to make of it a grotesque, meaningless structure, held up by pins and cords and undermined by frowsy pads.

The dress of this picturesque people never varies. The Burmese woman knows nothing about 'trimmings', nothing about 'style', and her mind is not kept in a state of unrest by the contemplation of the anxious problems which centre about hats.

Here is a country of intelligent women where there is no such thing as fashion, and, therefore, none of the hopes, the petty strivings, and the sorrows which depend upon the blind pursuit of what is fashionable. Women reputed to be more civilised have to dress as the gospel of the fashion-plate dictates. A mysterious being, with the wand of the 'latest style', drives them across the common of their little world, as a bumpkin drives a company of stiff-necked, cackling geese. No matter what the style may be so long as it is late. There is no option, no need of judgment; the fashion seekers will all go as they are driven so long as the gooseherd's stick embodies the last new thing.

The Burmese woman allows herself some latitude only in the matter of colour. Her silks incline to tints of pink and rose, of saffron and pale green. In the choice of these each follows her own taste. These dainty, delicate colours come as an agreeable relief to the unvarying blues and reds which seem to encompass the invention of the woman of India.

There are two other matters to be noted in connection with the woman of the country. She seems to be endowed with the privilege of preserving the youthfulness of her figure into advanced age. Indeed, it is hard to say with what lapse of years she will lose the quite girlish outline, the well-modelled shoulders and the slender hips.

Finally, she has at least one weakness, to wit, the smoking of Brobdingnagian cigars as large as wax candles from an

'A Burmese Lady', from Noel F. Singer, *Burmah*, Kiscadale, Gartmore, 1993.

altar. Some are white, some are green. They are compounded of tobacco and vague herbs, but however pleasant they may be to smoke, they spoil the pretty curves of a much pleasanter mouth.

The Other Side of the Lantern, Cassell, London, 1905, pp. 196–200.

36
Aung San Suu Kyi

MICHAEL ARIS

On 19 July 1947, a few months before the British transfer of power, the main architect of Burmese independence was tragically assassinated by gunmen in the pay of a political rival. The victim was Aung San, a figure still revered by a grateful Burmese people. At that time his little daughter Aung San Suu Kyi was just two years old.

When she was a fifteen-year-old schoolgirl she went to India with her mother, who had been appointed ambassador to Nehru's government. When the time came to further her studies she went to England where she stayed with British friends of the family. During her undergraduate years at Oxford she did some travelling, and soon after graduating went to New York and served in the UN Secretariat for three years. She then married Michael Aris and spent a year with him in Bhutan, where he had been working as a royal tutor, government translator, and historical researcher. Once back in England, the couple settled down to family and academic life, interspersed with trips to Rangoon to see Aung San Suu Kyi's distinguished mother, Daw Khin Kyi.

Then in 1988 Burma began to seethe with resentment at the continuing incompetence and brutality of the military regime headed by General Ne Win. The following passage is taken from Michael Aris' introduction to a book of his wife's writings. He outlines the way in which his wife came to unify and lead the popular movement for human rights and democracy in Burma.

IT was a quiet evening in Oxford like many others, the last day of March 1988. Our sons were already in bed and we were reading when the telephone rang. Suu picked up the phone to learn that her mother had suffered a severe stroke. She put the phone down and at once started to pack. I had a premonition that our lives would change for ever. Two days later Suu was many thousands of miles away at her mother's bedside in Rangoon.

After three months helping to tend her mother in the hospital day and night, it became clear to Suu and the doctors that her condition would not improve and Suu decided to bring her back to the family home in Rangoon. The familiar surroundings and the help of a dedicated medical team promised to ensure that her remaining days would be peaceful. When Alexander and Kim's summer terms finished at Oxford we flew out to Rangoon to find the house an island of peace and order under Suu's firm, loving control. The study downstairs had been transformed into a hospital ward and the old lady's spirits rallied when she knew her grandsons had arrived.

In the preceding months the students had begun to take to the streets calling for radical change. They had already met with lethal violence at the hands of the authorities. In one incident forty-one wounded students had suffocated to death in a police van. What ignited the whole country just the day after the boys and I arrived was an extraordinary and unexpected speech given by the man who had ruled Burma since he led a military coup in 1962. On 23 July, Ne Win, the general who had turned civilian, announced to a specially convened congress of his Burma Socialist Programme Party that he was resigning forthwith and that a referendum on Burma's political future would be held. I can still remember watching with Suu the scene in the congress as it was shown on state television. She, like the whole country, was electrified. The people at last had a chance to take control of their own destinies. I think it was at this moment more than any other that Suu made up her mind to step forward. However, the idea had gradually taken shape in her mind during the previous fifteen weeks.

In reality, from her earliest childhood, Suu has been deeply preoccupied with the question of what she might do to help her people. She never for a minute forgot that she was the daughter of Burma's national hero, Aung San. It was he who led the struggle for independence from British colonial rule and from the Japanese occupation. Trained by the Japanese during the Second World War, he and his associates among the legendary 'Thirty Comrades' entered Burma with the invading Japanese army who promised independence. When that promise proved false he went underground to lead the resistance with the Burma Independence Army he had created. He assisted the re-invading Allies, and after the war negotiated with Clement Attlee's Labour government for final independence. But he and practically his entire cabinet in the provisional government were gunned down on 19 July 1947 just a few months before the transfer of power. A jealous political rival masterminded the assassination.

Suu, who was born on 19 June 1945, has only the dimmest recollections of her father. However, everything she has learned about him inclined her to believe in his selfless courage and his vision of a free and democratic Burma. Some would say she became obsessed with the image of the father she never knew. At Oxford she steadily acquired a large collection of books and papers in Burmese and English about him. There is a certain inevitability in the way she, like him, has now become an icon of popular hope and longing. In the daughter as in the father there seems an extraordinary coincidence of legend and reality, of word and deed. And yet prior to 1988 it had never been her intention to strive for anything quite so momentous. When she left Oxford to care for her mother she had been set on writing a doctoral thesis on Burmese literature for London University. (A draft chapter is on this computer disk as I write, and I believe she is still registered at the School of Oriental and African Studies as a postgraduate student.) She had also entertained hopes of one day setting up an international scholarship scheme for Burmese students and a network of public libraries in Burma.

Nevertheless, she always used to say to me that if her people ever needed her, she would not fail them....

So it came as no surprise when Suu told me she was resolved to enter the struggle. The promise to support her decision which I had given in advance so many years ago now had to be fulfilled. Like Suu perhaps, I had imagined that if a day of reckoning were to come, it would happen later in life when our children were grown up. But fate and history never seem to work in orderly ways. Timings are unpredictable and do not wait upon convenience. Moreover, the laws of human history are too uncertain to be used as a basis for action. All that Suu had to draw on were her very finely cultivated sense of commitment and her powers of reason. But she was also blessed and burdened with her unique status as the daughter of the national hero. Although the regime has appropriated his image for their own purposes, his reputation was still inviolate in the hearts of the common people. Moreover Suu had never lost her Burmese identity and values through all the years abroad. Her knowledge of the Burmese heritage, her wonderful fluency in her own language and, very important, her refusal to give up her Burmese citizenship and passport despite her marriage to an Englishman—all these factors conspired with the sad circumstances of her mother's final illness to make her engagement unavoidable.

In the nationwide turbulence which followed Ne Win's resignation on 23 July 1988 and the immediate refusal by his party to agree to a referendum on Burma's future, Suu's house quickly became the main centre of political activity in the country and the scene of such continuous comings and goings as the curfew allowed. Every conceivable type of activist from all walks of life and all generations poured in. Suu talked to them all about human rights, an expression which had little currency in Burma till then. She began to take her first steps into the maelstrom beyond her gates. Alexander, Kim and I were behind her when she addressed a colossal rally at the Shwedagon Pagoda for the first time on 26 August.

Despite all the frenetic activity in her house, it never really lost the sense of being a haven of love and care. Suu is an astonishing person by any standards, and I think I can say I know her after twenty years of marriage, but I shall never quite understand how she managed to divide her efforts so equally between the devoted care of her incapacitated, dying mother and all the activity which brought her the leadership of the struggle for human rights and democracy in her country. It has something to do with her inflexible sense of duty

Aung San Suu Kyi addressing a rally.

and her sure grasp of what is right and wrong—qualities which can sit as a dead weight on some shoulders but which she carries with such grace.

By the time Suu's mother died on 27 December, nine months after her first stroke, it seemed as if several empires had come and gone. The carnival of mass demonstrations had turned repeatedly to bloodshed as the authorities tried to stem the tide of revolt sweeping the country. I shall not quickly forget the surge of hope and fear, the elation followed by near despair, the prolonged gunfire in the streets and the doves cooing in the garden through it all.

Three heads of state were forced by the people's movement to resign in quick succession, though ultimate power remained vested in the military officers loyal to Ne Win. The army controlled by those officers finally staged a coup on 18 September and brought in their State Law and Order Restoration Council (SLORC). They reiterated the promise of free and fair elections while clearing the streets with gunfire. Suu and her close associates promptly formed their party, the National League for Democracy (NLD).

It was the young people who already belonged to her party who brought order to the milling crowds of thousands who came to attend her mother's funeral on 2 January 1989. Having been forced out of the country some weeks earlier, I was allowed to return to Rangoon to be with Suu when her mother died. I flew in from Bangkok with our sons, whose school terms had again finished. Suu's only surviving brother was even allowed to come from America for the funeral, though he was now an American citizen to whom the authorities would normally deny a visit.

The negotiations and arrangements for the funeral of the widow of the national hero were conducted in exemplary fashion. It was the only occasion when the authorities offered Suu any co-operation, realizing that if they failed in this the consequences might be disastrous. Soldiers, students and politicians combined with Suu to make orderly plans in a way that made everyone realize what the country would achieve if unity could be won under her leadership. But the co-operation of the military was, alas, to prove very short-lived. Suu's growing prestige and popularity seemed to strike at the very heart of all that the army had come to represent. The constant appeals for dialogue and understanding which she issued before and after this occasion all went unheeded.

In the next seven months Suu consolidated her party's strength by touring almost the entire country. The boys and I were back at Oxford by then. Although Suu wrote as often as she possibly could, we were more dependent for news on the press reports than on her letters. We would read in the papers of the official harassment and vilification she endured at the hands of the authorities. The effect of this on the people was opposite to the one intended: the more she was attacked, the more the people flocked to her banner.

With hindsight it is easy to see why she and her party were perceived as the main threat to all the interests vested in the old system. The authorities had counted on the scores of new parties to produce a split parliament which they could dominate in any fashion they pleased. The head of state, General Saw Maung, was on record as saying he expected the next government to be a coalition of many parties. The prospect of a single party sweeping the board went counter to all they hoped for.

I shall not attempt to piece together here Suu's policies, movements and activities in this period. I was not with her and cannot speak from first-hand experience. The task must wait for future historians when time, distance and access to all the sources now hidden enable a dispassionate appraisal. But I do not think they will find cause to suggest that Suu acted with anything but dedication to a selfless cause. She brought overwhelming unity to a spontaneous, hitherto leaderless revolt. She insisted at all times that the movement should be based on a non-violent struggle for human rights as the primary object. She spoke to the common people of her country as they had not been spoken to for so long—as individuals worthy of love and respect. In a prolonged campaign of civil disobedience she flouted a great number of the Draconian measures introduced by the authorities. She wrote countless letters to the authorities complaining of their excesses—but with no response. At the same time she constantly begged them to open a proper dialogue—but to no effect at all.

Matters came to a head in July 1989. In the days leading up to the annual Martyrs' Day on the 19th, when the death of her father and his cabinet is traditionally commemorated, Suu had decided to point her finger at the main obstacle to political change. She voiced the belief, shared by many but never spoken in public, that the army was still being controlled by the retired general Ne Win. She expressed the doubt that the ruling junta ever intended to keep their promise of transferring power to a civilian government. When she announced her plan to lead a march to pay tribute to the martyrs, the authorities moved quickly to fill the streets with troops. Faced again with the prospect of terrible bloodshed in Rangoon, Suu called off the march.

Our sons Alexander and Kim had already joined Suu from their schools in Oxford, their third trip since the whole drama began to unfold. I could not come with them because my own father had just died in Scotland. On 20 July I heard the news that Suu had been placed under house arrest. I had absolutely no idea of her condition or that of the boys, but very fortunately I had a valid visa for Burma in my passport. I informed the authorities of my plan to come out to Rangoon right away.

As the plane taxied to a halt at Mingaladon Airport I could see a lot of military activity on the tarmac. The plane was surrounded by troops and as I walked down the gangplank I was quickly identified and escorted away to the VIP lounge. The British Embassy official who had come to meet me was unable to make contact. For twenty-two days I effectively disappeared from sight. Nobody knew what had happened to me. The British press carried stories about how an Oxford don had gone missing. My family in England was extremely worried. The British government and the European Community pressed very hard for consular contact, but to no avail. I had vanished.

The story of what really happened in those three weeks, perhaps the greatest single crisis we have so far had to face as a family, could occupy a whole book, but let me be brief. The very personable military officer who met me at the airport said that if I agreed to abide by the same terms under which Suu had been placed under detention I could stay with her and the boys. Those terms included no contact with any embassy or any person engaged in politics. I was able to say truthfully that I had only come to be with the family and saw no difficulty in abiding by these terms. We drove off from the airport to find the house surrounded by troops. The gates were opened and we drove in. I had no idea what to expect.

I arrived to find Suu in the third day of a hunger strike. Her single demand was that she should be allowed to go to prison with all of her young supporters who had been taken away from her compound when the authorities arrested her. She believed her presence with them in prison would afford them some protection from maltreatment. She took her last meal on the evening of 20 July, the day of her arrest, and for the following twelve days until almost noon on 1 August she accepted only water. On that day a military officer came to give her his personal assurance, on behalf of the authorities, that her young people would not be tortured and that the cases against them would be heard by due process of law. She accepted this compromise, and the doctors who had been deputed to attend her, whose treatment she had hitherto refused, immediately put her on an intravenous drip with her consent. She had lost twelve pounds in weight. I still do not know if the authorities kept their promise.

In all this, Suu had been very calm and the boys too. She had spent the days of her fast resting quietly, reading and talking to us. I was less calm, though I tried to pretend to be. Acting as go-between I had even been brought to a grand meeting in Rangoon City Hall in front of cameras to present Suu's demands to the Rangoon Command Commander and a room full of officers and through them to the SLORC leadership. At all times I met with nothing but courtesy. Eleven days after Suu ended her fast I was finally escorted to see the British Consul in a military guesthouse. In the presence of SLORC officials I confirmed the whole story of Suu's hunger strike which had already somehow leaked out. Indeed, I later discovered that the story had appeared in the Asia-Pacific edition of *Time* magazine with her picture on the cover.

Suu recovered her weight and strength in the days ahead. The crisis had passed and the tension eased. The boys learned martial arts from the guards. We put the house in order. I made arrangements with the authorities to send Suu parcels from England and to exchange letters with her. Things seemed to be on quite an even keel by the time the Oxford term loomed upon us once again. We left for England on 2 September.

It was the last time the boys were allowed to see their mother. Some days after we arrived in England the Burmese Embassy in London informed me that the boys' Burmese passports were invalid and now cancelled since they were not entitled to Burmese citizenship. All attempts to obtain visas on their new British passports have failed. Very obviously the plan was to break Suu's spirit by separating her from her children in the hope she would accept permanent exile. I myself was allowed to return once more to be with her for a fortnight the following Christmas. It seems the authorities had hoped I would try to persuade her to leave with me. In fact, knowing the strength of Suu's determination, I had not even thought of doing this. Perhaps at that moment they realized I was no longer useful to their purpose.

The days I spent alone with her that last time, completely isolated from the world, are among my happiest memories of our many years of marriage. It was wonderfully peaceful. Suu had established a strict regime of exercise, study and piano which I managed to disrupt. She was memorizing a number of Buddhist sutras. I produced Christmas presents I had brought one by one to spread them out over several days. We had all the time in the world to talk about many things. I did not suspect this would be the last time we would be together for the foreseeable future.

While I was there the authorities brought in papers from her party concerning the elections. She was to sign them if she agreed to stand for election in spite of her incarceration. She did so. But several weeks later it was learnt that the SLORC had contrived to rule that her candidacy was invalid. It made no difference in the end to the election results. On 27 May 1990 the people of Burma went to the polls and voted for the party she had founded and led. In an extraordinary landslide victory the National League for Democracy won 392 of the 485 seats contested, more than 80 per cent. Contrary to expectations, the polling was totally free and fair. The reason why the elections were allowed to take place at all seems to have been because the SLORC even then believed no single party could win. But Suu had always sensed that if a free election did take place, then her party would certainly gain the victory.... Again she appeared on the cover of *Time* magazine in Asia. The photograph must have been taken during one of her long campaign trips. Her lips are cracked and her eyes sore with dust.

The vote was a personal one for her: often the voters knew nothing about their candidate except that he represented Suu. Locked away for ten months before the elections, her place in the hearts of the Burmese had meanwhile only grown stronger. There is a great irony in this, for she had become the focus of a personality cult which she would have been the first to decry. Loyalty to principles, she had often said, was more important than loyalty to individuals. But she personified in the fullest measure the principles she and everyone else were striving for and so the people voted for her.

In the days which followed there was great expectancy that the ruling junta would release her from detention and announce a timetable to transfer power to the National League for Democracy. Back in Oxford I thought at the very least they might allow the boys and me to visit her again. But it was not to be. I received a final letter from her dated 17 July 1990 in which she asked me for copies of the Indian epics, the *Ramayana* and the *Mahabharata*. She commented on the fact that there was much more humour in the Thai and Cambodian depiction of the monkey-king Hanuman than in the original Indian version. Her letter was otherwise concerned with family matters and things she wanted me to send her. It was the last we received from her. Every attempt since then to regain contact has failed.

A great number of people have tried their best to persuade the junta to relent and allow us access to Suu, but so far to no avail. As I write these words it is more than two years since our sons last saw their mother, a year and nearly ten months since I was with her, and a year and nearly two months since she was last able to write to us. The SLORC does its best to conceal the completeness of her isolation, refusing even to call it house arrest but instead 'restricted residence'. They say she is free to rejoin her family at any time, refusing to accept that in spite of her British husband she is wholly Burmese, and that the Burmese people have amply demonstrated that they hold her as their own and as the talisman of their future freedom.

Events have proved her right. The regime appears to have no intention of transferring power in the foreseeable future. There is much official talk of the need for a new constitution before power can be transferred but no timetable has been announced to draw one up. The free elections took place, bestowing a clear mandate—but nothing has happened. Suu is still quite alone.

Postscript

(Seventeen days after writing these words Michael Aris received a telephone call from the Norwegian Nobel Committee to announce in advance that his wife Aung San Suu Kyi was being awarded the Nobel Peace Prize in recognition of her non-violent struggle for the restoration of human rights in Burma. She was by then in her third year of detention at the hands of Burma's military rulers, who had repeatedly offered to release her if she undertook to go into permanent exile. This she refused—and continues to refuse—to do. As she could not travel to Oslo to collect her prize for fear of being refused re-entry to her beloved country, her family attended in her stead. From May 1992 to January 1995 her husband and sons were allowed to pay her regular visits while her detention continued. Then, after nearly six years of house arrest, she was released on 10 July 1995. Her constant call for negotiated settlement of Burma's political problems has yet to be heeded by the military authorities.—Comp.)

Introduction by Michael Aris to *Freedom from Fear: and Other Writings*, by Aung San Suu Kyi, Penguin Books, Harmondsworth, 1991; 2nd edn., 1995; copyright © Michael Aris, 1991, pp. xvii–xxvii.

Some Elements of Burman Culture

37
Daily Life in the 1830s

HOWARD MALCOM

'*The* world *is the field over which the eye of the Christian wanders*', *thought Howard Malcom. Along with his fellow passengers, he was watching a great city recede as their sailing ship left Boston Harbour on a fine day in September 1835 and headed south in order to catch the trade winds that would carry the vessel eastwards. Not until 21 February 1836 did it cast anchor at Amherst (now Kyaik-kami) on the Tenasserim coast.*

He was an energetic American Baptist missionary, and soon he had visited all the major towns of Tenasserim which by now was British territory. On 14 June he and Mr Howard, an interpreter, set out from Rangoon in a 14-metre river-boat manned by Burmans; they headed upstream for Ava, the capital of the kingdom of Burma, and on the way they distributed Christian tracts in 82 locations and to 657 vessels. Everywhere people clamoured for these booklets, but Malcom soon realized that this was only because the tracts were novel in shape and were made of paper—not like the long folding documents of palm-leaf or black pasteboard that people were used to.

Arriving in Ava after a three-week voyage, Malcom stayed in the area for a month and later travelled through Arakan. In all his journeyings he was observant, carefully noting and sometimes drawing what he saw, and it was with the aid of such notes that he composed the account of his travels in Burma. In the extract below, he describes some everyday

272

features of Burman life in the closing years of the reign of King Ba-gyi-daw. (For a look at this king at the beginning of his reign, see Passage 8 above.)

THE favourite food, in common with all India and China, and universally used by all who can afford it, is rice. This is often eaten without any addition whatever, but generally with a nice curry, and sauces of various stewed melons, vegetables, &c. Except among the very poor, a little meat or fish is added. Sweet oil, made from the sesamum seed, enters largely into their seasoning. But the great condiment is chillie, or capsicum. From the highest to the lowest, all season their rice with this plant. The consumption is incredibly great, and in its dried state it forms a considerable branch of internal trade. The whole pod, with its seeds, is ground to powder on a stone (a little water being added if the peppers are dried), and mixed with a little turmeric, and onions or garlic, ground up in the same manner, and generally acidified with some sour juice: often, instead of water, the expressed juice of rasped cocoa nut is used to make the curry. In this the fish or meat is stewed, if they have any, and a very palatable sauce is made, at almost no expense. Sweet oil, made of the cocoa-nut, sesamum, or mustard seed, is a very admired addition to their various messes, and almost entirely supersedes the use of butter. The latter is used only in the clarified state, called *pau-bot,* and by Europeans *ghee.*

In the upper districts, where rice is dearer than below, wheat, maize, sweet potatoes, onions, peas, beans, and plantains, enter largely into the common diet. Indeed, a Burman seems almost literally omnivorous. A hundred sorts of leaves, suckers, blossoms, and roots, are daily gathered in the jungle, and a famine seems almost impossible. Snakes, lizards, grubs, ants' eggs, &c., are eaten without hesitation, and many are deemed delicacies, An animal which has died of itself, or the swollen carcass of game killed with poisoned arrows, is just as acceptable as other meat. Like the ancient Romans, the Burmans are very fond of certain woodworms, particularly a very large species, found in the trunks of plantain-trees. I have seen several foreigners, who had adopted it as one of their delicacies.

Though the law forbids the taking of life, no one scruples to eat what is already dead; and there are always sinners enough to keep the sanctimonious ones supplied with animal food. Indeed, very few scruple to take game or fish. Thousands of the natives are fishermen by profession. I asked some of these what they thought would become of them in the next state. They admitted that they must suffer myriads of years for taking so many lives, but would generally add, 'What can we do?—our wives and chidren must eat.'

Cooking is done in a thin, earthen pot, narrow at the mouth, placed close to the fire, on three stones. Very little fuel is used, and this of a light kind, often the stalks of flowers, reminding me of the remark of our Saviour (Matt. vi. 30), when he reproved unreasonable anxiety about raiment. The variety of modes in which the different kinds of rice are prepared is surprising. With no other addition than sugar, or a few nuts, or a rasped cocoa-nut, they make almost as many delicacies as our confectioners; and such as I tasted were equally palatable.

Though their wheat is of the finest quality, it is much less valued than rice, and sells for less money. Its name, 'foreigner's rice', shows it not to be indigenous; but when it was introduced is not known. Its being also called *gyōng,* which is a Bengalee name, intimates that it might have been received from thence. Animals are fed with it, and, in some places, it forms a large part of the people's subsistence; not ground and made into bread, but cooked, much as they do rice. The bread made of it by foreigners is remarkably white and good, the fresh juice of the toddy-tree furnishing the best of leaven. The bakers are generally Bengalese, who grind the flour, in the manner so often alluded to in Scripture, in a hand-mill. Wherever there are Europeans, there are some of these bakers, who furnish fresh bread every day, at a rate not dearer than with us.

In eating, Burmans use their fingers only, always washing their hands before and after, and generally their mouths also. A large salver contains the plain boiled rice, and another the little dishes of various curries and sauces.

They take huge mouthfuls, and chew the rice a good deal. Sometimes a handful is pressed in the palm till it resembles an egg, and is in that form thrust into the mouth. The quantity taken at a meal is large, but scarcely half of that devoured by a Bengalee. Only the right hand is used in eating, the left being consigned to the more uncleanly acts. They eat but twice a-day, once about eight or nine o'clock, and again towards sunset. They avoid drinking before or during eating, on the plea that they then could not eat so much: after eating, they take free draughts of pure water, and lie down to take a short nap.

The dress of men in the lower classes, while engaged in labour, is a cotton cloth, called *pes-só,* about four and a half yards long, and a yard wide, passed round the hips, and between the thighs, most of it being gathered into a knot in front. When not at work, it is loosed, and passed round the hips, and over the shoulder, covering, in a graceful manner, nearly the whole body. A large part of the people, especially at Ava, wear this of silk; and there is scarcely any one who has not silk for special days. A jacket with sleeves, called *ingee,* generally of white muslin, but sometimes of broad-cloth or velvet, is added, among the higher classes, but not habitually, except in cold weather. It buttons at the neck and bottom. Dressed or undressed, all wear the turban, or *goun-boung,* of book-muslin, or cotton handkerchiefs. The entire aspect of a respectable Burman's dress is neat, decorous, and graceful. On the feet, when dressed, are worn sandals of wood, or cow-hide covered with cloth, and helped on by straps, one of which passes over the instep, the other over the great toe. On entering a house, these are always left at the door.

Women universally wear a *te-mine,* or petticoat, of cotton or silk, lined with muslin. It is but little wider than is sufficient to go round the body, and is fastened by merely tucking in the corners. It extends from the arm-pits to the ankles; but labouring women, at least after they have borne children, generally gather it around the hips, leaving uncovered all the upper part of the form. Being merely lapped over in front, and not sewed, it exposes one leg above the knee, at every step. By the higher classes, and by others when not at work, is worn, in addition, an *in-gee,* or jacket, open in the front, with close, long sleeves. It is always made of thin materials, and frequently of gauze or lace. Labouring women and children frequently wear, in the cold season, a shorter gown, resembling a sailor's jacket, of common calico. Nothing is worn on the head. Their sandals are like those of men.

Boys go naked till they are five or six in cities, and seven or eight in country places. Girls begin to wear clothing several years earlier. Both sexes wear ornaments in their ears. They are not rings, or pendants, but *cylinders* of gold, silver, horn, wood, marble, or paper, passed through a hole in the soft part of the ear. The perforation is at first small, but the tube is from time to time enlarged, till it reaches the fashionable dimensions of about an inch in diameter. As in all countries, some are extreme in their fashions, and such enlarge it still more. I have seen some of these ear ornaments larger round than a dollar. The boring of a boy's ear is generally made, by those who can afford it, an occasion of a profuse feast and other entertainments. After the period of youth, few seem to care for this decoration, and the holes are made to serve for carrying a spare cheroot, or a bunch of flowers.

Men generally wear mustachios, but pluck out their beard with tweezers: old people sometimes suffer it to grow; but it never attains to respectable size. Both sexes, as a matter of modesty, pluck out the hair under the arm, which certainly diminishes the repulsive aspect of the naked bust.

Both sexes wear their hair very long. Men tie it in a knot on the *top* of the head, or intertwine it with their turban. Women turn it all back, and, without a comb, form it into a graceful knot *behind,* frequently adding chaplets or festoons of fragrant natural flowers, strung on a thread. As much hair is deemed ornamental, they often add false tresses, which hang down behind.... Both sexes take great pains with their hair, frequently washing it with a species of bark, which has the properties of soap, and keeping it anointed with sweet oil.

Women are fond of rendering their complexions more fair, and at the same time fragrant, by rubbing over the face the delicate yellow powder already mentioned, which is also found a great relief in cutaneous eruptions, and is often used for this purpose by the missionary, with success. They occasionally stain the nails of the fingers and toes with a scarlet pigment. Bathing is a daily habit of all who live in the vicinity of convenient water. I was often reminded, while sitting in their houses in the dusk of the evening, of our Saviour's remark (John xiii. 10), 'He that is washed needeth not save to wash his feet, but is clean every whit.' The men, having finished their labour, bathe, and clean themselves at the river, or tank; but walking up with wet feet defiles them again, so that they cannot with propriety come and take their place on the mat or bed. Taking up some water, therefore, in a cocoanut dipper, out of a large jar which stands at the door of every house, they easily rinse their feet as they stand on the step, and 'are clean every whit'.

All ranks are exceedingly fond of flowers, and display great taste in arranging them on all public occasions. The pagodas receive daily offerings of these in great quantity, and a lady in full dress throws festoons of them around her hair. Dressy men, on special occasions, put a few into the holes in their ears.

In all Burman pictures, it is observable that the arm, when used to prop the body, is curved the wrong way. This arises from the frequency of such a posture to persons who sit on the floor with their feet at their side, and from the great flexibility of the joints of orientals. It is deemed a beauty in proportion to its degree of flexure. I found the same fashion prevailing in Siam. The stories, in some books, of their dislocating their elbow at pleasure, and even putting up the hair, &c., with the joints reversed, are absurd.

The mode of kissing is curious, though natural. Instead of a slight touch of the lips, as with us, they apply the mouth and nose closely to the person's cheek, and draw in the breath strongly, as if smelling a delightful perfume. Hence, instead of saying, 'Give me a kiss,' they say, 'Give me a smell'. There is no word in the language which translates our word *kiss*.

Children are carried, not in the arms, as with us, but astride the hip, as is the custom in other parts of India. The cradle of an infant is an oblong basket, without rockers, suspended from the rafters. The least impulse sets it swinging; and the child is thus kept cool and unannoyed by the flies.

The custom of blacking the teeth is almost universal. It is generally done about the age of puberty. The person first chews alum or sour vegetables several hours, after which a mixture of oil, lamp-black, and perhaps other ingredients, is applied with a hot iron. When done by the regular professors of the art, it is indelible. At the metropolis, the practice is getting into disrepute, and still more so in the British provinces; and as intercourse with foreigners increases, the practice may become obsolete. Whenever I asked the reason of this custom, the only answer was, 'What! should we have white teeth, like a dog or a monkey!'

277

Almost every one, male or female, chews the singular mixture called *coon;* and the lackered or gilded box containing the ingredients is borne about on all occasions. The quid consists of a slice of areca-nut, a small piece of cutch, and some tobacco rolled up in a leaf of betel pepper, on which has been smeared a little tempered quicklime. It creates profuse saliva, and so fills up the mouth that they seem to be chewing food. It colours the mouth deep red; and the teeth, if not previously blackened, assume the same colour. It is rather expensive, and is not taken very often through the day. Smoking tobacco is still more prevalent among both sexes, and is commenced by children almost as soon as they are weaned. I have seen little creatures of two or three years, stark naked, tottering about with a lighted cigar in their mouth. It is not uncommon for them to become smokers even before they are weaned, the mother often taking the cheroot from her mouth and putting it into that of the infant! Such universal smoking and chewing makes a spittoon necessary to cleanly persons. It is generally made of brass, in the shape of a vase, and quite handsome. Hookas are not used, and pipes are uncommon. The cheroot is seldom wholly made of tobacco. The wrapper is the leaf of the then-nat-tree; fragrant wood rasped fine, the dried root of the tobacco and some of the proper leaf, make the contents.

Men are universally tattooed on the thighs and lower part of the body. The operation is commenced in patches, at the age of eight or ten years, and continued till the whole is finished. The intended figures, such as animals, birds, demons, &c., are traced with lamp-black and oil, and pricked in with a pointed instrument. Frequently the figures are only lines, curves, &c., with an occasional cabalistic word. The process is not only painful but expensive. The tattooing of as much surface as may be covered by 'six fingers', costs a quarter of a tical when performed by an ordinary artist; but when by one of superior qualifications, the charge is higher. Not to be thus tattooed, is considered as a mark of effeminacy. The practice originates not only from its being considered ornamental, but a charm against casualties. Those who aspire to more eminent decoration have another tattooing with a red pigment, done in small squares upon the breast and arms.

A few individuals, especially among those who have made arms a profession, insert under the skin of the arm, just below the shoulder, small pieces of gold, copper, or iron, and sometimes diamonds or pearls. One of the converts at Ava, formerly a colonel in the Burman army, had ten or twelve of these in his arm, several of which he allowed me to extract. They are thin plates of gold, with a charm written upon them, and then rolled up.

The upper classes sleep on bedsteads, with a thin mattrass or mat, but most people sleep on the floor. Some have a thick cotton cloth to wrap themselves in at night, but the majority use only the clothes worn in the day. Sheets are not thought of by any class: even Europeans prefer to have their mattrasses enclosed in the fine mats of the country, and sleep in suitable dresses.

Respectable people are always attended in the streets by a few followers, sometimes by quite a crowd. A petty officer of middling rank appears with six or eight: one carries a pipe, another a coon-box, another a water-goblet, with the cup turned upside down on the mouth, another a spittoon, another a memorandum book, &c. All classes use umbrellas when walking abroad. Peasants and labourers, when at work, generally wear hats two or three feet in diameter, made of light bark.

It is scarcely safe for travellers to attempt to pourtray national character. Calm and prolonged intercourse, at every place, with men long on the ground, and daily contact with natives, merchants, civilians, soldiers, and missionaries, gave me, however, opportunities for forming opinions such as fall to the lot of few.

The Burman character differs, in many points, from that of the Hindus, and other East Indians. They are more lively, active, and industrious, and though fond of repose, are seldom idle when there is an inducement for exertion. When such inducement offers, they exhibit not only great strength, but courage and perseverance, and often accomplish what we should think scarcely possible. But these valuable traits are rendered nearly useless, by the want of a higher grade of civilisation. The poorest classes, furnished by a happy climate with all necessaries, at the price of only occasional labour, and the few who are above that necessity, find no proper pursuits to fill up their leisure. Books are too scarce to enable them to improve by reading, and games grow wearisome. No one can indulge pride or taste in the display, or scarcely in the use, of wealth. By improving his lands or houses beyond his neighbours, a man exposes himself to extortion, and perhaps personal danger. The pleasures, and even the follies, of refined society, call forth talents, diffuse wealth, and stimulate business; but here are no such excitements. Folly and sensuality find gratification almost without effort, and without expenditure. Sloth, then, must be the repose of the poor, and the business of the rich. From this they resort to the chase, the seine, or the athletic game; and from those relapse to quiescent indulgence. Thus life is wasted in the profitless alternation of sensual ease, rude drudgery, and active sport. No elements exist for the improvement of posterity, and successive generations pass, like the crops upon their fields. Were there but a disposition to improve the mind, and distribute benefits, what majesty of piety might we not hope to see in a country so favoured with the means of subsistence, and so cheap in its modes of living! Instead of the many objects of an American's ambition, and the unceasing anxiety to amass property, the Burman sets a limit to his desires, and when that is reached, gives himself to repose and enjoyment. Instead of wearing himself out in endeavours to equal or surpass his neighbour in dress, food, furniture, or house, he easily attains the customary standard, beyond which he seldom desires to go.

When strangers come to their houses, they are hospitable and courteous; and a man may travel from one end of the kingdom to the other without money, feeding and lodging as well as the people. But otherwise they have little idea of aiding their neighbour. If a boat or a waggon, &c., get into difficulty, no one stirs to assist, unless requested. The accommodation of strangers and travellers is particularly provided for by *zayats* or caravansaries, built in every village, and often found insulated on the highway. These serve at once for taverns, town-houses, and churches. Here travellers take up their abode even for weeks, if they choose; here public business is transacted, and here, if a pagoda be near, worship is performed. They are always as well built as the best houses, and often are amongst the most splendid structures in the kingdom. Though they furnish, however, no accommodations but a shelter, the traveller procures at the bazaar all he finds necessary, or receives, with the utmost promptitude, a full supply from the families around. A missionary may travel from one end of the country to the other, and receive, wherever he stops, all that the family can offer.

Temperance is universal. The use of all wine, spirits, opium, &c., is not only strictly forbidden, both by religion and the civil law, but is entirely against public opinion. I have seen thousands together for hours, on public occasions, rejoicing in all ardour, without observing an act of violence or a case of intoxication. During a residence of seven months among them, I never saw but one intoxicated; though the example, alas! is not wanting on the part of foreigners. It is greatly to be deplored that foreigners, particularly Moguls and Jews, tempt their boatmen and labourers to drink ardent spirits, and have taught a few to hanker after it.

During my whole residence in the country, I never saw an immodest act or gesture in man or woman. The female dress certainly shocks a foreigner by revealing so much of the person; but no women could behave more decorously in regard to dress. I have seen hundreds bathe without witnessing an immodest or even careless act, though, as in the case of woman's dress, the exposure of so much of the person would, with us, be deemed immodest. Even when men go into the water by themselves, they keep on their pisso.* As to general chastity, my informants differed so greatly that I cannot speak. It is certain, that among the native Christians there has been much trouble produced by the lax morality which prevails in this respect among married people.

Children are treated with great kindness, not only by the mother, but the father, who when unemployed takes the young child in his arms, and seems pleased to attend to it, while the mother cleans her rice, or perhaps sits unemployed by his side. In this regard of the father, girls are not made secondary, though, as with us, boys are often more valued. I have as often seen fathers carrying about and caressing female infants as male. Infanticide, except in very rare cases by unmarried females, is utterly unknown. A widow with children, girls or boys, is much more likely to be sought again in marriage than if she had none. The want of them, on a first marriage, is one of the most frequent causes of polygamy.

Children are almost as reverent to parents as among the Chinese. They continue to be greatly controlled by them,

*Paso or longyi: a kind of sarong worn by both men and women.

even to middle life; and the aged, when sick, are maintained with great care and tenderness. Old people are always treated with marked deference, and in all assemblies occupy the best seats among those of their own rank.

They are called an inquisitive people, and may be more so than other orientals, but I saw no particular evidence of it. Perhaps much of what travellers call inquisitiveness is no more than the common form of salutation. Instead of 'How do you do?' their phrase is, 'Where are you going?' They certainly seem fond of news, but not less fond of their own old customs, to which they cling with great tenacity.

Travels in the Burman Empire, William and Robert Chambers, Edinburgh, 1840, pp. 56–8.

38
The Boat-race and the Pweh

H. F. PREVOST BATTERSBY

Henry Francis Prevost Battersby was born in England in 1862. After completing his secondary education he trained as an officer and, on receiving his commission, served as a war correspondent in South Africa, where he was wounded in 1900. As bad luck would have it he was also wounded early in the First World War and, while acting as Reuters correspondent in 1918 at the British and the American fronts, was gassed.

Both before and after these wartime experiences, he wrote poems, plays, and novels as well as factual articles and books, sometimes using the pen-name 'Francis Prevost'. Though he never achieved literary fame, he was sufficiently well known and well connected to accompany George, Prince of Wales, and his wife, Mary, when in 1905 the royal couple set out on a tour of the Indian Empire. The battleship HMS Renown *took them to Bombay, 'the gateway to India', and there followed a lavish and colourful progress through the subcontinent which included a huge military review of 100,000 troops serving under Lord Kitchener, the Commander-in-Chief.*

At the capital, Calcutta, the royal party re-embarked for Burma, landing at Rangoon amid a tumultuous welcome. In

Mandalay their Royal Highnesses were entertained on a lavish scale, with boat races along the moat on the north side of the walled city (or Fort Dufferin as the British had named it) and a pweh, *the nature of which is explained by Battersby. When in his account he reaches the entertainment towards the end of the races, he all but admits that his powers of description are somewhat inadequate; but he is clearly not too impressed by the* pweh, *which he writes as* pwé. . . .

THERE was an interesting difference in the entertainments which Mandalay offered the Prince from those which had been devised elsewhere for him; everything was Burman, and Burman as arranged by the Burmese. Elsewhere had always been the concession to English taste, or the white directing finger behind the local colour. Here there was nothing done for the Prince's amusement that the Burman would not have done for his own. We saw thus two most characteristic displays, a Burmese boat race and a Burmese pwé. The boat race, or boat racing, as one should more properly call it, since it lasted all the afternoon, was as well 'run' and as keenly followed as that at any regatta at home. The spectacle was not quite so dispersedly decorative as might be some racing festa on the Thames, since the water was sternly swept of all but the racing craft and the gilded karaweiks in which the starter and the judge were seated. But in the crowd that stood five and six deep along the northern side of the moat there was a gaiety and variety of colour that could not be matched in the whole of Henley.

Pinks, in a score of delightful distinguishable shades—for pink is the preponderant Burmese colour—hyacinth and rose and peach blossom and fuchsia, pale greens from reseda to eau de Nil, faint lavender and sky and succory blues, lemon and citron and amber yellows, all toned together by the little white jackets which intervene so happily between the bright scarf and petticoat, and all of them lustrous with the gleam of silk.

On the south side, too, along the machicolated[*] top of the red walls of Fort Dufferin, with its thirteen fantastic watchtowers of teak and gold, was a trimming of the same brightly dressed humanity, for the men's pasohs[†] are as gay as the

---

[*]The author must mean 'castellated', that is, having indented battlements.
[†]Or *longyi*: a kind of sarong worn by both men and women.

girl's tamehns; and on the water itself the long canoes with the brown rowers stripped to the waist, or wearing a coloured band about their breasts, or clad, as were the Intha crews, in gorgeous silks and plumed helmets, driving their painted paddles with wild cries and to the clash of cymbals, quite atoned for the absence of spectators afloat. The race-course was the north reach of the Moat, and the Moat is a rectangular belt of water, a hundred yards wide, which completely surrounds Fort Dufferin, each face of whose four walls is a full mile and a quarter. The racing boats were long narrow canoes, painted of a single colour, yellow, light blue, dull red, apple-green, and black being those one remembers as lasting longest in the contest. The rowers, who numbered about thirty, sat two abreast except the two bow men, the one on the inner side kneeling right forward, and driving in his paddle a foot clear of the stem, his body bending at each stroke like a snake striking. He kneels there, not only to get a longer drive on his blade, but because to win a boat race in Burma not only must the boat pass the winning-post first, but the bow oar must snatch from the post the trophy of victory as the boat dashes past it.

This trophy is a piece of rattan projecting at either end from a length of hollow bamboo lashed athwart the bow of the boat, moored in mid-stream, which marks the finish. Each boat is compelled to keep its own water by stakes fixed in the centre of the stream, and thus there can be no fouling nor hustling at the critical moment. It is no mean feat of steersmanship, especially down stream on a rapid river, to bring the flying boat within arm's length of the rattan, which only protrudes a few inches, and no easy task for bow to snatch the cane out as the boat passes, lurching, leaping, quivering forward, buried in the spray of the furious paddles. In a close race both the bow men may lay hold at once of the opposite ends of the rattan, in which case they are certain to be swept out of their boats into the water; when, unless one can hold on longer to the cane than the other, a dead heat, or thayay pwé, is declared. The boats, though they look rough, and are hollowed out of a tree trunk, have delightful lines rising slightly forward from amidships, and running to a high galley-shaped stem to which the steersman's oar is lashed.

The sides are drawn out by charring and wedging, and are so frail that the boat is practically held together by its thwarts and by the strand of twisted cane and wire running down the centre; and, though it looks somewhat crank when laden, carries its crew of thirty without drawing more than a few inches. A man standing upright on the centre thwart sets the time with the clashing of a pair of cymbals; and he also chants the recitative of the wild river songs, to which the rowers bark explosive responses.

The heats were rowed off, at a few minutes' interval throughout the afternoon, the paddles starting at about sixty, slowing down to between forty and forty-five, when the boat was well under way, and doing a tremendous finish at anything over eighty.

After the first round all the finishes were very close, a quarter of a length being the outside between any two canoes, and the win being more often a question of feet and inches. The Burmese are great gamblers, and boat racing is the form of gambling they most enjoy; but they are likewise great watermen, and the most exciting moments of their lives have been those spent at village races on the Irawadi. Swept as his country is by noble rivers from its uttermost boundaries to the sea, the Burman's highway has always been a waterway, the river his road. And, since where trade goes youth goes, and where youth beauty, all the sterner training of his young men has been on the strong waters, and the most reckless encouragement of his young women for the straining craftsmen of the canoe.

It is only at a boat race that a Burmese maiden is sufficiently excited to ignore what happens to her scrupulous neatness: to forget her sedulously powdered face, the set of the comb and flowers in her dark hair, and to risk the soiling of her silken skirts and the breaking of her long da-lizan necklaces in struggling along the edge of the water to get a last glimpse of the boats. Thus, though the Mandalay races were of a less breathless sort than an up-country contest, there was plenty of animation over them, apart from money lost and won. An advancing expanding roar of excitement followed the boats from start to finish, almost drowning the clang of the contending cymbals; and the acclamations were renewed as the winning crew in each heat paddled back up the course, chanting their savage boatman's songs and swinging their paddles to the curious broken rhythm of the music, their wet faces gleaming and their breasts swelling with excited pride. Well-made men they were, perfectly fit, with the full pectoral and firm loin muscles which the paddle breeds; but their notions of training did not preclude a big banana before a race or a big cheroot after it. Bananas in plenty were carried in the canoes, some doubtless offered, with rice, flowers, and betel, to propitiate the river nats [spirits], who otherwise might have shown their displeasure by hanging on to the keel, or even by upsetting the boat with a flip of their fingers.

The two most interesting crews engaged were the Inthas, Shan tribesmen, who had journeyed all the way from far Fort Stedman to compete. They paddle standing up in double rank, facing the bow, with the outer leg twined about the paddle and the outer hand on the head of it. The outer shoulder is swung forward for the stroke, the blade dipped well in advance of the body, the whole weight of which is used in driving the stroke through. It is a very taking style when the stroke is kept long, and all the gaily-dressed bodies with their tinsel plumes swing back right out-board together, and then bend forward with all their force against the straining blades, and perhaps over a longer course they would have worn down the Burmans. But they lost ground in trying to hold at the outset their quicker-starting opponents, and could never afterwards get on terms. Also they had to row in borrowed canoes fitted with a hand-rail to which they were unaccustomed, and this was sufficient of itself to account for the failure of either boat to work its way through to the finals. They and their Shan supporters took their defeat depressingly to heart, the elder rowers, some of whom, keen old sportsmen, must have been past fifty, looking quite childishly woebegone, for they had set all their hopes on beating the Burmans, who are disposed to look down on them as a people of inferior attainments, and who even rather resented their inclusion in the regatta.

Before the rowing of the final heats the Prince and Princess embarked in a gorgeously gilded karaweik, which is a barge with a pyathat or pyramidal roof to it and weird wyverns at the bow and stern, and were thus towed round the course by canoes manned by white-robed white-filleted rowers, with singing and strange music, to which in the central canoe a Burmese girl danced. Burmese dancing is one of those things for which very few Occidentals can report a ready-made liking. There was a Burman who danced in one of the canoes which towed the Prince's karaweik at the Rangoon illuminations just in the same way as did this girl at Mandalay; but, whereas she was all unbecoming clothes and fantastic contortion, his lean tightly clad body, with its angular spasmodic expressive posturing, and face flung up to the stars, seemed in some rapt inspired way like an incarnation of the uncouth music, a real interpretation of its barbaric vision and spell. But no other dancing that we saw came anywhere within reach of it, though there was a pretty touch on the lake the same evening, when, on the approach of the Prince's barge, great clusters of lotus blooms, pink and blue and white, seemed to rise from the water, from each of which floated as it came into view the sound of little cymbals and the thin reedy wail of the native clarinets and flutes, the central blossom opening as the music quickened, and a girl rising slowly from the heart of it like some entranced spirit of the flower.

Really it looked like that; and it is impossible, if you could expect a human shape to come out of a lotus, to conceive anything more appropriate than the affectedly fantastically decorative figure of a Burmese dancing-girl.

We saw all it could do and all it could not at the pwé given in the Prince's honour on his last evening in Mandalay. A pwé is a Burmese play, with which it is pronounced to rhyme, and it is the Burman's favourite amusement.

There is a pwé when he is born, when he is named, when he goes into a monastery, when he comes out again, when he marries, when he divorces, when he dedicates a pagoda, and when he dies. Pwés to celebrate a girl's ear-boring, a boat race, a horse race, a buffalo fight, a boxing match, the rice sowing and harvesting, the beginning of a house building, or a great haul of fish.

The pwé is given in the open air and is free to all, the giver roofing over and furnishing with a bedstead and a few rugs a space for himself and the friends whom he invites by means of little palm-leaf packets of pickled tea distributed by his sisters or daughters.

The neighbours shoulder their mats, and with a store of provisions and cheroots camp out all round him, and there they sleep and eat and smoke as the pwé draws itself out through the long hours of the night, since no pwé would be considered lengthy that only lasted for twelve hours, and

Karaweik Barge on Mandalay Palace Moat, photograph by Gerry Abbott.

there is nothing exceptional in one continuing through an entire week.

Pwés are of many sorts, sacred and profane, topical and classical, with marionettes or real figures. The puppet plays are very well dressed and done, and, even to a foreigner, occasionally amusing. The Burmese prefer them to the real thing, and the unseen actors in them become just as famous as those taking part in the legitimate drama. Also on to the mimic stage can come nats and belus, dragons and elephants, and all the spirit creatures of the woods, fields, and waters which occupy so large a space in the Burman mind. Thus it is possibly its air of superior realism which most commends the puppet play. To appreciate the drama proper—the zat-pwé—is a more considerable effort to one's insular intelligence. The music is immensely interesting, differing in its mode, its tone divisions, and its cadences from that of the West, so much so that much of it cannot be recorded by our notation, and is as difficult to repeat as the song of birds. Also the curious tone values of the instruments—from the great seing-weing, a circle of drums some eighteen feet in circumference, in which the player sits, to the wah le' khoht or bamboo clappers—brought the suggestion of music significantly nearer to the sounds of common things, and really to hear 'The British Grenadiers' played, as it heroically was, on this plaintive reed and dully resonant wood and skin was to register a new sensation.

But no assiduous patience could bring one to admire, nor even willingly to endure, the prima donna's nasal singing, and only an artist could take pleasure in the contorted ingenuity with which she danced.

The charm of a Burmese woman's costume is its gay simplicity. A pair of sandals, a few yards of bright silk wrapped round her waist and falling to her ankles, a short white silk jacket, and a gauzy silk scarf. That is all there is of it; and, though in decorative quality not to be compared with the Japanese, its dainty sufficiency cannot be beaten anywhere. The Burmese prima donna, who is likewise première danseuse, spoils it all by converting her skirt into a narrow sack by stitching it up the front, by fixing something like a lamp shade round her waist, and by wearing an elaborate and unbecoming head-dress. So handicapped she does wonders in the way of movement, but it is movement which can only seem seductive to the elongated Burman eye. Also she is often incredibly clever with her muscles: makes them talk, one might say, where ours are not only incapable but unconscious of speech.

Her bosom will be passionately convulsed while her face and lips and every other part of her remain absolutely placid, and she has taught muscles to contract and throb, over which we have consciously no control. Such feats are to us mere gymnastics, but to the Burman they speak conceivably another language; just as the kisses, which for us have so much meaning, say to him nothing that he would care to hear. Her acting, by our standards, is not more acceptable, and, seeing that she is often 'on' all night, one is chiefly surprised by its limitations. The 'funny man', who is a feature of almost all pwés, seems to have a wider range, and is amusing even when he is only funny in a Burman way, which is, alas! much more subtle and refined than ours.

There are other sorts of plays and other sorts of dances, with less of art and more of nature, some of them mere excited stampings, such as even stately dignitaries indulge in when the spirit moves them, at a boat race or a buffalo fight or a procession to the pagoda. And these really are the more attractive, as they are nearer akin to the nature of the people, attractive, at any rate, to those who find in that nature, light and lazy and laughter-loving, an unaffected charm.

India Under Royal Eyes, George Allen, London, 1906, pp. 200–23.

39
How to Make Lacquerware

MAJOR R. RAVEN-HART

When we last saw the good Major (in Passage 18 above) he and his companion had arrived by canoe in Pagán, an area noted for producing excellent lacquerware, and he was marvelling at some of the glorious architecture to be seen on the pagoda-studded plain.

He concludes the passage that follows by observing that he has the 'sort of useless mind' that made him puzzle for days on end about a mere gambling device. It would be fairer to say that he was endearingly inquisitive and, once in Pagán, he wanted not only to buy some lacquerware but also to find out exactly how it was made. We catch up with him just after he has entered the village via Pagán's east gate, which is set in the only surviving stretch of the ninth-century city wall and which has the two Mahagiri Nats ensconced on either side of the entrance as guardians, each in a well-tended niche....

I had two objects in the village whose gate they guard: to see lacquer-work made, and to buy some small pieces. After much walking and fruitless search, let me put it on record for others: to *see* the work done and learn about it, go to the Government school, not in the village at all; but to *buy*, go to Nyaungu, or the Arakan pagoda at Mandalay, or the Scott Market in Rangoon. The makers work here to order only, and keep no stocks: they will have hundreds of one particular article on hand but no choice whatever, and the school has very little for sale.

As several people told me different and incorrect stories as to the method of manufacture (one of them said it included baking in an oven!) and as at any rate one recent book on Burma gives a description which is ludicrously wrong, I think it worth giving a summary, learnt at that Government school. Besides, it may be a good thing to show how elaborate the process is, since some people in Rangoon appear to despise Burmese lacquer-work as 'cheap and nasty'.

Your foundation is of coiled or woven strips of split bamboo, an eighth or a sixteenth of an inch wide at most, or of bamboo interwoven with horse-hair—this latter gives the lovely flexible bowls, so thin that you can bend them between your fingers and let them spring back to roundness without the lacquer cracking. Some old bowls could be thus bent until lip touched lip and yet recover their shape: they sold for a couple of pounds apiece and seem to be made no longer. Papier mâché is used for more elaborate shapes, and linen, silk, cardboard, plywood, etc., can also be used as foundations, but bamboo is the classic. Women and girls usually make the woven bases, men the others: it is by no means easy, especially when a box and its lid have to be done, and allowance made for the thickness of the lacquer to be added.

Now let us tabulate:

1. Smear the outside of your foundation with rak and water, that is to say the gum of the *thitsi* tree (*Melanorrhea usitata*) which grows in the hill-forests and is tapped like rubber. Dry in a cellar for two to five days: lacquer sets hardest in a cool, damp atmosphere.

2. And the inside, and dry as above.

3. Shave the inside smooth on a lathe, using a special steel tool: the Government school uses treadle-lathes, the smaller makers the older bow-lathes, the bowstring taken two or three times round the shaft so that when the bow is moved backwards and forwards by the right hand the shaft and the object on it are rotated. Spread a mixture of rak and cow-dung (I heard 'kaudaung' as if a Burmese word, and asked what it was in English) on the shaved surface. Dry, always for several days.

4. And the outside, and dry.

5. Smooth the inside on the lathe with overburnt brick and clay and water, dry quickly in the sun, add a paste of rak with powdered paddy-husk ashes, smooth off, and dry.

6. And the outside, and dry.

7. Smooth the inside with fine-grained sandstone and water, dry in the sun, give one coat of pure rak; and dry in the cellar.

8. Smooth the outside in the same way, give three coats of pure rak in two days: apply them in the sun, by hand and not with a brush—and how those small boys at the school seem to revel in smearing on that sticky black mess! And dry as before.

9. And the inside; but the third coat is red, rak with tung oil and cinnabar; and dry.

10. Polish outside and inside with a knot of rope and finely-ground teak charcoal, and then with silicified wood.

That is the classic black-red type: a piece takes about two months to finish. The result is certainly cheap in the material sense, but hardly in the figurative: at any rate, Burmese kings regarded it as suitable for presentation to people like the King of Siam and the Emperor of China, and I agreed with Padre San Germano that 'the betel-boxes and the drinking cups of the Burmese would be regarded as curiosities in Europe' and loaded my exiguous hold with cups and plates and boxes, betel and other. (Betel-boxes are a lacquer speciality, by the way, because the leaves to be chewed keep fresher in it than in any other material.)

But if you want a coloured ornament, as is usually the case, you now start again. You draw the design, freehand, without a copy, flower-arabesques chiefly—this is about one day's work for the simplest small piece. You then grave, cutting away one layer of the lacquer where the red is to come, smear the *whole* surface with a red mixture of cinnabar and a vegetable-glue; and after a few days in the cellar rub and rub with paddy-husk and water until the red is left only in the graved parts, and polish with teak-charcoal, and coat with that vegetable-glue to protect the red. Then you grave for the green, smear on rak and tung oil, rub on green powder (of orpiment and indigo, nice names), dry in the cellar, and rub and rub as before—you will have to repeat this whole process three times or more before the green pattern is properly covered. And then the yellow (orpiment alone) three times or more, with of course the cellar-drying each time; and then the orange (orpiment and cinnabar) again three times or more. After a final polishing with teak charcoal the piece is finished: you can reckon on five to six months for this type.

Another classical type is obtained by adding ashes to the rak when putting on the penultimate layer on the outside in operation 8; and then over it a normal black layer. When this latter is hard you grave a design through it so as to show the grey below, with a very delicate effect.

You will note, by the way, that 'lacquer' as done here has nothing to do with 'lac': I got them mixed up, especially as lac is also a Burmese product and was once a very important one.

I fell in love with the gold-on-black lacquer, though not a classical style, both for the results and for one fascinating moment: after finishing stage 10 you put on your design in yellow on the black, not graving it, just painting it on with a Chinese writing-brush; you give it a sticky surface, design and all, with a thin coat of rak; you coat the *whole* thing with gold-leaf; and then you put it in a basin of cold water. Little by little the yellow paint dissolves, taking with it the rak and the gold-leaf: where you put yellow you now have black, and the original black is now gold. It is exactly like watching a negative develop, and as exciting.

They say the art started in Siam and came thence to Thaton: it was one of the things that Anawrahta brought back here to Pagan as booty. The other crafts died out—this fortunately survives.

Our way back from the Government school took us through the stall-streets again. A gambling-device interested me: an arrow revolved on a vertical pivot over a table with four colours. You staked a farthing on a colour: if the arrow stopped over it the bank paid four times. All very well, but where does the bank come in? There was no zero, no dead space: I could see no trick that enabled the banker to help his luck. It could not have been a magnet, nor any friction-operated device, as the arrow was at least a foot above the table, in the air: conceivably the pivot may be tiltable slightly, and the greater weight of one end of the arrow as compared with the other do the rest? It puzzled me at intervals for days: I have that sort of useless mind.

Canoe to Mandalay, Frederick Muller, London, 1939, pp. 171–4.

Flora and Fauna

40
Lost in the Jungle

CHARLES T. PASKE

Deputy-Surgeon-General Charles T. Paske, late of the Bengal Army, was a British surgeon who had gone to Burma—in his opinion 'one of the most promising of our eastern possessions'—during the Second Anglo-Burmese War (see Passage 28). Unfortunately it was not until forty years had passed that he published an account of his experiences there, and in consequence his narrative is generally somewhat lacking in immediacy.

One experience, however, clearly stood out in his memory and had no doubt become the subject of many an after-dinner reminiscence. To anyone who has wandered into the jungle only to lose one's way, the realization that one is lost comes heavily laden with dread—especially if it is known that tigers abound in the area. In the invading British Army there were some 'European' (that is, white) detachments, but it consisted largely of Indian troops (Sepoys) under the command of white officers. When the column that Paske was marching with managed without incident to reach its objective, an isolated spot near Pyé (Prome), the commander allowed four of his officers to indulge in a little hunting. Paske now takes up the story.

WE were encamped in a large open space by the side of a somewhat broad but shallow stream, which furnished men and animals with the best and most abundant supply of water that we had come across since our departure. Nor did its advantages end here, for, besides to some extent protecting one side of the camp, its rippling music was very refreshing to our ears as we rested during the heat of the day.

As the result of a conversation, in which sport was the leading topic, it was agreed that four of us should go in a body and see what we could make of the jungle-fowl, which had, as usual, been crowing away that morning all along the line of march.

Accordingly, towards sunset we sallied forth, the two officers belonging to the European detachment and their orderlies, the officer in command of the Sepoys, and myself, with a Burmese lad to carry my ammunition.

A few minutes' walk brought us to the jungle, which we at once entered, on the *qui vive* for whatever small game might turn up, the idea of encountering anything larger having, strange to say, never occurred to any of us. We were soon threading our way through an exceedingly pretty part of the jungle, amid gigantic trees with gnarled trunks, festooned with creepers, and inlaid with delicately-tinted and waxy-looking orchids, that peeped out everywhere from a profusion of spotless green leaves. These beautiful flowers, which always appear to me to be gifted with more expression than perhaps any other, seemed to warn us of dangers lurking within that tangled mass of vegetation, the haunts of the cruel python and other formidable creatures. There is much to be said in favour of the orchid, in spite of its lowly position in the vegetable kingdom as a parasite, or, to let it down more easily, an epiphyte. It is, in point of fact, a veritable robber, though not to the extent generally supposed; for, though it derives its sustenance from the tree on which it grows, yet this is extracted from the effete bark, and not from the juices. In this respect, therefore, orchids are more sinned against than sinning; sinners or no sinners, they are worthy of adoration, whether abroad in their sylvan haunts or as exotics at home. Exquisite in themselves, they show how, on so frugal a diet, they can rival any of our favourites, on which animal and other manures have been lavishly expended.

The forest now resounded with the report of double-barrelled firearms, and jungle-fowl were falling on all sides. Reloading, I followed, as I thought, in the track of the others, but their reports sounded further and further away as I advanced, and at length died away completely. Now and again I hailed them by name, but I might just as well have searched for a needle in a haystack as my companions in such a labyrinth, so I soon followed an independent course. That we had scattered was not to be wondered at—indeed, unavoidable; twisting about and facing every point of the compass in order to avoid trees and to steer clear of patches of thorny, low-growing jungle, both for their own sake and for the sake of what they might harbour, anything like keeping in touch was impossible. I found myself, therefore, alone, but for my little ammunition-bearer, who kept as close to me as he could, bounding forward whenever I fired, and every bit as interested in the proceedings as I was myself.

I had been creeping along cautiously for some time, looking to right and left and listening attentively, when it suddenly dawned upon me that it was time to get back to the camp. I accordingly did so with every feeling of confidence, but a few attempts convinced me of the fact that I was lost.

In my perplexity I took my boy into confidence, but, either owing to my imperfect knowledge of the language or his timidity, he proved but a Job's comforter. Nor was there any help to be derived from the position of the declining sun, as it was completely hidden from view by the thick foliage overhead and everywhere around; so I proceeded at random, all interest in the excursion having vanished, and my every thought centred on how to get clear of the forest.

Having performed the operation of 'right-about-face', I must surely be making progress; and it is astonishing how, under such circumstances, a straw seems sufficient to clutch at. I was still fresh, which was something; a trifle warm perhaps, and well disposed towards a pint of the *dimidium dimidiumque** of the ancients had such been available, but, in default of nectar, I sought another comforter, that had often helped me to pull myself together and look an unpleasant situation in the face. My companion looked as if he would

---

*'Half and half': a mixture of two alcoholic drinks.

liked to have followed my example, but I had not even a cheroot to offer him.

Barely ten minutes after this the jungle terminated abruptly, and we came upon a green sward of considerable extent, and fringed with trees and undergrowth. It almost resembled an artificial clearing, inasmuch as not even a shrub intercepted its continuity; and I was on the point of crossing it when a terrific roar on my right sent all the blood back to my heart, and a magnificent tiger trotted into the enclosure. I was too taken aback to move; my pipe dropped from my mouth on to a stump, scattering its lighted contents over my feet. The tiger was a grand specimen—graceful, sleek, and beautifully marked, but for the moment his beauty concerned me far less than my own slight chances of escape. My thoughts involuntarily wandered for an instant to that farce in which the pariah-dog enacted a leading *rôle*—what a contrast to this awful reality! and I was just resolving to pour the contents of both barrels into his face, in the hope of blinding him, when he snarled at me and disappeared, lashing his tail.

This was a great relief, for the perspiration was streaming down my face, and my teeth were clenched as in death. I recovered my pipe, and looked round for my boy. He was gone, and my calls received no answer. I would have signalled to him by firing, but the young absentee was in possession of both powder and shot, leaving me with only two charges to depend on in case of further emergencies. I was therefore compelled to proceed alone, coming to the conclusion that he had bolted on hearing the tiger roar, and had either made off to his own village or else succumbed to fear, or to *something worse*, the bare possibility of which I dared not contemplate.

Absolutely alone! Lost in a tropical forest, with night coming on apace, and no ammunition other than the two charges of small shot already in my gun. This was truly an enviable position, especially as the forest was known to be swarming with wild beasts, such as I had just encountered. I shouted once more for my boy, and plunged again into the thicket at haphazard, and in a state bordering on desperation. Anxiety and fear quickened my steps; my eyes seemed to penetrate further than usual, and my ears detected the faintest sound. I was startled by the snapping of a twig under foot, while the cry of a jungle bird terrified me. How I wished they were all

'The Hunter', from Noel F. Singer, *Burmah*, Kiscadale, Gartmore, 1993.

defunct, or that I had never attempted to molest them in their hidden retreats.

In addition to my gun, I carried a stout branch, which I hurled at every suggestive clump likely to harbour any kind of animal. I realized to its full the couplet of the poet—

As in the night imagining some fear;
How easy is a bush supposed a bear:

in my case a tiger. Hope was ebbing fast, so I scanned the trees around, with a view to taking up my position in one of them for the night.

Even then I should not be beyond the reach of tigers, snakes, and black ants; while, if I fell asleep, I might have occasion to prove the literal truth of the words: *Periculosior casus ab alto!*[*]

The outlook, both above and below, was certainly as bad as bad could be, and I felt sick with anxiety, and so weary

[*]'It might be more dangerous to fall from a height.'

with suspense that I almost wished the end would come and leave me at rest.

It was, however, decreed otherwise, and to my intense satisfaction the trees became further apart and the undergrowth less dense, and—oh, joy!—a familiar sound smote my ear, and I once more stood on the brink of a stream.

This was a relief in many ways. First and foremost, I lay my gun down, tucked up my sleeves, and drank greedily, for I was both hot and thirsty; and then I once more lighted my pocket companion and considered my position. Though matters had decidedly improved, I was still on the horns of a dilemma. We were encamped, it is true, on the banks of just such a stream as this; but, even if this were the identical one, ought I to follow its course up stream or down? The pleasing thought also occurred to me that animals are wont to make for the water to slake their thirst during the first watches of the night, but this troubled me far less than the choice of direction.

The ultimate result of my calculations was a decision in favour of moving with the stream; so I advanced with extreme caution, looking on all sides whenever I was following one of the many bends of its tortuous course.

Once, a large moving object loomed some way ahead, leaving the water's edge and striking inland; it was probably a tiger, but the increasing darkness rendered identification impossible; and my attempts to ascertain the nature of its footprints when I shortly afterwards crossed its path were equally fruitless.

Save for the rippling of the stream perfect silence reigned around, a few stars twinkled overhead, and the dark line of the forest looked more gloomy than I had ever yet seen it. Doubtless my feelings painted the surroundings in unusually gloomy colours.

It was now half-past-six by my watch; and on making the next bend, I saw a light not very far ahead. It might of course belong to a party of the rebels out reconnoitring, in which event I should be between two fires, Stooping down and gliding inland from cover to cover, I approached cautiously; while, as I neared the place, other fires came in sight, and figures flitted past them. I crept closer and closer, resting for a few seconds behind each convenient bush; the figures were in the 'shadowed livery of the burnished sun', though taller and slighter than the average Burmese. Still more cautious, and bent almost double, I traversed the remaining distance, soon making out every detail of the camp I had quitted the same afternoon. Not sorry to stand upright once more, I sauntered gaily into the place, whistling a tune, answered the challenge and proceeded straight to my tent.

The others were just sitting down to dinner, at which I soon joined them; after which, in return for their consideration in allowing me to enjoy the meal undisturbed by questions, I gave them a full account of my adventures, and was heartily congratulated on my narrow escape.

Comparing notes with my fellow-sportsmen, I found that the whole party had scattered, returning separately, but in good time. Captain H.—the 'long one', as we called him—had also encountered a large tiger asleep, and was just pushing a bullet down over the shot, when the animal awoke, snarled at him, and walked unconcernedly away. Considering how these animals rest during the day and prowl about in the evening, there was every reason to suppose that his tiger and mine were identical; if so, its experiences that day, encountering no less than three white faces—the captain's, his orderly's, and my own—were indeed probably without precedent.

Life and Travel in Lower Burmah: A Retrospect, W. H. Allen, London, 1892, pp. 150–7.

41
Denizens of the Forest

ALICE HART

Like many countries, Burma is rapidly being denuded of much of her flora and fauna. The teak forests that once supplied the world's navies with shipbuilding timber are drastically depleted: the Bengal tiger is scarcely ever seen; and the rhinoceros has gone.

As a dutiful Victorian wife Alice Hart, who expressed her admiration of Burmese women in Passage 34, would have seen little of the wildlife she describes in the passage below. But as in other matters, she certainly gathered a great deal of information not only from books but also from the Burmese and from the expatriate British community. The General Fytche that she mentions was a cousin of Albert Lord Tennyson who had first served in Burma as a young officer and had eventually left the country in 1871 as Chief Commissioner; one of his ancestors was Ralph Fitch, the author of Passage 4 above. Mrs Hart also refers to Mr Theobald, a deputy superintendent of the Geological Survey of India who was something of an authority on Burmese zoology and botany.

THE banana or plantain tree grows freely, and furnishes its wholesome fruit all the year round. Peepul and banyan trees cast their broad shadows in the forests, where tamarind, sassafras, ebony, tobacco, lac, cinnamon, mango, and indigo trees grow in profusion. The open underspace is filled by the golden-green plumes of the feathery bamboo, and the branches above are bound by creepers into an impenetrable tangle. Some of these are of gigantic size, with grand flowers, producing Brobdingnagian pods, which in the case of the *Entada Pursætha* measure no less than five feet in length. The great leaves of the *Pothos gigantea* measure two feet long and half a foot broad. From the branches of the forest trees hang festoons of delicate and brilliantly coloured orchids, and the barks are feathered with ferns. The rattan grows everywhere: the strong canes furnish ropes with which to drag timber, and the finer ones are used for basketwork.

The pride, however, of the forests of Burma is the teak tree. There are said to be twenty varieties of teak, but the most abundant is the *Tectona grandis*. It comes to maturity in about eighty years, and attains a girth of twelve to sixteen feet, with a bole of eighty to ninety feet to the top of the branches. Splendid baulks of timber sixty feet in length, and as much as twenty-four inches square, are frequently shipped from Maulmain. The wood is of a light brown colour, and amongst its valuable properties it contains a resinous oil which preserves iron from rust and resists the action of water as well as of insects. It is quickly seasoned and easily worked, and from its combined strength, elasticity, and endurance is considered to be the most valuable timber for shipbuilding in the world. The tree comes to perfection on the southern and

'Greater Moth Orchid', from F. W. Burbidge, *The Gardens of the Sun*, John Murray, London, 1880.

western slopes of the hill forests, where it is exposed to the rays of powerful sun. It does not grow on northern slopes. The trees are not found in large numbers together in the same area, the proportion being generally one teak to every five hundred, or in the so-called teak forests, one to three hundred other forest trees. The teak is of rather rapid growth, and in eight years it reaches a height of twenty-five feet or more. The leaves are very large, and have been compared by Oriental writers to elephants' ears. They are from ten to

303

twenty inches in length, and from eight to sixteen in breadth. The tree is deciduous, and seeds at the end of the rainy season. The seeds are contained in a hard shell, and, owing to the lateness of the season when they are produced, they lie dormant for a considerable time.

The teak forests are strictly preserved by the Government; no tree can be felled, even by those who have purchased the right, till it has been girdled by the Government forest officers. The rivers down which logs are floated must be kept free from all obstructions; no hill gardens are allowed to be made in the reserved districts, and cutting, marking, or felling of any trees or shrubs of any kind without express permission is penal; even roads and bridle-paths may be closed if it is thought that giving access to the forests endangers the valuable teak trees. All these elaborate precautions are taken to prevent the calamity of forest fires, which are easily kindled by the nomadic tribes of the mountains, who wastefully burn down the jungle to effect a clearance previous to the primitive sowing of their crops. In the days of Burmese rule, the forest lands were free to anybody who chose to make a clearance, and the strict laws now enforced over the extensive tracts of forest reserved by the British Government are felt as a great hardship.

There are many other fine timber trees in the forests of Burma, among which may be mentioned the *Dipterocarpus lævis* and the *D. turbinatus*, which are, however, more valuable for the wood-oil which they produce than for their wood. The oil is extracted by making a triangular excavation in the bole of the tree, in which a fire is lit; this causes the oil to flow freely into an earthen vessel, suspended to collect it. A single tree is said to produce as much as from thirty to forty gallons in a season without injury to its vitality.... The tree is of magnificent proportions, springing to a height of 180 feet, with a girth of sixteen feet, the trunk being often buttressed with mighty offshoots extending over an area of fifty feet.

Though the greatest part of Burma is within the tropics, it is a subject of constant surprise to travellers to find the fruits of temperate climes growing wild in the forests, not in the high altitudes, but on the coast. Wild cherries and pears have been found, and are stated to be of good flavour. The bramble grows wild in Burma, the English brake fern (*Pteris aquilina*) is common on the hills, and the silver fern of Kamchatka has been met with. There is an abundance of tropical fruits; the pineapple is as plentiful as are apples in England, and oranges, lemons, pomegranates, guavas, and mangoes supply the vegetarian Burman with fresh fruit all the year round; while wild peppers, cayennes, chillies, and leaves of the forest trees, provide him with the hot curries in which he delights. But the fruit which is execrated as warmly by some as it is delighted in by others is the dorian, celebrated of old as it is at the present time for its evil smell and its exquisite flavour. The explorer Linschoten's description of it, four hundred years ago, is identical with that given of it by every traveller since; for he says, 'In taste and goodness it excelleth all kinds of fruit, and yet when it is first opened it smelleth like rotten onions, but in the taste, the sweetnesse and daintinesse thereof is tryed.' If one can become reconciled to the odour of rotten onions, the dorian is acknowledged to be 'beyond question the finest fruit in the world'. In appearance it is like a large melon covered with spikes, so that it resembles a hedgehog.

Great as are the wonders of vegetation in the forests of Burma, the animal life with which they abound is still more astonishing, for here the wild elephant of colossal size roams at will, the man-eating tiger makes its lair, the monstrous rhinoceros wallows in lonely pools in the cool of the evening, and herds of buffaloes and deer find illimitable grazing-grounds. Here monkeys in countless crowds chatter among the trees, gorgeous parrots scream, gentle turtle-doves coo, the solitary tucktoo calls, and the hungry vulture watches for its prey. Here the deadly cobra lies in wait for its victim, and the hamadryad rears its head to strike and kill, the chameleon changes the colour of its coat unobserved, and the deadly pangu spider strikes the serpent with its poison fang, and outvenoming the most venomous in hate, sucks the brains of its victim. Every spot is filled with beautiful, terrible life, and it is not surprising that to the imaginative Burman the forest glades are peopled with demons and fairies, and that even the double-headed serpent is to him an object which he believes he has seen with his own eyes.

The elephants which abound in the forests of Tenasserim, Pegu, and Bassein are said to be larger than they are in any part of Asia. They are held in so much veneration, that if a baby elephant is captured and brought in, it is considered honourable and an act of 'merit' for the women to suckle it from their breasts. Elephants congregate in herds, of which the largest and strongest tusker is generally the lord, but not always so, for sometimes the position of leader is taken by a strong-minded and cunning female elephant. The herd is always devoted to its leader, who is implicitly obeyed and followed. If a young male elephant becomes too obstreperous, he is driven out of his own herd, in which case he either fights the lord of another for the leadership or else becomes an outcast. Such a bachelor elephant is always called a 'rogue', and is a most vicious and destructive creature. General Fytche tells an entertaining story of a 'rogue' elephant of immense size with which he did single combat in the Bassein district. For more than two hundred years this 'rogue' had been a terror to the people far and wide; native huntsmen had failed to shoot him, and he was believed to be under the special protection of the Nats [spirits]. Indeed, once when a native huntsman had shot at him with a magic silver bullet, specially cast by a 'medicine man', the gun had burst in his hands, which was proof positive of the protection afforded to the wicked elephant by the demons of the forest. General Fytche determined to rid the neighbourhood of the 'rogue', which had killed many men in his time. He tracked him to a dense forest, where he saw him rubbing his back against the bole of a gigantic tree, and fanning himself with some branches which he held in his trunk. Fytche fired, the elephant fell on his knees, but he was only stunned, and getting up, made straight for his enemy. The General dodged his quarry behind the trunks of trees for some time, but finally took up his position at the foot of a large tree, and awaited the charge of the immense beast. When the elephant was within twelve paces he fired, and the 'rogue' sank dead at his feet. This elephant was 11 feet high, with a girth of 15 feet, and with tusks measuring 7 feet long. . . .

The man-eating tiger is common in the forests of Burma, and is the terror of the inhabitants of the jungle villages, so that tiger-shooting on foot, a sport of real danger, can be enjoyed by those who like the excitement of risking their lives in this particular way. The tiger is often accompanied in his nocturnal expeditions by the wolf-like jungle dog (*Canis rutilans*), with which it shares its prey.

Ponderous rhinoceroses wander through the glades; in the daytime they seek high ground, and at night they descend where there is a pool in which they may wallow. The rhinoceros of Asia differs from that of Africa by the presence of well-defined incisors, by means of which the bark is stripped off trees and plants uprooted for food. The one-horned species or *Rhinoceros unicornis*, the unicorn of Scripture, is also found in Burma. Its horn was highly valued as a sovereign remedy against poison, and merchants used in the olden days to come to Pegu to barter with the King for this commodity, 'whereof the King onely hath the traffique in his hands'.

Herds of buffaloes wander at will; the male leader is a fierce and courageous fighter; not only will he charge a man, but it is said that a herd will surround and kill a tiger. In the open spaces of the forest immense herds of deer may be encountered, particularly the large-horned *Cervus frontalis*, peculiar to Burma and Manipur. The natives kill deer, not by shooting or chasing them in the ordinary way, but a party of ten or twelve men go into the woods at night in a buffalo cart; in front two or three lighted torches are carried, and two persons walk beside the cart bearing great wooden bells which are constantly beaten. The deer seem dazzled by the light and dazed by the noise, so that they remain motionless, and are then easily killed with swords, spears, and knives. Wild boar and porcupines are common in the woods, but the lion, the king of beasts, is not a native of Burma. The bear is found in the mountains of Martaban; the orang-outang is said to be met with in the forests of Pegu.

Apes are very numerous, and I have seen them gambolling in crowds on the banks of the Irrawaddy. Sangermano describes how 'they leap from tree to tree with such agility as to seem birds rather than quadrupeds; they fight with each other and mock the lookers-on, and chase the fish and crabs that have been thrown on dry ground in the most ludicrous manner.'

But perhaps the Burmese forests are more remarkable for their wondrous snakes, vipers, and venomous creatures than for other specimens of natural history. The stories told of the hamadryad (*Naja Elaps*) are numerous. This deadly snake is from twelve to fifteen feet long, and if attacked, or if its nest is interfered with, it will pursue a human being with great rapidity of movement and persistency of intention. When it raises its head, it is taller than a man, and it is said to strike at once at the head of its victim....

An old story is told of a hamadryad which established itself near a village and became the terror of the inhabitants. A reward was offered to anybody who would kill it, but no one cared to make the attempt. At last an old woman declared herself ready to undertake the daring deed. She placed a pitcher of melted pitch on her head and started alone to meet the hamadryad. It raised its body and struck as usual at the top of the head of its intended victim, but unawares it plunged its head into the melted pitch, where it stuck fast and was suffocated. Mr Theobald tells, however, that he has seized with his own hands one of these large and deadly snakes on two occasions.

The cobra capello is very common in the forests, but it is outdone in venom by the cobra ceras, the deaf viper, which no noise can rouse, but which, 'if confined so that it cannot fasten on its captor, will in its rage bury its long fangs deep in its own body'.

The python makes its huge meal undisturbed in the forests, and all travellers tell stories of its power to swallow whole deer, and even great boars. It is said to strip off the skin and flesh from the head of its prey, cover the whole body with a glutinous saliva, and swallow the animal entire, head foremost. It kills by constricting the animal in the coils of its immensely strong body before swallowing it. Notwithstanding its dangerous tendencies, the python is believed to be the embodiment of a Nat. The Burmans have a tradition that the boa was in the far-away past the most venomous of snakes, but that on being once teased by an impertinent crow, he became so angry that he spat up all his poison. Other snakes ate the poison, and thus became venomous, but the python was henceforth harmless. In Tavoy the huge reptile is made a domestic pet, and is kept amiable by being fed on rice and eggs. He becomes, in fact, an inmate of the household, 'so that the cat, the dog, and the baby may be seen curled up together in a corner with the boa, making one another mutually cosy'. The strange favourite has, however, its uses, and the Tavoy fishermen look upon the python as the most weather-wise of beings. He is always carried with them when they go fishing, and remains coiled in the bows so long as the weather is fair; but if a storm is coming on, the python quietly drops into the sea and makes for land, and the fishermen look upon this as a signal that they also had better make for port. Tigers are fond of making a meal of a python, and Fytche describes how he shot a tiger which was in the act of devouring one....

In the delta, crocodiles are very numerous in the estuaries of the Irrawaddy and Salwen rivers, where the water is brackish. They often become most formidable as animals of prey, and a single alligator will, after having made several victims, become so emboldened that he will usurp dominion over a certain portion of a river, where he is the terror of every boat's crew that passes. In a Burmese dug-out the steersman sits very low, often only a few inches above the water's edge. The crocodile's mode of attack is to glide up silently to the bow or stern of the boat, and then with one stroke of his powerful barbed tail close to the top of the low boat, he sweeps into the water whoever may by within reach, when he is seized and devoured. Burmans wear nodules of iron pyrites as a charm against crocodiles, but they do not prevent the monster from swallowing man and charm together. Dr Price, the American missionary, was present when one of his crew was seized by an alligator on the Irrawaddy. The man had gone overboard to do something to the boat, when he was seized by a crocodile of extraordinary size, and quietly dragged under water in sight of his helpless and horrified companions. Presently the monster reappeared close to the boat's side, holding the still living man by the waist in his terrible jaws, just as a dog holds a stick. Rising with his prey several feet out of the water, he brought it down with great force and a loud crack on the surface, with the object probably of breaking up the body; the red stain on the placid water giving a silent sign that the murderous intention had been carried out.

It is pleasant to turn to the consideration of the kinder relations often established between man and the denizens of the rivers. At a holy island on the Irrawaddy above Tsengoo, a colony of large fish live a tranquil life in a pool under the shadow of a phongyee-kioung, and are fed by the solitary monks. On the boatmen calling 'tet-tet', a number of large fish, three or four feet long, crowd round the boat's edge to be fed with pellets of rice, and seem to be delighted to have their backs stroked. These fish are considered sacred, and to do them royal honour, they are sometimes caught by the people on festival days, and brought into the boat to have gold leaf attached to their backs, and are then returned to the river.

I must conclude this short account of some of the natural wonders of Burma by telling of the floating islands on Lake Nyoung-we, beyond the Taungu country. The surface of the water is covered by a great number of floating islands. They are produced by the interlacing roots of a coarse grass or reed, which in dry weather shoot downwards to the bottom of the lake. When the floods come, they are separated from the soil, are floated up and become free. The inhabitants on the borders of the lake build fishing cottages on these islands, which they anchor to the bottom by long bamboos. They undulate in an alarming manner with every step, and in a squall a man's house may face every point of the compass.

Burma, with its marvellous forests, rivers, and mountains, would prove such a mine of fruitful research to the naturalist and man of science, that it is most earnestly to be hoped that the Government will, at no distant date, send fully qualified men to investigate the flora, fauna, geology, and the natural history of this wonderful land, so that we may have accurate knowledge within our reach, and not depend, as now, on the observations of missionaries, military men, and travellers for our scientific knowledge of the country.

Mrs E. Hart, *Picturesque Burma Past and Present*, J. M. Dent, London, 1897, pp. 90–8.

42
The Case of the Flowering Bamboo

GORDON HUNT

Despite being a member of the grass family, bamboo may grow taller than many trees, some of the several hundred species reaching 20 metres in height while others do not exceed a few centimetres. Although the species are widely distributed, being by no means limited to the tropics, and yield some of the oldest and most important materials used by humankind—for building, furnishing, weaving, making weapons, and even eating—the Bambuseae are still not adequately classified. Bamboos grow very fast and, like all grasses, are flowering plants; but the flowering occurs at indefinite and unusually lengthy intervals, in some species as long as 120 years, and may result in the death of the plant.

In 1928 at the age of twenty-one, having left school and worked for four years in the timber trade in England, Gordon Hunt went to Burma to begin a career in forestry. Fourteen years later he would be forced to escape from the advancing Japanese forces and trek for more than 1400 kilometres from Bhamó to the Chinese city of Kunming. Here, however, we join him in 1930. After two years' hard work in Central Burma he has been transferred to take charge of a large mixed forest, and has hardly settled in when there comes a terrible heatwave and drought; and the flowering of the bamboo is giving rise to unexplained fears.

FOR months I worked harder than ever before. The rains came and went. Then Central Burma experienced one of the worst hot periods ever recorded. The entire countryside became parched and the earth scorched. Rivers, normally with a perennial flow of water, dried up. The village cattle began to die. Anxiety showed on the faces of the local peasant folk and almost daily I heard their pathetic stories of wells drying up and their struggle to find sufficient water even for their own use.

Everywhere there was suffering and a growing atmosphere of utter despair. Nature was really being cruel. Only those who have experienced real drought will understand its utter tragedy. Even where I was camped, sixteen miles upstream from where the water shortage was causing such concern, we also had to struggle to find enough to make a cup of tea. In the dried-up river-bed my men would scour out holes in the sand and before dawn collect the pint or two that had seeped through during the night. But we were not a village. Our requirements were small and fortunately I was well stocked with beer, tinned milk, soups and so on. We suffered no real hardships. Almost every evening I would shoot the pigeons which driven by thirst would flock in near our water-holes in the river-bed. Bathing was out of the question. A ladle or two from the shell of a coco-nut was my daily ration.

But in that fateful year 1930 nature had even worse things in store for a drought-stricken people. God knows they were suffering enough. One morning my head clerk appeared and I had only to take one look at his face to sense that he was the harbinger of ill news. Immediately I thought that in the wake of the water shortage cholera or some similar epidemic disaster had hit below the belt of a people already at a low ebb.

'What is it, U Thein?' I asked him. 'Why are you so worried?' 'Thakin,' he answered, 'it is far worse than disease. What I have seen this morning may mean starvation. Please come with me and I will show you. Perhaps you can help.'

A mile from my camp, where the hillsides by the thousands of acres were covered in bamboos, the old greyhead tried to tell me whence his fears of starvation stemmed. I saw that the bamboos had yellowed but this, at least to me, was understandable under such conditions of drought. Even at that hour of the early morning the heat of the sun was almost unbearable. But U Thein was determined that I should listen to his fears that this meant famine. I did my best to tell him that for a season his people would have to face up to a shortage of the growing bamboo. I knew how much they relied on it—what it meant to them as a supply of building material and all manner of household uses, even down to carrying water to their rice fields and the little fertile patches where they did their market gardening. Now great clumps of bamboo drooped downwards, the forests of bamboo were dying. In my own way I tried to comfort this ageing Burmese clerk by telling him how for every stick of bamboo that died thousands more would spring up once the rains came, and the forest would once again burst into new life. But my words were of no avail. It was the floor of the forest that concerned him. It was strewn with tiny yellow flowers. They lay inches deep. Underfoot they crinkled and crackled on the dry leaves shed from the trees. They were everywhere and already starting to turn into yellow dust. It was sad to see a forest dying but nothing I saw indicated famine.

Walking home I questioned U Thein about his fears but he confessed that all he knew came from stories handed down from father to son as to what happened if the bamboo flowered. I knew from some technical journal I had read of the vagaries of the flowering cycle of bamboo. From what I recalled it occurred about once a century. It varied from district to district but was spaced between seventy and ninety years. But what it had to do with famine had occupied no part in the journal. Yet my clerk could talk of nothing else but jungle rats descending from the forest like locusts and devouring every grain that the villagers had raised. According to him they had invaded and terrorised whole villages, gnawing their way into the storage bins where the paddy was kept to sustain whole families from one harvest to the next.

U Thein went on to tell me that his father, now well over eighty, remembered the day when the bamboo had flowered in his district. Would I care to come and talk to the old man? By this time my colloquial Burmese was pretty fair, but so fascinated had I become with this weird story of the invasion of rodents following in the wake of the flowering of the bamboo, that to help me out with the old man I enlisted the aid of my senior assistant, a Eurasian, not particularly bright but who spoke the language like a native.

We met the old gentleman and he told us his story. Yes, it was perfectly true that as a child living near Toungoo the bamboo had flowered. There had been famine. Whole fields of grain had been devoured before they could be harvested and rats by the million had invaded the villages. Many, many people had died of hunger. But question him as, between us, we did, there was no logical conclusion to be drawn between the flowering of a plant and an invasion of rats. We tried to reason it out ourselves. Did the forest rats live off the young bamboo shoots and when deprived of them seek food elsewhere? It made no sense, because for all we knew that land laid bare by drought would burst forth into a new and glorious lushness after the first weeks of the monsoon. Nothing added up.

But quite unknown to me the problem of the flowering bamboo was attracting attention elsewhere. The Department of Forestry was deeply concerned, and completely out of the blue I received word that the Chief Entomologist in Burma was coming to inspect my forest within a matter of days. Nothing could have pleased me more. Dennis Atkinson (known to his colleagues as the 'Provincial Bugger') was a dear friend of mine. Ten years my senior he had nevertheless opened doors for me which without his influence might have been shut. Because I was keen on forestry, from a sylvicultural aspect as well as commercially, I had on his behalf carried out a series of experiments mainly connected with the activities by night of certain tree-borers, particularly the bee-hole pest that was making such serious inroads into plantation-grown teak. I do not think for a moment that I was able to contribute much to the academic war being waged in scientific circles but at least I had established that when the moon was full these pests were more active than at any other period in the month.

This, however, was of no great importance to me at this time, my curiosity about rats following the flowering of the bamboo was all that mattered. Who better than Dennis to give me the answer. He was far beyond being a hunter after bugs. This man was first and foremost an ecologist, one of those rare birds who, in simple language, could analyse and correlate any form of phenomena, be it plant, animal or human, with its environment.

Dennis duly arrived, hot and tired after climbing round my hills. Apparently to the south of us the position was even more serious. We talked while with a pint or so of discoloured water he did his best to remove some of the dust of his journey. Fortunately I was able to offer him a cool beer, for in spite of the heat we had our own somewhat primitive but nevertheless effective means of ensuring cold drinks. It was no more than a wicker basket packed with damp straw and it dangled by a cord from the floor of the hut. Always there was someone to give it the occasional swing and to keep the straw moist.

It took a drink or two to drag Dennis from his tree-borers to my rats. He was one of those people it is impossible to hurry. He had to tell his stories in his own way—that of an ecologist—but as he developed the theme of nature and the queer tricks it sometimes played, he gradually led up to the problem of my rats and what the flowering of the bamboo had to do with causing such consternation and fear.

'I will tell you why these peasants for miles around are so panic-stricken. They have every reason to be. Apart from the old man who remembers when the bamboo flowered in his district there are few alive today to tell of how the rats came and devoured all their grain. The same thing is likely to happen again, unless within the next two years my Department finds some means of either exterminating the rats or containing them in some way.'

I was now completely out of my depth. What had two years to do with famine and the look of fear on my clerk's face when he had shown me the carpet of yellow on the forest floor.

Dennis must have seen the blank look on my face for he hurried on, 'It's quite simple. We have both seen what is happening; within a matter of weeks the bamboo forest will be dead. But that is only the beginning of what could be a frightful calamity. Every pretty little flower you saw today contains seed. For some reason that we have yet to discover this seed provides such a high protein diet to jungle rats that they gorge themselves and flourish as never before. It is probable that to rodents the seeds contain some highly reproductive vitamin or hormone. All we know is that they breed and multiply by the million. Their progeny wax fat and fast, and they in turn multiply in terrifying numbers. For two years this goes on and then comes the day of famine. The bamboo forest has turned green again and there is no longer the food to sustain the vast, increased rat population. Nature has robbed them. The days of plenty are over. They begin to starve and die as quickly as they multiplied. Mind you,' Dennis went on to say, 'we in the service have little more to go on than the story of your old man. But from such recorded evidence as we have on our files, his version of what happened in the Toungoo area nearly a century ago is not wide of the mark.

'Driven by hunger the rats descend from the forests like soldier ants on the march, and, having laid waste the growing crops before they can be harvested, they then storm and eat their way into the village storehouses. What they don't eat they foul with their droppings. It's then that the peasants are faced with starvation. Thank God that what you and I have seen today will not be repeated here in our lifetime.'

I never knew for certain whether science averted a large-scale plague of rats in this area as shortly after the flowering of the bamboo I was transferred hundreds of miles away. I can, however, confirm that rats are not alone in gorging the flower seeds when they fall. Wild jungle fowl in untold numbers are equally attracted as later I was to witness in another forest. In this case there was no danger to crops or the threat of starvation as the flowering occurred in a remote district in Northern Burma which was practically uninhabited.

The Forgotten Land, Geoffrey Bles, London, 1967, pp. 37–42.

43
Creatures Great and Small

GERRY ABBOTT

In Passage 22 we met a Danish traveller who became a novice monk. The novitiate is something that almost all male Burmans undertake, often when they are still young boys, though their stay in a monastery may well last only a few days. The novice-to-be (maung shin) is dressed in princely style and is by tradition carried to the ceremony, whether on a bullock-cart or on a pony or even, if the parents are sufficiently well-off, mounted on an elephant. Nowadays this last option is usually not only impracticable but very expensive—costly enough for two families to share the hiring costs, as was probably the case in the following passage.

As we saw in the introduction to Passage 26, the author of this extract was teaching in Mandalay University in 1988. At that time the main means of transport across the town was the cycle, and during rush hours the whole width of certain streets was occupied by cyclists all heading in the same direction. As if this did not make driving hazardous enough, there were also various animals to contend with; and here we are concerned with Mandalay's fauna rather than with its traffic conditions. In this extract Abbott deals mainly with the creatures he saw in the vicinity, not only on the streets but also in the garden and in the home—creatures varying in size from elephants to tiny ants; and as usual, it was the smallest that caused the most problems.

WHILE driving to and from the university, I had at various times narrowly avoided flattening humans of various ages, dogs of various shapes and colours, pigs of all sizes from frisky pink piglets to lengthy mud-covered sows, goats, bullocks and—biggest of all—great, placid buffaloes that lumbered across the roads, slow, single-minded, unstoppable. (I had long ago in Thailand learned that when hit at, say, twenty miles an hour by a decelerating car, a water-buffalo will often just walk away, leaving the vehicle badly damaged.) I thought I had encountered all the jaywalkers that Mandalay had to offer—human, canine, porcine, ungulate—but I had not. The road to the university, 73rd Street, was beginning to get busy again and, driving towards the main gate, I was behind the usual group of five lads cycling in line abreast, talking and laughing as they dawdled along, each with one arm on another's shoulder. I accelerated round them in second gear, then stood on the footbrake as hard as I could to avoid a head-on collision with an elephant. Fortunately, there was just room to pull over and let the towering beast pass. The man leading the creature out of the campus gave me a look that left me in no doubt that he was questioning my sanity, and I realised what I had done: as I overtook the cyclists, I had sounded a warning hoot which must have appeared to be for the elephant. As is so often the case, one sees the humour of the situation only after the event. Had I run into the poor elephant and been squashed into a subsequent existence, I like to think that some latter-day Orwell would have written my obituary and entitled it 'Hooting an Elephant'.

Some time later, I saw the elephant coming back past my room with a Burmese-style howdah on its back. The *oozi* or mahout sat in the centre of the howdah, and on either side of him sat a boy resplendently dressed in *shinbyu* robes—the finery worn before entry to the novicehood in a monastery. On either side of the elephant walked a young man holding a traditional red-and-gold umbrella to shade the boy riding above him; the handles must have been about ten feet long. The elephant passed out of sight, carrying the two young *maung shin** on a triumphant yet solemn journey that symbolises the relinquishment of the riches and vanities of this world which Prince Theidat (Siddhartha) had achieved when he left his aristocratic comfort, first to become a wandering mendicant and then, on attaining enlightenment beneath the *bodhi* tree, to become the Lord Buddha.

* * *

Summer had arrived. A week earlier, the temperature in Rangoon (where it was generally much cooler, though more humid) had reached 104 °F. I had no means of knowing what

*Young man about to become a novice monk.

the local temperature was, but all the symptoms of high summer were in evidence. The street corner by Mingala market was once more melting and folding itself, like something out of a Geology textbook, into hills and valleys of hot and wrinkled tarmacadam. The city's cyclists were more dazed and dozy than ever, so I constantly reminded myself: 'There is nothing around a Mandalay cyclist.' My colleagues, whose diet was far poorer than mine, were complaining of the heat, though it was not bothering me yet. In our garden, various birds were courting and nesting, and the mangoes were now an inch or more long; and some other trees had shed many of their leaves. It felt as if spring, summer and autumn had all arrived at the same time.

And the reptiles had reappeared. The turquoise blue lizards dormant in all the gardens were now to be seen on almost every tree-trunk, sunbathing or nodding vigorously to themselves or chasing dowdy little brown females up and down and round about; I had seen a couple of vipers on the road in the last few days; and the first domestic snake of the season had been seen at the water-tap in the back garden. I had received a copy of a circular sent to the friendly group of Australians working on the Mandalay Water Project, who seemed to have made us honorary Aussies. I had known before coming to Mandalay that Burma had the world's highest incidence of death by snake bite. This circular pointed out, among other things, that 90 per cent of snake bites in the Mandalay area were those of the Russell's Viper, one of the world's more deadly snakes. This creature and the cobra were common enough and venomous enough to warrant caution. I made a mental note to be more careful now when scrambling about on hillsides, and especially among old pagodas, whose sun-warmed bricks and cool crevices provided near-perfect living conditions for snakes.

The python is non-venomous and kills by constriction. But unlike its cousins, it grows to be quite a size and has made a name for itself in Burma over the years. In the Thaton district in 1927, for instance, a twenty-foot specimen swallowed a sleeping hunter whole, feet first, presumably after first crushing the poor fellow. The python was discovered in a state of post-prandial lethargy and killed. In 1972 a python of similar dimensions ate an eight-year-old boy. Fortunately, the city was not crawling with pythons. However, the Russell's Viper was fairly common and, although the hospital had a supply of the right serum, there were likely to be unpleasant side-effects, the nature of which remained unspecified. (About rabies, the circular was less optimistic; the hospital possessed only the old type of serum, which had to be administered in a lengthy series of painful injections into the stomach lining. I had already decided that, since one had twenty-four hours in which to get initial treatment, if I got bitten I would fly straight to Rangoon for the quicker, less painful modern treatment.)

Another creature that had recently emerged was the tucktoo, a largish lizard that inhabits trees, roofs and walls, usually outside rather than inside buildings. I preferred the more onomatopoeic Thai name—*took-eh* is the nearest I can approximate to it in English spelling. The name comes from the series of hiccups-cum-belches that these lizards produce from time to time, day or night, but more noticeably at night. They warm up with a short crescendo of single syllables (took-took-Took-Took-TOOK-TOOK) and then stop this stuttering to announce TOOK-EH! TOOK-EH! for up to a dozen times in a slow decrescendo. On this particular day, the one outside my office produced eight hiccup-belches; thirty years earlier, my Thai colleagues had told me that seven brought good luck to the hearer—seven, no more, no less. They had also told me that if a *took-eh* bit your finger you would never be able to free it from the creature's mouth without killing the lizard and cutting its jaws away. They never told me why or how anyone might contrive to get his finger stuffed down a *took-eh*'s throat in the first place.

The *took-eh*'s lesser cousin, a small house-gecko called in Thailand *chingchook* and in Malaysia *chichak*, is *ein-myaung* in Burmese. No room is complete without a dozen or so of these semi-translucent putty-coloured lizards. They scurry up walls and across ceilings—especially near lights, where insects gather—and snap up, often audibly, mosquitoes, flies, beetles, insects of many kinds. I had once watched a three-inch *chingchook* in my Bangkok house catch and deal with a resting dragonfly whose wingspan was almost twice as broad as the lizard was long. It was a long and noisy struggle, the *chingchook* chattering occasionally between its clenched teeth, the dragonfly's wings vibrating against the kitchen wall and all but lifting the lizard into the air. For fifteen minutes the stricken insect buzzed its four powerful iridescent wings in an attempt to take off; but whenever it rested for just a moment the reptilian jaws jerked the insect's thorax a fraction deeper into the gecko's throat. Two wings floated to the floor. The two opposite ones continued to vibrate for a minute or two before dropping off. The *chingchook* then bashed the dragonfly's body repeatedly against the wall by swinging its head in a paroxysm of triumph. The dragonfly's large head flew up in an arc and clattered across the stone floor of the kitchen. The *chingchook* had then wriggled the remaining thorax and abdomen slowly and voluptuously into its gut.

These little house-lizards will tackle almost any insect except ants and certain species of beetle. Being indoor creatures, they do not hibernate during the cool weather. They occasionally fall on you as you open a screen door or move a curtain, whereupon you feel a brief cold wriggle like a weak electric shock; then you hear a faint 'splat' on the teak floorboards and you see a dazed little thing that you feel sure must be badly injured; but as you look it scuttles to the skirting-board, leaps on to the wall and scurries behind a picture or a bookcase or whatever to nurse its headache. Occasionally, you wake up to find that you have rolled over in your sleep and squashed one; sometimes you crush one between door and jamb; and once as I opened the door of the freezer compartment of our fridge I startled a young *ein-myaung*, which leapt into the ice-box and quick-froze itself. But, on the whole, the creature cannot count homo sapiens among its natural enemies. The ones that inhabited my room at the university were a bit of a nuisance in that every morning I had to sweep their droppings off my books and papers; on the other hand there was one in my study at home that appreciated my guitar playing and would chirrup as soon as it heard the first strumming.

I don't much mind snakes and other reptiles, though naturally I was always wary of snakes because unless you are an expert you can seldom tell whether a particular specimen is harmless or deadly. (An old Indian handbook of mine says that 'a certain amount of precision in its identification can only be acquired by noting the characteristics of some of the important scales'—which means getting well within striking distance.) A lot of harmless snakes are therefore needlessly killed all the time. But harmless or harmful, snakes don't make my blood run cold. Large spiders do. I went one morning down the garden of our temporary house to look at a well that supplied us with all our water. Lifting off the corrugated-iron cover, I could see nothing at first but the reflection of a bright sky, motionless palm fronds and the silhouette of my head. Then there was a minute movement of a point of light a foot or so from my right eye, on the brick-lined wall of the well. A huge spider was watching me. It was the colour of dark soil and had the squat body and powerful legs of a small crab. And it was bristly. Two of its eyes were glittering at me, taking in the sudden foreign light and refracting it like tiny shattered windscreens. I was being eyed with circumspect efficiency by a born killer that was much too close for my liking. Gently I straightened up and gently I lowered the cover into place and allowed myself to breathe again.

We weren't often bothered by spiders, fortunately, but scorpions were a constant problem. I narrowly missed scooping up with my bare hands a large dark one that had taken up residence under some emptied-out packing material. Discovered, it scampered straight for my bare foot, whereupon I executed a standing leap towards a broom and then executed the scorpion by using the broom as a sledgehammer. Sweating, I swept the bits outside. I always sweat when I have to kill something. . . .

But, as usual in the tropics, it was the smallest creatures that did the most damage. Mandalay could probably boast of dozens of species of ants; the ones we suffered from were some normal-sized ones that ran like the wind and some minute reddish ones that bit like tigers. Close-packed hordes of these little red devils had long ago succeeded in achieving all the usual feats, invading the kitchen, colonising the cupboards, committing mass suicide in pots of jam sealed with screw-top lids and drowning in an alcoholic stupor in the dregs of wine and beer. Then for a fortnight or so they disappeared. Had they moved on? Was the ant season over or something? No. One morning I moved my radio cassette-recorder and found under it a heap of black dust. The ants had pulverised the cassette-to-cassette recording mechanism.

When the really hot weather came, the ant High Command decided that an airconditioned bedroom might be preferable to a sweltering kitchen. Patrols and search parties were sent out under cover of darkness into the bedclothes. Encountering vigorous resistance and chemical warfare, they retired to regroup elsewhere. This new rendezvous turned out to be the study, where they found huge reserves of edible glue in book-spines, lampshades and furniture joints. When they took to climbing up the chair I was sitting on and marching into my shorts armed to the mandibles with formic acid, it was my turn to retire for a drink. I found their dark, fleet-footed cousins living very comfortably in our ancient, dying refrigerator.

Back to Mandalay, Impact Books, Bromley, 1990, pp. 95–102.

Other Oxford Paperbacks for readers interested in South-East Asia, past and present

* *Titles marked with an asterisk have
restricted rights.*